It Was Too Soon Before...

ALSO BY DIRK VANDEN

Who Killed Queen Tom? - 1969

Leather - 1969

The Leather Queens - 1969

Twin Orbs - 1969

I Want It All - 1969

All or Nothing - 1970

All Is Well - 1971

I Want It All - Revised - 1995

Chapter 9 from *I Want It All*
in Simon Sheppard's *Homosex* - 2007

All Of Me (Can You Take All Of Me?) - 2010

Down the Rabbit Hole - 2011

All Together (*The All Trilogy* in one volume) - 2011
Nominated for a Lambda Literary Award for Best Gay Erotica, 2012

"Once Upon a Time in 1969"
(Chapters 11 & 12 from *I Want It All*)
in Richard Labonté's *Best Gay Erotica of 2012*
The anthology was nominated for a Lammy in Gay Erotica, 2012

It Was Too Soon Before...

The unlikely life, untimely death, and
unexpected rebirth of Gay Pioneer,
Dirk Vanden

By Dirk Vanden

LETHE PRESS
MAPLE SHADE NJ

Author's note: Some of the names of the people in my life have been changed to protect the guilty as well as the innocent. Other widely-recognized names have been used to provide a realistic and recognizable background for my otherwise true story.

www.lethepressbooks.com   lethepress@aol.com

Book Development & Design by Toby Johnson
Cover art and interior photographs by Dirk Vanden
Photos of Mike Davis & Al Parker courtesy of COLTstudiogroup.com.
    Used with permission

Published as a trade paperback original
by Lethe Press, 118 Heritage Avenue, Maple Shade, NJ 08052.
First U.S. edition, April 18, 2012

ISBN 978-1-59021-354-4 / 1-59021-354-8
e-isbn 978-1-59021-415-2

Library of Congress Cataloging-in-Publication Data

Vanden, Dirk.
    It was too soon before-- : the unlikely life, untimely death, and unexpected rebirth of Gay pioneer, Dirk Vanden / by Dirk Vanden.
       p. cm.
    ISBN 978-1-59021-354-4 -- ISBN 1-59021-354-8
    1. Vanden, Dirk. 2. Authors, American--20th century--Biography.
3. Gay authors--United States--Biography. I. Title.
    PS3572.A4275Z46 2012
    813.54--dc23
    [B]
                                   2012014177

Acknowledgments

A sincerely grateful *Thank you* to: Chico, for being my "#1 fan," and your continuing help and encouragement; to Wayne Gunn for encouraging me to continue trying to find a publisher for this autobiography; to A.B. Gayle for sending me where I never would have gone on my own; to Maitland, for helping me promote myself; to Toby, who helped me say what I needed to say; to Tom, my "adopted son, for everything; and to everyone else who has helped shape my life and get me to where I am today: Thank you all very much!

Last but not least, I need to thank my beloved dog Buddy Jr. for his ten years of love and devotion. Had it not been for him, I would have given up many times. He was 14 or 15 years old, and had developed hip problems during the last six months of his life. When he finally couldn't walk by himself, I took him to his doctor and held his head as he died peacefully around 4 PM on March 20, 2012. Thank you, dear Buddy, for your love and your life. I miss you most of all.

Introduction

The story is told that after the Holy Grail appeared marvelously to King Arthur and the Knights of the Round Table and then, just as marvelously, disappeared, the Knights of Camelot all agreed that they should enter upon a quest to rediscover the Grail and so bring heaven to their land. And they also agreed that in this effort it would be unseemly to follow in another's footsteps and that they should each pursue their own paths, beginning in that place in the forest which was darkest and most alone, and follow a path that no one had ever blazed before. In this way, they would achieve the Beatific Vision symbolized by the Grail cup and, in the process, do good deeds throughout the land, making it heaven on earth. Comparative religion and myth scholar Joseph Campbell loved to recount this story, calling it the archetypal example of the modern, Western spiritual hero's journey—an adventure beyond belief and orthodoxy, beyond membership in religion, beyond obedience to convention, even respectability in society, true to one's own path. This is, almost always, also the Gay hero's spiritual journey.

Dirk Vanden's heroic and earnest quest to be true to himself led him to reconsider everything he'd been taught by the religion that had shaped him as a devout youth. His "spiritual path" demonstrates how Gay consciousness exemplifies and helps bring about an evolution of consciousness and a "spirituality" beyond the myths and religions of old. Vanden's life story shows how Gay men necessarily transform their religious upbringing to create a kind of personal new vision of their own, based in personal experience and deep intuition, that fulfills their zeal to be good and contributing persons, offers them a life of adventure and discovery and, most importantly, that makes sense in the modern, scientific, post-mythological world. No one else will follow Dirk Vanden's path; it is his alone. But all of us can be inspired by him to follow those lone paths of our own.

—Toby Johnson, author of *Gay Spirituality: The Role of Gay Identity in the Transformation of Human Consciousness*

It was too soon before;
It isn't too soon any more.

***

I must follow the path I'm on,
No matter where it may take me.
It goes where I need to go
To learn what I need to know,
When the path ends,
And I get to where I'm going.

The Wit & Wisdom Of Gabriel Horny

Milestones on the Path

It Was Too Soon Before...

The Little Bastard, home from Sunday School, age 8

MILESTONE 1: "A Miracle"
1932, AGE 0

I was conceived in a one-bedroom "tourist cabin" in Kansas City, Missouri, early in June, 1932. Nine months later, on May 7, 1933, I was born in a little one-room cabin on my paternal Grandfather's farm, on a high-desert alkaline plateau in eastern Utah called *Myton Bench*, near the center of the Ute Indian Reservation and a tiny Mormon town called Roosevelt, the only child of a middle-aged Mormon couple, Van and Afton Fullmer; he was thirty-two and she was thirty. I grew up in not-quite blissful ignorance of my true beginnings and only solved that mystery many years later, after my mother died at age ninety-six—which made me sixty-six when I figured it all out. It answered all the questions.

I'm fairly certain that my life began when the man I believed, for most of my life, was my *"father,"* was in school, and my *"uncle"* was home, sick that day, and couldn't go to school, and my mother was in *estrus*.

I'm also convinced that this shameful secret explains why my "father" treated me with frigid disdain all his life and why my mother punished herself with excruciating headaches all of hers. I also believe that it has had a great deal to do with my particular version of homosexuality.

Although I wasn't to solve *the unmentionable mystery* until much later in life, my maternal grandmother gave me the first clue. Grandma Vernon was surely the most religious person I've ever known. She was as close as anyone can come to being a *latter-day saint*. She was good and kind and loving and giving, and she spoke with a conviction that, as far as I was concerned, could only come from being *absolutely right*. She adored me and I returned the adulation.

I can vividly remember sitting at the big round table in Grandmother's kitchen, which smelled like vanilla, as I drank milk or lemonade and ate cookies or freshly-baked bread with homemade butter and jam, listening raptly as she bustled around the large room, cooking something (in my memory she is always cooking something), telling one of her many stories. She knew all sorts of wonderful stories—from the Bible, from her life as a young Mormon girl, whose parents had crossed the plains in covered wagons—but my favorite of all was about *me*.

"We had all but given up hope," she would say, "hope that your mother would *ever* have children. She and your father had been married for *ten long years* before you came along." Grandmother had brought forth eleven children of her own. She knew well enough that women without children were considered practically useless by the Mormon Church, and therefore, also by Mormon friends and Mormon relatives as well. She would look at me and smile—the kind of radiant smile that only *holy saints* and *Jesus* could smile; sometimes she would squeeze my arm or pat my hand. "But then," she would say, *"a miracle occurred!* God answered our prayers. *You* were born."

She would hug me tightly and whisper how much she loved me, and I would press as close to her as I could get, and tell her how very much I loved her, too. Then she would say *"Praise the Lord!"* And I truly believed I was talking to *The Lord* when I answered *"Amen!"* I truly believed that I was *God's Miracle*.

I grew up mostly in my mother's home town of Vernal, Utah, way up in the northeast corner of the state, high in the Rocky Mountains, on coast-to-coast Highway 40, about twenty miles west of the Colorado border, and about thirty miles east of my "father's" home-town, where we spent a few early years—Roosevelt was the center of the *Ute Indian Reservation*.

It turned out that the *Ute* tribe of *Native Americans* had much more to do with me than I had been led to believe—until Van lost his cool one day when we were arguing and snapped: "You never knew your great-grandmother was a *'Squaw,'* did you?" He spit the word out like it tasted nasty. I said "Really? Which tribe?" He said "Oh, shit" and walked out of the room.

When the Mormons took the state away from the Native Americans who lived here, at least deigning to name the state after the Utes, they *"converted"* many of those people—mostly women—and the Mormon men married them. There was a surplus of unmarried Mormon men in those days of polygamy. My great-grandfather must have been such a man. In her older years, my grandmother Fullmer was obviously Ute. Which makes me one-eighth *Native American.* Unlike my "father," that makes me very proud.

Vernal was a small, all-white, 99% Mormon town, nestled in the middle of a beautiful, broad, fertile green valley, near the source of the *Green River*, crisscrossed with small farms and ranches, all surrounding a "downtown" of about four blocks, in the center of a town about four miles square, with a population of just over fifteen hundred—for the entire valley, not just the town.

At various times during my childhood, I had probably heard many clues about things that had happened before my birth, but I didn't assign them any particular significant, or *secret,* meaning until after Mother had died at age ninety-six, in a *"Convalescent Hospital."*

I couldn't even *think* such things until they were *both* dead.

Going through her remaining belongings, I found references to her marriage: *"What fun we did have."* (How unlike my parents, *having fun.*) And cryptic notes about the first ten years:

"1922 - Married in Temple, SLC."

"1932 - Kansas City, Missouri, rented tourist cabin. Van started school. Also Bud."

"1933 - Roosevelt, Utah, Dale born May 7. There was snow on the roses outside my window."

My given name was *Richard Dale Fullmer*; I was called *Dale* at school and by all my relatives. I hated the name because I thought it was a girl's name; Dale Evans, Roy Roger's singing cowgirl wife, was the only other Dale I knew about. When I started high school, the teachers called me by my first name, so I gladly went by *Richard*, or *Dick*. I think I probably enjoyed having a nickname that also had a sexual connotation. In college, I shared a class and a coffee break with a hunky student from Holland named *Dirk Van der Elst*. I liked his name better than mine—

Dirk for *Dick*—"short knife" instead of "penis"—so I adopted it as my *nom-de-plume: "Dirk Vanden."* My *nom-de-paintbrush* was *"Dirk,"* and later, when I lived in San Francisco with Herb Finger (ne "Irving,") my *"chosen name*, rather than my given name" *was "Dirk Fullmer."* That's still me.

I now believe that the man listed on my birth certificate as "father" was actually my uncle—Van Fullmer, Jr., who did not want, or couldn't make babies. He had grown up as the eldest in a family of nine, eight of which he had helped raise from newborns, one per year, one year after another, until he was sick and tired of babies, and had probably decided he did not want any *"damn kids"* of his own. He definitely didn't like children. He often referred to me as "the damn kid" to his co-workers.

That is not to say he was a *"bad"* man, in any other way; he was a *very good* man, helpful and kind—to everyone but me. Everyone loved *Vannie*. Everyone but me. He paid my expenses until I had graduated college, but it wasn't because he loved me. He was not the kind of father the other kids had, or that I'd read about in books, or seen in the movies, or heard on the radio, in the stories we listened to every evening (instead of talking) and I didn't have a clue about *why*.

Automobiles were just becoming popular in the 1920's and Van had a talent for keeping them running. He knew that if he went to an Automotive Certification school, he could take his *"Certified Auto Mechanic"* certificate and get a job anywhere in the country—*anywhere besides Utah.* They both hated Utah. He and Afton, my mother, had saved up for ten years so he could go to such a school in Kansas City, Missouri. Just before they left, Van's younger brother, "Bud" (Von—two years younger) decided that he wanted to go get *certified*, too.

A week before the school started, the three of them drove to Kansas City, in a Model-A Ford, and rented a tourist-cabin, close to the school— two rooms, with a single bedroom for them, and a fold-up bed for Bud. In the spring of 1932, Van and Von started Automotive School and Afton got a job as a waitress. He was thirty-one, she was twenty-eight, and Bud was twenty-nine.

They had been there only a few months when Mother announced she was pregnant. Having already spent most of their savings on Bud's tuition and daily needs, and without mother's salary and tips to finance their stay, and with a baby on the way, they had to quit school and move back to the farm in eastern Utah.

I was born in the old one-room cabin on my grandfather's farm, where Van had been born thirty-two years earlier.

It does not take a mathematical genius to add $1 + 1 = 2$. For ten years, *for whatever reasons*, Mother had been unable to get pregnant. She knew, as did all of her friends and relatives, that she could only prove her worth as a woman by producing children. Barren Mormon women are considered worthless. Mormon women were not supposed to have "fun" but were expected to have lots and lots of kids. Then, after ten long barren years, wonder of wonders, a *miracle* happened: the answer to prayers: *Me!*

Within *weeks* of my "uncle's" moving in with them, *"a miracle occurred!"*

My guess is, Van was probably sterile from a childhood disease—he'd had several and they'd had little or no medical help as he was growing up—just prayers. Maybe he knew he was sterile, probably not. Doctors didn't test for those things in those days. I doubt that he had deliberately avoided impregnating her for ten years. Mormon men are supposed to be prolific breeders, and are valued for adding to the number of potential tithe-payers they produce. But for whatever reason he hadn't become a father yet, surely he had reason for being suspicious when I was announced.

It is also very possible that Bud raped her—something neither of them would have talked about. There was no way, short of face-to-face confrontation, that he could ever prove the baby wasn't his, and I'm sure that never happened. Von was only two years younger than Van and they looked enough alike to be twins. Their DNA's would have been virtually identical, so *I* would have come out practically the same, one father or the other.

At least my grandparents remain my real grandparents.

After their failed attempt at Certification, they returned to hated Roosevelt, Utah, and Bud went on to sire eight or nine kids he could claim as his own. Half of them were blue-eyed towheads, like me. The other half were dark like their Native American (Ute) mother. And Grandmother.

Now I understand why "Dad" hated me. No wonder Mom punished herself with debilitating migraine headaches the rest of her life. I was her *sin*—her *bastard*. They had been married in the Mormon Temple in Salt Lake City, so divorce was not an option. They were chained together *"For time and all eternity"* by their temple vows. I'm certain that they never talked about it with each other or anyone else. No one ever talked about sex in those days. It was a terrible secret between the three of them, all their lives. *Did she or didn't she? Was I or wasn't I?*

I am not accusing my mother of being a tramp. I'm quite certain she never was. Except for that one deviation, she was a *"good Mormon woman"* all of her life, even though she only went to church now and then. She respected her temple-marriage vows and wore holy-underwear, as did Van, all of her life. But something happened in that cabin, in Kansas City, Missouri, and she gave in to her physical needs during estrus, and *"cheated,"* or *"sinned"*—just *once!* But that's all it took. If she hadn't, I wouldn't be here, so I can't say it was a *"bad"* thing she did, but that one *"sin"* in her life haunted and tortured her all the rest of it. It soured their love and their lives, *and mine.* Every single day of my life, I was a reminder to her of that terrible, unforgivable *sin* she had committed. *"Adultry!"* Even Jesus condemned it.

Every time my supposed father looked at me, he wondered if she had cheated or not—or felt a gnawing hatred for me, suspecting the truth but unable to prove it.

Having loved someone and lived with him for eighteen years, I know that what my *"parents"* had was not love; it was love in the beginning: *"What fun we did have."* But by the time I came along, it had become a *religious contract* they were both too terrified to break. The penalty was eternal damnation. Divorce was not an option.

I'm convinced that Mother lived to be ninety-six, partly because of her fear that Van was *"over there, on the other side,"* just waiting to make Heaven a Hell for her, just as he had her life on Earth. Mormons believe that their marriage will never end, but will go on-and-on for "time and all eternity," chained together forever. How much like Hell would that be?

One final thing he did to let me know that I was no son of his: When he died of a heart-attack at age seventy-three, he left a will with a lawyer, who summoned Mother and me to his chambers to read that Van Fullmer, Jr. had left his entire estate—*less one dollar*—to his wife, my mother. To me he left that *one dollar*— but *only* if I didn't contest the will. The lawyer gave me a dollar bill—my "father's" legacy.

Even now that I've reasoned it all out—especially now that I realize what *hell* they both went through *because of me*—I wish I could somehow go back in time, when he was still alive, and yell at him, *at both of them*: *"IT WAS NOT MY FAULT!"*

I often asked Mother: *"Why does Daddy hate me?"* To which she always replied: *"Daddy doesn't **hate** you, dear. That's just **his way**."*

Now I think I know why that was his way.

MILESTONE 2: Mama, What Does "Fuck" mean?

1942, AGE 9

It was late in the summer of the year I turned nine. I had been out in the hills west of our home, in Roosevelt, in the high desert country of northeastern Utah: red sandstone hills, low, twisted cedars and pinion pines—with my cousins, Ronald and Ginger, two and one years older than I, riding our bikes along the canal road.

They were from a very large family, six other children besides them, and they knew a lot about *"The Facts of Life."* I, on the other hand, was an only child and knew nothing at all about sex. This now seems very strange, considering that I grew up on a series of farms, where we had horses and cows, dogs, cats, pigs and chickens, but I obviously ignored their sexual behaviors, or repressed them. Most likely, Mother distracted me and said: "They're just playing. Never mind."

We had stopped by the old swimming hole, in the shade of a grove of cottonwood trees. Ronnie told us a joke he had heard at school. It had to do with a boy asking a girl if he could "fuck" her. At first, she refused, so he offered her a piece of fruit and so she let him. This went on through four different fruits, and, finally, the punch line was: "Apples, peaches, pears and plums, I won't get off 'til the baby comes!"

They both laughed like it was the funniest thing they had ever heard.

I didn't get it.

"You are the stupidest person in the whole world! You don't know what *'fuck'* means, do you?"

"...no...."

"That's how *babies* are made, dummy! By *fucking!*"

I was quite certain that they didn't know what they were talking about. I had no idea what "fucking" really was, but believed that God made babies, and delivered them in the same way Santa Claus made and delivered Christmas presents: Miracles, plain and simple.

I protested. They insisted, then proceeded to demonstrate how it was done. Ronnie was eleven and, to my amazement, could make his little dink get hard and bigger, and with Ginger leaning back against a tree, her dress held up to where she could peer over it to watch, Ronnie put his stiff little prick up into her pussy. They moaned and gyrated briefly, acting as if they were having a wonderful time, and then disengaged and suggested that I try it. My poor little dink simply wouldn't get hard at all: it had shrunk up so tightly into my body that I couldn't possibly get it up inside hers.

It was the first time I had seen a girl's "privates," and I was shocked and frightened. It looked like she was missing something. I had seen other boys naked, but had never seen an erect pee-pee! It had never occurred to me that such a thing could happen. I was fascinated and terrified at the same time.

I was also amazed at the casual way Ron and Ginger were acting, as if this was something they did all the time. I couldn't help feeling that, in spite of my failure, I had taken part in something terribly wrong, if not downright sinful.

They were too disgusted to go on playing with me, so they got on their bikes and went home. I wandered along the canal road for several hours, feeling utterly miserable and useless.

It was true, what they said, I told myself: I was stupid. Things like this happened to me all the time, especially at school. All the other children seemed to know enormously more than I did about life, things they had learned from their older brothers and sisters. I grew up very much alone, even though I went to school with more than a hundred other children. I had no one to tell me the secrets they had discovered in the process of living, no one to warn me that adults lied—even parents.

There was, of course, the distinct possibility that my cousins had tricked me. It certainly wouldn't have been the first time. I was a completely gullible child and very often the other kids, and sometimes my older relatives—especially my uncles and their kids on both sides of the family—made a fool of me, using my innocence as their weapon against me.

I felt like such an idiot because I didn't know things I should know—if for no other reason than to understand when I was being teased. My Dad teased me for being "stupid." Maybe he was right.

Mother was out on the front porch of our house when I returned, mending one of her dresses (we were very poor, and she made or repaired most of our clothing). "Where on earth have you been?" she asked, not really angry. "I was starting to get worried."

"Mama…" I was frightened, but I needed to ask somebody, someone I could trust to tell me the truth. "What does *'fuck'* mean?"

She caught her breath and stared at me, speechless for a long, terrible moment, her eyes wide with shock and outrage. Then, very slowly and carefully she put down the needle and crossed her hands in her lap. *"If you ever use that word again,"* she said in a voice like winter, *"God will strike you dead!"*

After a long, intense silence, she asked in almost a whisper: "Who taught you that word?"

I hated tattling on my cousins, but I had never in my life lied to my mother, so I said "Ronnie and Ginger."

The very idea seemed to strike her dumb for another awful silence as she considered the implications of what I'd just told her. "I don't want you to have anything to do with them—ever again! Do you understand me?"

I managed to mutter "Yes," but I was so frightened I could hardly speak; I had never seen my mother so angry about anything!

She sent me to my room, and said Dad would punish me when he got home from work.

I didn't believe that Dad would actually spank me. First of all, I'd heard him use the word himself—several times—when he was talking to his brothers, when he didn't know I could hear what he was saying. Some of the men he worked with at the turkey-farm east of town, said it all the time: They said *"Fuck this,"* or *"Fuck that,"* or *"Fucking right!"* Also, the very house we were living in had had *"FUCK YOU"* written on some of the walls before we moved in. Mother had very quickly painted those rooms, covering the words, but no one had said anything about God killing whoever had written them.

Dad had spanked me only once in my life: a little over a year before, when I had refused to go to school. We had moved three times that year, during my second grade, because Dad couldn't find a good job: from Roosevelt to Rock Springs, Wyoming, then to Sacramento, California, then finally to Baggs, Wyoming, where he worked doing odd jobs on a sheep ranch. In Baggs, I had been even more of an outsider than usual. A one-room school housed all of the twenty or so children who lived in or near the tiny town, and all the kids knew one another—half of them were related. In Baggs, we were the only Mormons, and I was teased mercilessly about being a "Moron." I was ridiculed and ostracized until I couldn't take it any longer. One morning, I told my parents I would rather die than go back to that hateful school, where even the teacher acted like there was something wrong with me. Dad spanked me then, so hard and so long that I passed out. When I woke up, mother was crying and told me I wouldn't have to go back to that school again—we would be leaving Baggs and moving back to Utah, back to Roosevelt, Dad's home town, into my Uncle Howard's old house in Hancock Cove.

The thing I couldn't understand was why God would strike me dead, and not Dad, or Ronnie, or Uncle Bud, or Uncle Glen, or any of the others I'd heard use the word. Was I special, for some reason?

I was hoping that Dad would explain it all to me. Maybe it had something to do with the difference between men and women. I wasn't sure what that difference entailed, but I had no doubt now that it was real. For one thing, women didn't swear, or weren't supposed to. Maybe *"Fuck"* was a swearword that men could say, but women couldn't.

Shortly after our old pickup rattled past my window, I could hear them arguing in the kitchen, but I couldn't make out the words. It was the first time I had ever heard them argue. When he came into my room, he was grinning. He sat on my bed and patted his knee.

I went to him, feeling very conspiratorial, and I bent myself over his knee, expecting a pat or two—but his hand smacked against my butt so painfully I yelped and started to cry; this seemed to encourage him, and his hand slapped even harder, and went on and on until I was screaming "Don't! Please!"

Finally, mother came into the room and told him to stop! That was enough.

They left me crying, cringing painfully on my bed, my mind a jumbled chaos of fear and confusion. I felt more alone than I had ever felt before. I felt betrayed and abandoned. And something new, a feeling I'd never had before, of being, somehow, unclean in the sight of God! Without meaning to, without even knowing what I was doing, I had *sinned.* That meant I was a terrible person.

That evening, no one said a word during supper. When I had finished eating, Mother sent me to my room again. Usually I was allowed to listen to the radio with them for an hour or so after supper, but the radio wasn't even turned on that night. Instead, I could hear their voices, from the kitchen, arguing again, low at first, then louder until I could hear him yelling something but couldn't understand the words. Something crashed! Then the kitchen door banged open and Mother ran out, through the living room and out the front door, sobbing as she ran. Dad yelled: *"Come back here!"* From outside she called: *"I'm never coming back!"*

He ran out after her, slamming the front door behind him.

I followed them, terrified, crying, stumbling in the darkness, along the rutted dirt road that led into town. I could hear her sobbing, and I followed the sound until I could see the two of them, darker silhouettes against a background of shadows, huddled in the ditch beside the road. He was kneeling, holding her as she cried, sounding utterly heartbroken.

I ran to them, my arms open to embrace them, ready to beg their forgiveness, and to plead with her not to go away.

Dad furiously shoved me away and I stumbled backward, falling in the dirt. "Get out of here!" he yelled at me. *"This is all your fault anyway, you little bastard!"*

The next morning, we all acted as though nothing had happened. Mother woke me at six o'clock, as usual, and we fed the pigs and chickens while Dad milked the cows, and turned them out to pasture, as always. We had breakfast together—silently—and then Dad went to work. I started to help Mother wash the dishes, as I had done for several years, but she said, "No. I'll do them. You go on out and play."

I wanted her to say she was sorry for getting so upset, and I desperately wanted to tell her that I hadn't meant anything bad when I asked her that terrible question, I had merely wanted to understand. But she never mentioned the incident, nor did I, nor, as far as I know, did Dad, ever again.

Up to that point, Mom had been my best friend—I had been with or near her almost every hour of my life, except for school—I would go with her everywhere, doing the chores, weeding the garden, shopping, to Church, visiting relatives, and we would laugh and sing songs and play games; she would hug me or hold my hand and smile with a smile that let me know that she loved me very much, and everything was all right. I thought she was the most wonderful person in the world, and that had made me feel very special indeed, because she had so obviously adored me.

But after that day, we became strangers. It was as though she had turned something off. From that day onward it seemed to me that she never allowed herself to feel anything for me besides obligation: she had been responsible for bringing me into the world, so she cooked my meals and washed my clothes and cleaned my room, and she always made sure I had enough money to buy clothes and essentials, but she never again praised me or encouraged me or seemed to care whether I got an A or a C, passed or failed a test, got promoted or demoted or kicked out of a class. As long as I didn't involve her in my life, she paid me no mind. Or seemed not to, no matter how successful I was at school.

Dad had never paid me much attention anyway, but after that night, it seemed he had even more than his usual contempt for me. Although I lived with them for nine more years, that night we each moved away and apart from each other, and there we remained for the rest of our lives.

MILESTONE 3: Me and Jesus

1942-49, 9-16

It is easy to understand how I got swept up in a passion for *Religion* at age nine—after that horrible day and sleepless night, hearing my Dad's furious voice, echoing over and over in my head: *"This is all your fault, you little bastard!"* I desperately needed acceptance and approval, which was definitely not coming from either of them.

It never occurred to me, at the time, to think "bastard" meant anything but a "dirty, rotten, nasty" person. It took many years before I even started to consider that I might not be "legitimate." Instead, it was just a word he used to hurt me, like "Sissy," and "Coward," and "the Damn Kid."

I didn't understand what terrible sin I had committed to have them treat me like they were doing, which was mostly ignoring me, as though pretending that I didn't exist. Even though both sets of grandparents were Mormons, my mother's, the Vernons, were all very religious, while the Fullmers rarely went to Sunday School—although they did have a framed map of the Mormon Trek across the plains, from Illinois to Utah, and a framed lithograph of the Mormon Temple in Salt Lake City. My mother's family, the Vernons, believed that God answered the prayers of those he considered Good Mormons

We moved again, shortly after that incident, and probably as a result of it. My mother surely confronted her sister about her nasty children teaching me things she didn't want me to know. It must have made her wonder if my true beginnings might be family-gossip. *How many had wondered or guessed where I came from?*

We moved from Roosevelt, near my paternal grandparents to Vernal, next door to my maternal grandparents' house in the western end of the valley. They had a little "Guest House" for visiting relatives, across the yard from the much larger main house, which had seen ten children grow up and move out to have big Mormon families of their own. It had a tiny bedroom, a living room and a kitchen. I slept on a rollaway bed in the living room. The bedroom was closed off by a red velvet curtain that pulled across an archway on a large wooden rod.

All of my aunts and uncles, on both sides of the family, were producing large Mormon families of their own. I was the only "only-child."

I often wondered why my mother hadn't had children before or after me. It wasn't because she couldn't have children. Having me proved that she could—but she never did again.

In Vernal, they both got jobs, Dad as a lineman for the *Utah Power and Light Co.* and Mother as a cook in her brother's diner, downtown, called *The Rite Spot.*

We stayed in the little house by Granddad's until Dad could build a house for us to live in. He had already built one of our homes, back on the Myton Bench. He bought five acres from Grandfather and within a year, they had built a very nice, livable house, a mile down the street.

I wasn't encouraged to *"get in the way"* in the building process. Dad thought I was *"too stupid"* to help. *"Aw, for cryin' out loud, not that one! That one! What the hell's the matter with you?"* Etc.

While Grandmother Vernon was welcoming and loving, Grandfather V. was just the opposite. Grandmother had described him in her journal as "a handsome young convert from Kentucky," but by the time I moved next door, he was an angry, bitter old man, who hated everybody. He had once donated a stained glass window to the local *Mormon Tabernacle* (where I was confirmed, under the *"W. P. Vernon window"*), but things had gone wrong in his life and he did his best to be unpleasant to everyone, probably especially to my mother—for coming back home—with a baby of questionable parentage. He probably treated Dad like a loser. They never acted like friends. Neither one of them went into a church house in my lifetime, except for funerals. They both treated me as an unwanted presence.

Grandfather Vernon died of cancer several years after we moved out of that little house. I can remember Dad getting dressed in a dusty blue suit to go to the funeral. It was the only time I'd seen him in a suit or in the church house. And there was Grandpa, also in his *Church suit,* down in front of the altar, in an inappropriately ornate casket, surrounded with shiny white satin and beautiful flowers.

It was the only time I'd ever seen my Grandfather smile.

Both Mom and Dad worked weekdays, which left me alone much of the time. Grandmother saw the need and did what she could to fill it. She took me under her wing and taught me about *God and Jesus.* She had studied *The Bible* and knew many of the stories by heart. Everybody in the Ward knew *Sister Vernon* and loved her. I was loved and accepted because I was her grandchild—and I did everything I could to live up to her expectations.

In the process, I fell in love with Jesus, meek and mild, loving and forgiving. In Sunday School we often sang *"Jesus wants me for a sunbeam,"* and I sang it like I meant it. I *became* a Sunbeam for Jesus. At school, the kids called me *"Goody-two-shoes,"* and a *"pansy,"* but I didn't care. I was doing *The Lord's* work and that was much more important than worrying about being called bad names. I was helping my Church pave the way for Jesus to return and turn the earth back into *Paradise,* the way it once was in *The Garden of Eden.* That's what Mormon lives were all about, or were supposed to be, getting Jesus to come back.

Even though the indoctrination process starts early, for toddlers in Sunday School, and then "Primary," young Mormons are not considered *real* Mormons until they are baptized and confirmed at age eight, or later. At that age, they are considered old enough to decide whether or not they want to become *"members"* of the *LDS Church.* (As though any eight-year-old Mormon-born kid would say "No, I don't want to be a Mormon like everybody else around me.") Kids get a lot of attention and love as they prepare themselves for membership in *The One and Only True Church on Earth.* I studied and memorized the Mormon *Articles of Faith* and *"The Gospel of Jesus"* became part of my life.

In that closet He told me to go into to pray, I repented many times for uttering *that* word which I would not even allow myself to *think*, let alone say aloud. Jesus quickly became my mentor, my adopted, perfect father-figure, the one who forgave me for being stupid and a terrible *sinner*— whatever my Sin was; Jesus didn't care; He forgave me because he loved me. He welcomed me into His heart and home with all the love I could possibly want. Over and over, I listened to, and read, and incorporated, His advice in my quest for something to believe in that didn't involve feeling guilty for reasons I didn't understand.

I didn't trust my parents any longer. At age ten I discovered they had lied to me about Santa Claus, and that embarrassing revelation ended my confidence in them. Once I realized they had lied to me, about so many things, it wasn't difficult, setting them apart from me—like in a separate room of my life—and adopting my Grandmother as my substitute mother and Jesus as my substitute father. Although He was absent, physically, from my life, He had left His words in a book, especially for me. And His *"spirit"* definitely seemed to be with me twenty-four hours a day.

For the next six years, between 1943 and '49, I became intensely religious, spending every spare moment contemplating Mormonized-Christianity, imagining what it would be like, preparing myself and my soul for the *imminent Second Coming of Christ*. My mother had showed me a "Patriarchal Blessing," she had received as a girl, which promised her that she would live to *"hear His sweet voice,"* when Our Savior returned. I read and reread the *Bible* and *Book of Mormon*, the *Doctrine and Covenants* and various Church books and magazines. I prayed often for God to forgive me whatever terrible sins I'd committed, and to be for me what He was for Grandma—a source of incredible strength in the face of adversity—a source of love and understanding, when all the world misunderstood and hated me.

I took part in all the church-boy-programs, *"Primary,"* *"The Boy Trail Builders,"* *"Blazers"* and *"Trekkers"* and *"Guides."* I was ordained a *"Deacon"* at age twelve, a *"Teacher"* at age fourteen, and an *"Aaronic Priest"* at sixteen. I planned on becoming an *"Elder"* when I went on my Mission, and joined the *Melchizedek* Priesthood.

I definitely intended going on a Mission when I got out of high school, or maybe after graduating from *BYU*. I wanted to spread the *True Gospel* to the *Heathens* of the poor, disadvantaged countries, Mexico and South America. I planned to lead hundreds, perhaps thousands of *questing souls*, to *The True Church*, saving those souls for Jesus in the process. When I came home from saving souls, I would get married to a good

Mormon girl and raise a family of good Mormon children (but not just one alone—I would never subject a child of mine to that affliction—but not nine or twelve either; two or three maybe). We would all go to Church together, and sing the hymns, tell the stories, praise Jesus and God and Joseph Smith, and rejoice together as we marched arm-in-arm into the Millennium. Then, me and the missus would fly off to some planet, far, far away, where we could try our hands at being God, ourselves. God and Mrs. God, as One, to see if we could do better than Jehovah.

I had no idea what I would do to support my anticipated family, except that it wouldn't be by farming. I trusted that God would make clear to me what He wanted me to be and do when the time came.

I had decided that when I was drafted for service in World War II, I would tell them I was a "conscientious objector." That wasn't an official Mormon designation, but I didn't understand the concept of *"Praise the Lord and pass the ammunition,"*—lyrics of a popular song during The War. I hated that song! With absolute clarity the Bible said *"Thou shalt not kill."* Period! He never said *"except for Germans or Japs or Eyetalians,"* no matter how terrible they were—and Jesus had commanded: *"Forgive your enemies,"* without excepting Italians, even though they were Catholics—*"the Great Abomination,"* according to Mormonism.

The only trouble with my ideas was that nobody agreed with me. I was amazed how many supposedly religious people were sending their sons and grandsons to kill or be killed by *"the enemy."* They would become very angry with me if I tried to say what we shouldn't be killing anybody. I was being *"unpatriotic"* and even sinful. I couldn't understand the concept of Jesus leading an army of "Christian soldiers, marching as to war." Jesus leading us into mortal battle didn't make sense to me. His mission was to save souls, not waste them.

It was like that with just about everything. The more religious I became, and the harder I tried to be *"good,"* the more people avoided me, kids as well as adults. They started calling me "Goody-Two-Shoes." For some reason I couldn't fathom, someone who really practiced what they preached was regarded as simple-minded. Someone who tried to be *good* and *honest* and *pure* was treated as *"holier than thou,"* and shunned, not cherished. It didn't make sense. The harder I tried, the less people liked me!

In 1947, at age fourteen, I became a freshman at *Uintah High School*, on the outskirts of Vernal. Across the street from the high school was the LDS *"Seminary*," a small church-like building housing a schoolroom and two teachers' offices. Once a week, all the Mormon children in the ninth grade studied *The Old Testament*. Sophomores studied *The New Testament*, and juniors studied *The Book of Mormon*. In each grade, I applied myself to Seminary with much greater interest than regular schoolwork. I diligently perused all of the books of The Bible and was one of the few students who could actually discuss the various books and chapters and characters. I could recite all the names of the books.

My other major activity and interest besides Mormonism was in *The Theatre*—acting, directing and finally writing plays. As a freshman, I had discovered acting and loved pretending to be someone else, escaping from the restrictions that was Dick Fullmer, Boy Saint. I could memorize the words someone else had written and was guaranteed to make an audience laugh at me when I spoke them loud enough.

I was good at all of them, acting, directing and writing, and they called me "talented" and gave me awards.

All of my extracurricular time was spent at Church or onstage, in one capacity or another.

I was allowed to skip Phys Ed and any of the sports that involved running because I couldn't run more than a few steps without developing a "stitch" in my groin. I later learned that it was the same feeling, as being kicked in the balls. It was agony, but no doctor could figure out what caused it. I just couldn't participate in sports.

This gave me even more time to immerse myself in religion and theatre.

Even though I was *good-looking*, not quite handsome, but not ugly, girls didn't like to go out with me, even though they were Mormon virgins looking for husbands. All I wanted to do was talk about *God* and *Jesus*. I rarely had a second date.

At the end of the third year of Seminary, in the spring of 1949, the "graduating" class was rewarded with a trip to Salt Lake City, where we would all be *"Baptized for the Dead"*—a Mormon innovation and tradition—in an enormous marble font on the backs of twelve life-sized golden oxen, symbolizing the twelve tribes of Israel, in the holy inner-sanctum of the Temple. We would then eat supper together, see a John Wayne movie, and stay overnight in one of the largest hotels in town, the *Hotel Newhouse.* All we had to pay was a small share of the room cost—we split up four to a room, two to a bed—and for meals, souvenirs, movies, or special treats.

Grandmother had often told me the story about the boy who was being baptized for the dead in the Temple: When he came up from each of the immersions, he could see the spirit of the person he had just helped join the Church, until finally all twelve were standing in the air around the rim of the font, transfigured, smiling gratefully at him. And then, suspended above everything, Jesus, *Himself,* his arms outstretched, silently thanking the boy for the wonderful work he was doing.

I prayed night and day that something like that would happen to me. More than anything else in this world, I wanted to see Jesus, and to know for certain how much He loved me.

In the white marble dressing rooms in the Temple basement, we were given white loose coverall-like garments, which covered us from ankle to chin, and concealed any trace of sexuality—at least, when dry. In groups of twelve, we were guided into the font, which looked like a huge bathtub resting on the backs of the gold-plated oxen. There were cold, wet steel steps going up, then warm marble steps leading down into the warm water, where the baptizer would take each of us in turn and prepare to dip us, saying loudly: *"Richard Fullmer, on behalf of...."* He would pause as an invisible reader pronounced a carefully researched name from an unseen list, *"John Jacob Jones,"* and the baptizer would repeat it, *"John Jacob Jones ... I baptize thee in the name of the Father, the Son and the Holy Ghost. Amen!"* Dip, rise, move one space around the font. Around and around we went, getting dunked for a dozen dead people apiece, and as I worked my way around the tub, I prayed fervently to be allowed to see Jesus—but by the end of the session, I had seen nothing, not even any grateful ghosts.

I tried not to be disappointed. I tried not to read any "hidden meaning" into the non-answer to my prayers. But it was hard not to think that maybe God was still angry with me for that word I had said, seven years ago. Or, maybe the truth was, *God just plain didn't like me*, and wouldn't answer my prayers no matter how good I was or tried to be. He hadn't answered any of them yet—as far as I knew—so maybe He never would.

After supper in the hotel cafeteria, we all went to see *Red River*, starring John Wayne and a new actor, Montgomery Clift, and I felt curiously *guilty* for thinking he was handsome and very exciting. After the movie we all bought snacks and headed back to our hotel rooms, about ten o'clock.

My roommates happened to be three of the most popular boys in high school, all athletes, all members of practically every club in school, and all presumably good Mormons. Arnie, Max and Dell shared another distinction, I discovered, when Arnie produced a pint of *Old Grand-Dad Whiskey* from a sack of fruit and sandwiches he had brought from home— and *I* was the only one who had to be asked if he wanted a swig.

At first I refused, righteously indignant, and not a little amazed— these were three of the "best" boys in town. Our religion strictly forbade alcohol; without a doubt, they were breaking a sacred law. But they passed the bottle around between them, as though it were nothing more than a bottle of root beer. Impulsively, I decided to risk everything I had gained during my six years of devotion, and accepted the bottle the third time around. It became a way to get back at Jesus for not showing up when I had prayed so hard. It was like saying *"I don't care. So there!"*

I had never tasted whiskey, or any alcohol, not even beer, but I managed to swallow the first searing gulp before it made me nauseous. The second one went down much easier. By the time the bottle was empty, I was feeling very light-headed and giddy.

When Dell drunkenly produced a package of *Lucky Strikes*, I excused myself and went into the bathroom. *"Well, fuck you!"* he called after me, then, *"No, never mind!"* They all laughed and started coughing. Tobacco was forbidden, just like alcohol! I was extremely apprehensive about breaking so many laws at the same time. I was also still surprised and shocked that the three Good Mormon Boys, who had just been Baptized for the Dead, in the Holy Mormon Temple, were out there drunk and smoking cigarettes, and talking about which girls' tits they had seen under those wet coveralls.

I hadn't noticed any tits; I had been preoccupied with the lumps I could see, through the warm clear water, in the crotches of the boy's coveralls. Some had looked like they might be hard.

I turned on the water in the bathtub, so I wouldn't have to hear what they were saying, then decided to take a bath. It seemed a little ludicrous, after having spent half of the day submerged to my shoulders, but the thought of a steamy, soothing bath was very inviting—and I had to get away from the smell of tobacco. I wanted very much to share that cigarette they were passing. After a little trouble undressing, I slipped into the warm water, quite drunk and relaxed. By this time, the boys in the next room were talking quietly, occasionally laughing, probably telling dirty jokes.

For a few minutes I relaxed in the warmth and buoyancy of the water, almost distracted from the events and disappointments of the day. Then someone coughed! It sounded like he was there in the room with me, but the door was closed, and there was no one behind me. The cough came again—from someplace directly in front of me. Then water splashed, as though someone had just moved in the tub—but it hadn't been me.

Then I noticed a tiny hole, slightly larger than a pencil, in the wall, carved through the plaster just above the water knobs and spigot. I knelt in the tub and leaned close to look through.

I saw a naked, handsome, well-built young man, his hair cut short, almost certainly a sailor or soldier, in a bathtub like mine, on the other side of the wall; he was facing me and I could clearly see that he was playing with his cock! As soon as I started watching, it got hard. He knew I was watching. I could tell, because he put on a show for me, arching his muscular young body above the water, stroking himself almost casually, until suddenly he groaned and shuddered and came, squirting all over himself!

I sat back on my heels, amazed, terrified—and more aroused than I had ever been! I had jacked off before, and had wet-dreams, of course, but nothing had come even close to the excitement I was feeling at that moment. It took only a few quick strokes and I shot more than I ever had before, and almost passed out from the thrill of it!

Guilt overwhelmed me immediately. I quickly soaped up and rinsed off—making sure that none of my semen remained on the tub—then hurried out to where Arnie and Dell were passed out on one of the two beds.

Max was sitting in the middle of the other bed in his shorts and t-shirt, smoking a Lucky. I secretly had a crush on Max. He was handsome and muscular, one of the school's star athletes I felt a frightening desire to get close to him, as close as possible, to press our bodies together and kiss each other. Instead, I quickly I picked up the package, lying beside him on the bed, and tapped out a cigarette. Max grinned and held out a lighter and flicked it for me. I took only one deep drag and the room started spinning and I almost toppled over. Max caught me, laughing, and then drunkenly guided and carried me back to the bathroom, where I threw up in the toilet.

He waited for me to clean up, then tucked me into bed and whispered "Sweet dreams, little buckaroo, you've had a busy day."

I had an almost overwhelming impulse to pull him close and kiss him, but I passed out instead.

I had a terrible hangover the next day.

MILESTONE 4: My First Catholic
1949, 16

A round the same time as the Seminary trip to the temple, during the spring of 1949, for all of my involvement in theatre-arts, I won a scholarship to a six-week summer Theater-Workshop at Denver University, in Denver, Colorado.

It marked the first time I had been away from home, by myself, for more than a day or two, and I had been eagerly anticipating my escape from Mom and Dad, and an association with other young people who excelled in some form of *Theater Arts*. In Vernal, I was the only student contemplating a career in "show business," and that choice was considered more or less insane by most of the kids I knew. This workshop would give me the chance to meet my real peers, and talk with someone who understood the excitement and fulfillment of *acting.*

The male scholarship winners, twelve of us, stayed in one of the fraternity houses, just off campus. We were not all actors; there were debaters, orators, stage-managers, etc. We would all be involved in the many different aspects of Theatre. It was D.U.'s method of recruiting students—and to use unused classrooms and frat houses during the summer.

On the evening of my first day there, I had just unpacked my suitcase, and was sitting at the foot of the small bed assigned to me, looking out the window of my little room, trying to decide what to do next, when a deep voice behind me said "Howdy there, new neighbor. My name's Ray. I'm from Kansas. Like Dorothy."

I felt a very strange rush of sensations as I turned to look at him. It was like going down in an elevator, or going very fast over a bump in a car. Ray Evans was a potential "leading man" if ever there was one:

brown wavy hair, in the currently-popular "duck's-ass" cut, very chiseled features, with a small dimple in his angular chin. He could have played Cary Grant's younger brother. He was wearing the national high-school uniform: Levis and T-shirt, penny-loafers and argyle socks.

For some reason, I felt almost giddy, knowing he was talking to me. "Looks like we're the early birds." he said. "I'm headed down to the Rec Room. They've got machines with sandwiches, and candy and all sorts of stuff. Also got a pool table. Do you play?"

"No. I don't know how." *Playing pool* was considered a *sin* in Vernal.

"Well, then, I'll teach you. C'mon."

He seemed like a very nice, intelligent, outgoing, friendly person— *and* he was interested in me. He seemed fascinated by my stories about where I lived and went to school, and what I was planning to do with my life. I had never had anyone pay that kind of attention to me and my plans or desires. I told him all about wanting to be the first in my family to graduate college. Then I would either go to New York or Hollywood and make my living (to rave reviews, of course) as an actor.

He told me about his life in Hutchinson, and his plans to go to college, except that he was considering a career in television.

All the time he was teaching me *eight-ball*, it seemed as though he kept posing for me. He would lean back against the wall, watching me, with his arms crossed and his hips thrust forward so that I could plainly see a *bulge* in his crotch. Now and then he would rub the lump, not at all secretly, but when he knew I was looking. I tried to ignore his actions, but found them very exciting.

After several games of eight-ball, which I learned to play fairly well, we bought sandwiches and *Cokes* (cola drinks, like coffee and tea, were forbidden by the Mormons) and went upstairs to his room to eat. We talked long into the night, our first night in Denver. I had no doubt that Ray had something on his mind that he wasn't saying aloud, and I guessed that he, like me, would like to do something more to express this feeling that we obviously shared. But neither of us made the move.

The next day, we got together at the student union for lunch and chatted like old friends as we went through the cafeteria line. As we started to eat, he crossed himself! I was seventeen years old, and only in the movies had I ever seen anyone actually make the *sign of the cross.* According to Mormon dogma, the Catholic Church was what the Bible called *"the abomination of desolation sitting in the holy place"*—shortened to simply *"The Great Abomination"*—the reason the rest of the world couldn't make Christianity work. Even the Jews, who had killed Jesus, were friends by comparison. Catholics were considered *The Enemy.*

According to my religion, this wonderful, charming, handsome, exciting new person in my life was my mortal enemy. I felt like something invisible was ripping me apart, like a tornado crashing around inside me.

I avoided Ray for the next few days, and on Sunday went to the nearest Mormon chapel for Sunday School. In class, taught by the Bishop of that Ward, I introduced myself as a Brother from Utah, at D.U. on a scholarship, and said that I had met someone in the workshop who seemed like a nice person, but that I suspected he was one of those *"you know, men who 'like' other men.* What should I do?"

The Bishop rocked back on his heels and squared his shoulders and clenched his fist and shook it at me as he said: *"Run from that man as you would run from a snake! He is an abomination in the sight of God!"*

Afterward most of the class avoided me, as though I frightened them, but one girl patted my arm and said: "It must be *the most terrible thing in the world, to be one of those people.* You should pray for his *poor tortured soul!"*

Of course, the question had not been just about Ray, it also had been about *me.* And I went back to the Frat house that Sunday, feeling absolutely wretched, knowing that, if I *ever* gave in to those *forbidden impulses,* my church would consider me an *abomination.* That would make Ray—if he really was *"one of those people"*—a double-abomination: a Catholic Queer!

When I finally got up the courage to approach Ray again, he had found a new friend. They were both polite, but distant, as though they had decided I wasn't worth bothering with.

I felt terrible. I had turned to my religion for help and comfort about something that was happening to me, and my religion had only gathered its skirts and screamed *"Sinner!"*

It hadn't helped me understand why I was haunted by ideas and images of what might have happened, had I not refused to recognize his overtures, that first night. In my imagination, I undressed and hugged and kissed Ray Evans, night after night—but we hardly spoke for the rest of the six weeks.

I gave all my time and energy to my role as Papa in *I Remember Mama*, and a tiny role in *Richard III*, which was presented in an outdoor theater for two weeks of balmy summer nights, as the "graduation" for the workshop. Then I got on a bus and went back to Vernal, knowing that something *monumental* had happened to me, but *terrified* of understanding just what that something had been.

As soon as I got home, I called Gwen, my girlfriend, for the last year, whom I tentatively planned to marry—when the time came—and suggested we get together soon, for a movie or something. Mostly I wanted to talk to her and, maybe, ask some "innocent" questions. She suggested that we go to see a new actor, Marlon Brando, in a movie called *The Men,* which was playing at one of Vernal's two movie theaters. We made a date for the next night.

The movie was about a wounded soldier, played by Brando, in a hospital, trying to adjust to normal life. *Marlon Brando looked almost exactly like Ray Evans!* All I could see, for two hours, was Ray. All I could think of was *Ray.* Leaving the theater, I had no idea what the story was about.

After the movie, I deliberately picked a fight with Gwen and took her home, suggesting that we split up.

I was angry and excited, and I jacked off as I drove home, imagining what it would be like to be with Ray, to touch him…kiss him…! But as soon as I came, I felt as though my world was about to come tumbling down on me!

I went back to see the movie again, the next night, to see what I had missed the night before, and as I walked into the semi-darkened theater, before the movie started, I noticed Leon Elkins was sitting in his usual seat, the second one in on the last row in the center.

It looked like he was waiting for someone to join him, and I had heard that was exactly what he was waiting for; whoever sat there next to him would be "accidentally" touched, then, if that person didn't get up and move, fondled, and then be asked for a ride home. Whoever took Leon home from the movies got a blow job. Leon was Vernal's *resident Queer*, and most of the boys in high school seemed to know about his services.

Instead of sitting next to him, I sat in the seat across the aisle, and throughout the movie, kept turning to see if he might be looking at me. He did, several times, but gave no sign that he wanted me to join him. After the movie, he got up and went out and started walking along Main Street, toward his home, east of town.

I ran to my car, my heart pounding, and followed him almost a block before he turned to look back, then I pulled up beside him. He didn't say a word, but just looked at me. "Would you like a ride?" I asked.

He studied me for a moment, then shrugged. "Sure. Why not?" I had never seen Leon outside the movie theater, and was amazed that, up close, in the light of the streetlight, he looked just like anyone else—a twenty- or twenty-five-year-old man. (Being *queer* had kept him out of the Army; he was one of the few young men his age left in town.) His voice wasn't *lispy*—as it was made out to be, when the boys told each other about their adventures with Leon. He had a nice voice, and a pleasant smile. But he didn't touch me.

We drove out into the boondocks, listening to romantic music on the radio. When I parked in a secluded place, my heart almost stopped when I looked over and saw his pants open, his cock arching up out of his fly. His smug grin seemed to dare me to touch it. He even turned in the seat to make it easier for me to get to. *"Suck on it,"* he whispered. *"You know you want to."* It looked like he was offering me a popsicle.

"No!" I was shocked that he would even suggest it. I wanted to tell him *he* was the *queer one, not me*, but I couldn't get the words out. That was what I had wanted *him* to do to *me*—and once he mentioned it, I couldn't stop wondering what it would *feel* like?

How would it feel to take that satiny-headed thing in my mouth? The idea made me nauseous, but it also made me tingle all over!

He reached over and took my hand and guided it to his cock, which jumped when I touched it! It was the first time I had ever touched another man's penis, and it felt like a kind of raw electricity was flowing between us!

"Jack it off," he ordered, as he unzipped my pants and fumbled to get my cock out of my shorts—but I came before he could get it out!

It took several more minutes for him to come. I was fighting nausea as I fumbled to masturbate him. Finally he pushed my hand away and finished himself, catching the stuff in his handkerchief. He gave a long, satisfied sigh, stuffed himself back into his pants, grinned at me, and said, *"Now* you can take me home."

Driving home with my shorts soaked with semen, guilt and remorse settled over me like a thunderstorm.

I spent several days and nights thoroughly depressed and confused. I knew I couldn't discuss it with either of my parents. They were certain to over-react—or, even worse, not react at all. I had no close friends I could talk to, or even distant friends who wouldn't instantly despise me if they found out what I had done. It was driving me crazy and I had to do something.

I finally decided to go to my Bishop, supposedly the most spiritual, understanding man in the Ward, and once again risk a humiliating rejection, to ask him *why* God would allow such a terrible thing to happen to someone as devout and faithful as I had been?

I rode my bike to his house, about two miles away from ours. His wife said he was out in the barnyard, fixing something in the stable. She said to go on back and talk to him there.

As I approached the corral, I could hear his voice, low, but sharp and angry, before I could make out the words. I could also hear a cow, bellowing and gasping. I could see, through the wide, low, stable feeding-window, Bishop McKee, with a pitchfork in his hand, stalking after a cow that was running away from him, bawling and limping, around and around the corral, with bright red trails of blood running down her flanks from where the pitchfork had obviously pierced her skin. He didn't see me looking through the manger.

"I'm gonna *kill* you!" the Bishop snorted furiously. *"You Goddamned fucking sonofabitch!"*

I backed slowly away from the window, his words echoing over and over in my head, then ran to my bicycle, and peddled as fast as I could, back home.

It was mid-afternoon and my parents were both at work in town. I marched out into the field where we had recently cut and bunched the hay. It was dry and hot and the air seemed to be humming. I planted my feet wide and looked up toward Heaven, and yelled *"Fuck!"* as loud as I could.

Nothing happened.

I had hoped for lightning, but *absolutely nothing happened.*

I clenched my fists and shook them at Heaven, took a deep breath, and yelled *"Fuck God!"*

In the silence that followed, my whole world wavered and then collapsed into ruins all around me—but there in that hayfield in Vernal, everything else went right on, *exactly as usual*, as though nothing at all had happened.

PART TWO

MILESTONE 5: The New Me
1950-52, 17-19

My last year of high school was very schizophrenic. Almost everyone treated me like the person I had been, before that catastrophic summer, and I pretended that nothing unusual had happened, but secretly, I had changed drastically. I had stopped going to church and was trying to stop judging myself and the world by Mormon standards. I stopped believing that I, somehow, owned the world just because I was a Mormon.

I had decided that I no longer wanted to associate with bigots and hypocrites who lied and cheated and swore worse than sailors, then went to church and pretended to be pious and holy. I had discovered that there were good people in this world who were not Mormons, who were often not even religious, and that, just because a man is supposed to be saintly, that is not necessarily, or even probably, what he really is.

More and more doubts and questions had come into my mind, over the years, and I finally decided, at age eighteen, that religion was all a bunch of lies, designed to control people with their fear of the unknown, and to keep them tithing. I hated to admit it, but Dad had been right, when he had remarked, every spring as long as I could remember, when he loaded the manure-spreader to fertilize the fields: "Well, I gotta go spread the gospel."

God was simply the adult version of Santa Claus.

Even so, I felt guilty and vaguely apprehensive, as though delayed lightning might yet strike. It wasn't that easy to get God and Jesus out of my life. There was an emptiness where comfort had been, questions for which there were no pat answers. There was a gnawing awareness that I had been duped, and I felt like the same kind of fool I had been as a child, tricked and cheated by those I had trusted most.

Even worse was the future. Suddenly, my expected exaltation with the resurrected Saints in Paradise was replaced with an enormous emptiness.

I decided that nothing in life was certain. And no one could be trusted. I was forging ahead into the unknown, all by myself.

And my parents didn't even notice.

Now, secretly, I looked at people in a brand new way—I was fascinated by penises, cocks, dicks, pricks, and felt terribly ashamed for it. Now I looked at boys' and men's crotches the way other boys looked at girls' breasts. I was amazed at the number of barely-concealed erections displayed by teenage boys. They got hardons at the strangest times. And whenever I saw the telltale protrusions, I felt a delicious but disturbing tingling in my own groin.

I pretended that I, too, went bonkers over big tits, but I had no comprehension of what that fascination was about. I secretly admired the flat, firm pectorals and muscular arms and legs of the basketball players and other athletes—like Max—and, of course, felt like a "Godless Sinner" because of it.

All of my life I had felt like something was "wrong" with me, but had never understood exactly what that was. Now I knew what was wrong: I was *Queer.* I was something that everyone hated and feared. I was something that most people thought was evil and "abominable." I was also a *criminal*, illegal in most of the civilized world. I had heard men say they would kill a Queer who made a pass at them. Or they'd kill him, even if he didn't make a pass, just because he was Queer. Everyone seemed to agree that it was perfectly okay to kill or beat up Queers, because they deserved it, *just for being Queer*. I had heard frightening stories about marines or sailors beating up on some pervert who had somehow got into the service by mistake.

Now, *I* was that *Pervert,* a *Deviate,* a *Sodomite,* an *Abomination in the sight of God,* wretchedly and *unforgivably Sinful*—according to most religions around the world. Even though I vowed and consciously tried to do everything I could to become something else, everywhere I turned were bulging crotches.

I tried masturbating to pictures in National Geographic of naked native girls with huge breasts, but nothing would happen until I ignored the magazine and closed my eyes and thought about Ray—or Leon, or Max!

Or that guy in the bath tub!

One amazing and likewise-memorable incident happened during my senior year, when I was directing and producing *The Uintah Thespian Society's Radio Show*, dramatizing children's stories, which I would adapt for radio, on our local station, *KJAM*, whose offices and studios were in the basement of the *Hotel Vernal*.

The parking lot was behind the hotel, and my car's windshield pointed directly at a first-floor hotel room window, with the blind and drapes open.

I was giving a ride home to two teenage girls who had been voices in the radio-play we had just finished. We had just got into my parents' car, all three of us in the front seat, and slammed the doors, when a man's hand and a hairy naked arm reached out from the left side of the window in front of us, using the drape to hide him as he reached for the cord to pull the blind down.

The window was wide and the hand couldn't reach the cord, so it reached up to a corner of the bottom of the blind, and pulled it down. You could see the man's shadow move across behind the blind as he held it down. After a moment, he released it—apparently thinking it was locked in place—and started to stand up, but the blind zipped up and went flapping around the top of the window, and there he was "in Vista Vision," good-looking, well-built, stark naked, with a large erection that curved upward.

He wildly scrambled to grab the flapping blind, or the dancing cord, which he finally did, then pulled the blind down and apparently knelt down behind it until he was sure it would stay pulled. It did this time.

I have often wondered if it really was an accident that exposed a horny naked man, or if maybe it was something he did on purpose, as an exhibitionist, and could claim "it was all an accident" if anyone complained.

I started the car and backed out of the parking space. None of us said one word about what we had all seen, as I drove away from the hotel parking lot, heading the car away from an incredibly vivid image. In a kind of "memory snapshot," the naked man's arms and legs are spread wide, jumping and flailing frantically as he tries to catch the flipping pull-cord, his balls and cock bouncing with each move. He looked like a spider, a naked human spider, a well-built and very well-endowed spider, scrambling for his web. It gave me a hard on and I jacked off after taking the girls home.

In the movies, instead of watching the faces, I found myself watching the crotches. Errol Flynn and Tyrone Power often displayed exciting bulges in those tights. All the other boys went crazy over Jane Russell's big tits in *The Outlaw*, but I got thrills and chills and a hardon over her unknown costar, Jack Butel, as Billy the Kid, who showed practically everything encased in skin-tight denim.

I hated myself for even noticing, let alone gawking at the bulges and protrusions in all the men's trousers and swimsuits, but I could not stop looking. (John Wayne and Roy Rogers and Gene Autry never showed anything.)

As a "fuck you" gesture to Mormonism, at age sixteen, I started smoking and drinking: *Fatima* or *Wings* cigarettes (fifteen cents a pack) and *Coors* (3.2 alcoholic content) beer. And, of course, if anyone at an unofficial high-school party offered it, any of the *hard stuff: "Yes I do, thank you very much!"* I was still too young to buy cigarettes legally, so I stole them from the drug store, or got them from a machine in the bus station—Lucky Strikes, Camels and Kools—or later, had someone else buy them for me.

That was the year *Alaric Alexander* came to UHS to teach Drama and Civics. He explained that his name was Teutonic, a family name after his great-great-great grandfather, or something. *"Rick"* smoked *Pall Malls*—secretly, of course; he would have been fired very quickly had the all-Mormon school board discovered that he smoked cigarettes, or drank beer, or secretly read *George Bernard Shaw* to his two favorite students, at his house, while all three of them smoked Pall Malls and drank Coors—or

Hills Brother's coffee, or Lipton tea, or Dr. Pepper, or "real" eggnog for Christmas and champagne for New Year's!

Rick was probably the first bisexual I'd met, although, at the time I had never heard of that particular sexual identity. He had come from a Good Mormon home, but had "strayed from the path." He was very interested in me, and in several of the other boys in the plays and drama class, and always managed to be in the dressing rooms back-stage, when the boys were changing costumes—but nothing ever happened that I knew about. He was equally fascinated by one particular girl, a senior, Mary Alice Warren, new also to UHS that year; her father was a doctor who had opened a new practice in Vernal that summer.

Mary Alice had grown up in Salt Lake City, and was extremely cosmopolitan, compared to the bumpkins of Vernal. She too smoked—Pall Malls, of course. Eventually, I heard, they got married.

My last year of high school, we became a threesome, "The Three Mousecatchers." We read plays together, saw movies together, drove all the way to Salt Lake City to see plays at the University of Utah, or touring companies at the Rialto Theater downtown. We also presented three very sophisticated plays that year: *My Sister Eileen, Years Ago,* and *You Can't Take It With You.* I student-directed the first, played "Papa" in the second, and was a Russian ballet teacher in the third. That year reconfirmed my decision that I wanted to be "An Actor," a Professional. Acting was fun. It was pretending to be someone else other than myself. It was a kind of temporary escape, or even "therapy." I was very good at it. I loved doing it.

I won a drama scholarship that year, to Brigham Young University, for a "reading" (a ten-minute monologue) of *Hamlet,* Act I. It was a major triumph for me, but I had no desire to go to the Mormon school, or to anything even vaguely connected with the church. I decided I would prefer to go the University of Utah, and Rick and Mary Alice encouraged me.

Mom and Dad were not at all impressed with the scholarship. They had promised to send me to college if I wanted to go. They would pay my bills, scholarship or not, until I could get a job and support myself. They didn't seem to care about honors or scholarships. Neither of them asked me why I had chosen the state university in preference to the religious one.

Less than a week after I graduated high school, in June, I hitchhiked to Salt Lake City to register for Summer School at "The U." I wanted to get as far away from Vernal as I could, as quickly as possible.

I was picked up by a traveling salesman, in his forties or fifties, much too old to arouse any interest in me. We stopped for coffee at a truck stop, about halfway to SLC, where the grouchy old man behind the counter annoyed me for some reason.

When we were on our way again, the salesman said "You don't like old men very much, do you?"

It was quite true, I hated old men: they were grumpy and mean and judgmental, but I said "I don't know... Why?"

"Did you know that homosexuals don't like old men?"

"I'm not a homosexual!" I snapped.

"Oh, really?" He paused meaningfully, looking sideways over his shoulder at me. "Well, I am."

Neither of us said another word for the rest of the trip. I sat hunched against the door, ready to open it and leap out if he tried to touch me. He let me off near a bus stop at the eastern edge of the city. As I got out of the car he called "See you in the park—sweetie!" He blew me a kiss as he drove away.

I was seething, and terrified. Apparently there was something about me that made people think I was Queer, but I didn't know what it was. I had often heard "It takes one to know one," but what unconscious signal had I given the salesman?

I didn't really believe that my dislike of old men had anything to do with it.

I didn't think I looked Queer. I thought of myself as "very average." While I didn't look like a "jock," or a "stud," I wasn't effeminate. Having grown up on a farm, I had a naturally lean and fairly muscular body, and I had very deliberately maintained a "masculine" attitude and carefully avoided doing anything that would label me unmanly. Rick had directed me in the finer points of looking and acting "butch" in the plays. ("Don't put your hands on your hips. Never raise your pinkie. Keep your voice deep, and slur your words just a little; do not articulate.")

I found a place to live that afternoon, an upstairs room in a boarding house only a few blocks from the university. Since it was summer, most of the students were away for vacation. There was only one other boarder in the house, a "Graduate Assistant" in Physics. Dick Rogers was very tall—maybe seven feet—very friendly and helpful, with a deep resonant voice, and a very large bulge in the tight tan pants he always wore. Within a week he had invited me into his bed, and I masturbated the biggest cock I had ever seen—and the next day moved out of the boarding house in a huff, telling the landlady that her other boarder and I "didn't get along."

She seemed to understand what I wasn't saying, but refused to refund any of my rent.

My next living quarters were in the barracks at Fort Douglas, at the far-east end of the university's campus, right up against the mountain. It was still summer, and the soldiers and cadets who usually lived there were off on some kind of maneuvers involving Korea. I had two tiny rooms, one with a bed, the other with a desk, and shared common bathrooms and showers with three or four other summer students, whom I rarely saw. I very deliberately avoided any situation that would put me with anyone in the showers or at the urinals.

It was there that I started writing my first novel, *To Themselves Unknown,* about a young college student discovering that he had homosexual desires, briefly exploring the "tortured 'Gay' lifestyle," but then finding the right woman, who would take him to bed and make a man of him. (I think by that time *Tea and Sympathy* had opened on Broadway, so I probably borrowed the improbable ending from that propaganda piece for the impossible ending for my story.) That ending got tossed before I finished college.

The window behind my desk looked out over almost the entire city, all the way out to the mountains by the lake, and I spent many nights sitting at my Royal portable typewriter, looking out over an ocean of sparkling lights, trying to tell my story—trying to figure out just what my story really was.

At the end of summer and the beginning of the new school year, the regular occupant of my rooms returned, so I had to move. I found a basement "Pullman apartment"—two rooms connected by an arch, one with a tiny kitchen-dinette with a hot plate for a stove, and the other with a couch that opened into a bed, plus a small bathroom with just a toilet, a tiny wash basin and shower that smelled of mildew and Clorox. From across the hall came the scent of cheap perfume.

Lyle Granville, about thirty, and almost ugly, worked as a clerk at Woolworth's downtown. He would come home from work, to the rooms opposite mine, and get "dressed up to go out," dousing himself with *Evening in Paris*. At first, I thought it was his sister I kept meeting in the hallway between us. Then it dawned on me that he went out—to dinner, or the movies, or wherever "she" went at night—dressed as a woman. (It didn't really do much good—he simply looked like an ugly woman.) I avoided him, but he didn't seem to care, or even notice.

One afternoon I went home at a time that I usually spent studying at the Student Union. As I fixed a sandwich in my kitchen, I heard strange noises coming from the rooms across the hall. There was a crash and a thud, and then something that sounded like a lost soul, crying for help.

Lyle's door was locked. I knocked and called "Is anything wrong in there?" At first there was silence, then a faraway voice moaned: "Outside! Please!"

I ran up the stairs and around to Lyle's side of the house, and there, sticking out of the ground-level half-window, was a pair of denim-encased muscular legs, and a picture-perfect butt, with a belt loop snagged on a nail in the middle of the window-frame. His weight and the head of the nail kept him in that position, unable to move backward or forward. I grabbed him under the legs and lifted him to unhook the loop, then guided the legs through the window, which swung closed behind him.

I went back to my rooms, leaving my door open, wondering if I should call the police, or the landlady?

In a few minutes, a very sheepish-looking young man, about my age and kind of cute, came from Lyle's apartment and paused in my doorway. "Hi," he said. "Hello, again." He grinned guiltily. "I guess you're wondering what I was doing."

"I guess you could say that," I said.

"Well...actually...uh...I was going to wait...for Lyle."

"He doesn't get home for several hours."

"I know. I mean...well...usually...I go to sleep...I just got off work... and he wakes me up...when he gets home...you know what I mean?"

I was fairly sure I had figured it out. "I'm not really sure that I do," I said. "What do you mean?" I was beginning to enjoy this little cat and mouse game. Usually I was the mouse, but this time I was the cat. "Come on in and tell me about it."

His expression changed from a defiant glower to a wide grin. He stepped inside quickly and closed the door behind him.

"Would you like a beer?" I asked, taking one for myself from the small refrigerator, built into the kitchen cupboard.

"Sure! I'd love a beer! Helps relax me, you know?" He remained by the door, his hand still on the knob.

"Right. Oh, I know all right." I gave him the beer. "So sit down and relax." I pointed toward the very-worn overstuffed chair, then sat on the couch. He took a long swallow of beer, then sat beside me on the couch, spreading his legs until his knee touched mine. At the same time he leaned back and groaned, and I could see the outline of his hard cock under the denim. My own cock was responding. Here was a masculine-seeming young man, very obviously inviting me to have sex with him. And I wanted to, desperately, but at the same time I was terrified of what I wanted to do for him.

He took my hand and placed it on his erection, then he leaned back, his arms across the back of my couch, and waited. I wanted to be angry with him. I wanted to stop doing what I was doing, and tell him to go away, but it felt so good. It gave me a strange sense of power: he wanted something that I could give him. I could give him pleasure and release. So I unbuttoned his jeans and pulled out his cock and jacked it off. He caught the semen in his hand and bounded into the bathroom, slamming the door. I heard the water running for a long time and began to wonder if maybe he'd slashed his wrists or something. Then he came out and walked straight to the door, without looking at me. "Please don't tell Lyle about this."

"I won't," I promised. And I didn't. But I moved out at the end of the month. I discovered that Lyle had several other young boyfriends, and I would not allow myself to be caught in another situation like the last. It was humiliating how I so easily gave in and did what they wanted, without getting a thing done to me in return. I had to take myself out of harm's way.

I didn't succeed, of course. I ended up in an apartment building, right next door to Alex and John.

Alex had a beard and almost white, wild Albert Einstein hair; he was a graduate student, working on his doctorate in music. His thesis was on Bach's *Art of the Fugue.* John was very tall and thin and almost handsome; he was a waiter in Salt Lake's poshest restaurant on the top of the Hotel Utah. They invited me to Christmas dinner, and we ended up, drunk on wine and eggnog, on the plush white rug in front of their twinkling Christmas tree, listening to Bach, sucking each other's cocks while performing very athletic twistings and turnings to the music.

It was my first "threesome." It was also the first time I had actually put one of those things in my mouth, and I was amazed when I didn't throw up! I discovered I could take it all the way down my throat and still breathe. There was something incredibly intimate and thrilling about it, and, in fact, it excited me more than anything ever had, especially when someone else was doing the same thing to me at the same time. As they were, to *Jesu, Joy of Man's Desiring!*

But as soon as I came, the guilt and remorse returned, and I quickly excused myself, got dressed and hurried next door to my own bed, where I cried myself to sleep because I had defiled Christmas.

At the end of spring quarter, I decided to take the summer off. My parents had sold their home in Vernal, and were packing to move to Citrus Heights, California, a farming and citrus-growing community about 20 miles east of Sacramento, where another of my Dad's brothers and his family had a little farm. I decided to help them move. Afterward, I planned to spend the summer exploring San Francisco and the seacoast, coming back to Utah in time for the fall quarter.

We had worked it out that I would meet Mom and Dad on a Saturday morning, in Salt Lake, where I would take over driving the rental truck, and they would follow in the Buick and trailer. That left me Friday night with nothing to do. I decided to go to a movie, but after wandering around downtown, trying to decide what to see, I passed by a place I had heard about: The Beehive Lounge, across from the Hotel Utah. Supposedly, it was a "semi-Gay" bar, where the college crowd hung out. I was still under age, but I looked older—I had definitely "aged" my first year in college; for one thing, my hair was beginning to recede.

After an hour or so, walking around and around the block, I decided to take a chance and go inside. I had a fake ID if I needed it (I'd changed the date on my draft card) but nobody ever asked. It was so dark it was hard to tell how old or young anybody was. I sat at the bar, and when my eyes finally adjusted to the darkness, I noticed, in the mirror behind the bar, a pair of eyes looking directly into mine.

I turned away, then looked back, and he was still staring straight at me, or, my reflection in the mirror.

I turned to look toward him, sitting on a stool down the bar, and he turned toward me, grinned and nodded. I nodded back.

He bought two bottles of beer, then came over to me. "Let's sit over here." He led me to a dark booth. We sat across from each other and his leg tentatively pressed against mine. "Hi! I'm Dave," he said. "I've seen you at school. I work in the Union cafeteria. I guess you haven't noticed me."

I studied his face; it was unlikely that I had noticed him before; I would have remembered. His deep-brown eyes were incredible. They seemed to be sparkling. His grin was contagious. He laughed as though he was truly having a good time, and I laughed with him. I was captivated. He was wooing me. And he was certainly succeeding in getting me excited.

Finally we left the bar and got into his car, which he drove out west of the city and parked.

The springtime air was crisp and brilliantly clear—you could see the twinkling lights of towns many miles away. The radio was playing, and Rosemary Clooney was singing *"Come on-a my house."*

He moved across the seat, but instead of grabbing my crotch, he took my face in his hands and kissed me. I had never been kissed like that by anyone, let alone another man, and the most incredibly sweet sensations started cascading through my body. I wrapped my arms around him and kissed him passionately, feeling I had waited all my life for this. He responded with equal excitement.

With the doors open, we jockeyed into a sixty-nine position, where we took each other all the way down, and came into each other at the same time, and then lay there tenderly holding each other for what seemed like hours as Doris Day sang *"Once I had a secret love..."*

MILESTONE 6: My First Lesbian

1952, 19

All the way from Salt Lake to Citrus Heights, driving the rental truck, all I could think of was Dave Smith. I was in love. There was no doubt about it. He was gentle and sweet, but not soft or effeminate, and was very good at sex. The best I'd ever had. He was bright, and pleasant, and most important, he had liked me enough to give me his name and phone number. I assumed that meant that he wanted to see me again. I convinced myself that he might even be feeling about me the same way I was about him.

I had never felt anything quite like the sensations and emotions we had seemed to be sharing last night, and I couldn't imagine his not feeling the same things.

As soon as we had unloaded the truck and trailer into the old farmhouse Dad had rented, I caught the train in nearby Roseville, and went back over the mountain and the desert to Salt Lake City, where I called the number Dave had given me in the train station phone booth. His mother answered and went to get him.

"Hi, this is Dave. Who's this?"

Just the sound of his voice made my heart jump and skip a beat. "Hi," I said, "It's Dick."

"Who?"

"Dick Fullmer."

"I'm sorry. Do I know you?"

"Last Friday!" I said desperately.

"Oh. Oh, right…yes…right. I remember." He paused uncomfortably. "I thought you were in California."

"Well, I was, but I decided to come back."

"*Why?* I mean, you were *right there*, almost to *The City!* I mean, why come back *here?*"

It was not the response I had wanted. Clearly he was not overjoyed to have me back. It even sounded like he might be wishing I had not come back at all.

I tried to think of a reasonable excuse for making such a stupid mistake. "Well…I, uh, decided…to…uh…try to…you know, *find a job?* Remember, right at first, we talked about working this summer? You said you were a *supervisor* at *Lagoon*, and maybe could get me a job, *remember?* Well…I decided I needed the money more than I needed to see the ocean."

"Oh…." he said flatly. "Well…okay. I'm going to be out there hiring all week. Why don't you come on out? I'll try to make sure you get something, okay, but I can't guarantee what. Okay?"

"Sure. Thanks a lot."

"Okay. Well, listen, they're waiting supper for me, so I gotta go. Nice talking to you…Rick. See you."

I sat in the large empty waiting room of the train station and wondered if I ought to just heave myself under the next locomotive to come through. What an idiot! I had thrown away a vacation in San Francisco for nothing. I didn't want a summer job at Lagoon. I wanted a lover!

Something inside me seemed to harden. A door closed. I had made a fool of myself once again. *Love*, I decided, like Santa Claus and God, didn't exist. If you believed in any one of them, you opened yourself to disappointment and pain. Obviously Dave hadn't felt any of the emotions I had experienced. He had no desire to do it again. He didn't even remember my name. He'd called me *"Rick."*

I finally decided that somehow I had made it through the deaths of Santa Claus and God, and somehow I would make it through this similar crisis. And, maybe, some day, somehow, there was a chance that Dave would change his mind if we worked together every day.

I bought a paper and found a small apartment for rent, close to the railroad station, where I would have to catch the *"Bamburger Car"* (an electric trolley that ran between Salt Lake and Ogden, passing Lagoon on the way) to work. The apartment was in the basement of a typical sturdy Mormon brick house like those lining the streets of most Utah cities and towns.

Lagoon was an amusement park, halfway between Ogden and Salt Lake City, which boasted an enormous swimming pool. Signs along the highways and all around the park proclaimed *"Swim in water fit to drink."* (The *inside joke* was "Pee in water not fit to swim in.") They hired mostly college kids, for very low wages and small percentages of the "take." There were carnival rides and games, a dance pavilion and a funhouse where a woman's recorded voice laughed raucously, constantly, endlessly, over and over and over, from ten in the morning until ten o'clock at night. (Alfred Hitchcock used it in one of his movies.)

My game booth was right next to the funhouse, and right across the midway from the dance pavilion. I had charge of the *"Greyhound Races"*— eight metal *"dogs"* which "raced" in jerky progress up a track, according to which player could bounce his ball through the hole fastest. Winners received tickets called *"points"* which they could eventually trade for ashtrays or kewpie dolls, or, for the really big spenders, a giant stuffed Panda or Teddy Bear, at the Prize Center.

Dave was my boss that summer—he was Supervisor of Games—and he treated me like all of the other employees, as though we had never shared those incredible hours, which had been for me some of the most exciting of my life. "I'm not really Gay," he told me. "I was just out for a little fun that night." Actually, he was engaged to a beautiful girl named Donna. He was perfectly friendly, and helpful, and encouraging, but he was like that for all his charges. Everybody liked working for Dave. I wanted to hate him, but I couldn't—he was too nice a guy. So I hated myself instead.

I felt more rejected than I ever had before. Apparently I had been born with some kind of flaw which made me unpalatable to most people. Everyone from my Dad to Dave Smith considered me less than important. I seriously considered suicide.

I also started hanging around the Beehive Lounge, hoping that lightning might strike twice. It didn't, but one night, after the bars had closed at two o'clock, I was drunk and horny, walking alone on an empty street, headed back to my basement room near the train station after several frustrating hours at the bar. I noticed a car driving slowly past, turning at the corner ahead, then, in a few minutes, driving past again. There were five passengers in the car, and they all looked like teenage Mormon boys. They drove around the block three or four times, then finally pulled over to the curb and one of them leaned out the window and told me "We're looking for a Queer to suck our cocks."

With hardly a hesitation, I told them they had found what they were looking for, and they took me to the City Cemetery, where I sucked off each one of them, as they took turns lying on one of the graves. I fully expected to be at least beat up, if not killed, but something I did or said— or didn't do or say—changed their minds, and they even took me back to where they had picked me up. I wished, then, that they had killed me because I felt like the most contemptible whore on earth and wanted to die.

A few nights later, after everything in the park had closed except the dance pavilion, I was sitting at the train stop, waiting for the next trolley into Salt Lake. It was after midnight, and most of the park's workers had gone home. Suddenly a huge dark shadow stepped out of the darkness and sat beside me. "Why are you looking so fucking depressed?" It was Chris!

"Chris" Christensen worked *"the Whip,"* an adult version of the *Tilt-a-Whirl*. It had huge levers and gearshifts that usually required a man to manipulate, but Chris was bigger than any of the men at Lagoon. She was about six-foot-six, and exercised with barbells. In the pool, she wore men's trunks and a woman's brassiere.

I was terrified of her and tried to be polite but distant. "Oh...hi, Chris. It's okay. You wouldn't understand."

"Oh? Wouldn't I?" she asked. "You're Gay, aren't you? You know I am, don't you? What makes you think I wouldn't understand?"

"You're *Gay?"*

"What'd you think I was?"

"I didn't think anything!" I declared defensively.

"Yeah, right. Some people think I'm a *hermaphrodite*, but I'm not. I'm just a Lesbian. You know about *Lesbians*, don't you? What am I, your first *Dyke?"* She laughed and squeezed me so tight it hurt. "Hell, you're

still wet behind the ears. You need to learn a lot more stuff about the world before you kill yourself."

"I wasn't really going to."

"No, but you've been thinking about it. I've been watching you."

"You have?" I was almost flattered. "Why?"

"You reminded me of me a few years ago, when I first figured it all out. I used to sit right there where you are and look at the trolley car coming, figuring I could jump right in front of it, and they wouldn't be able stop in time to keep from running over me. What a messy way to go. And you might just get mangled and not die, y'know? Have your arms or your legs cut off, or something else, and then where would you be?"

I couldn't help laughing. "Nowhere I want to be!"

"You bet your ass! C'mon, I'll give you a ride home."

"But you ride a motorcycle!"

"It rides two. C'mon. You'll love it!" She practically dragged me into the parking lot. I was terrified the entire way into town. It was a *"Harley Davidson, top of the line,"* with shiny black fenders and lots of chrome, but still, it had only two wheels, and I knew that a little tilt too far on either side could send it spinning. I sat scrunched on the hard little seat behind her, over the rear wheel, with the wind screaming past my ears, holding on for dear life. It was a thrilling experience, but not one I was eager to have again.

I could hardly move when we finally stopped—not in front of my apartment, but in front of a bar on State Street, one I'd heard about but had never had enough courage to go inside. *The Crystal Lounge* was where the hard-core homosexuals hung out—Salt Lake City's *"dykes and faggots."*

"You been here before?" Chris asked.

"No!"

"Well, prepare for *baptism by immersion*, sweetie. In we go!" She pulled the door open and ushered me into a new world.

The *Crystal Lounge* was physically similar to most of the other "lounges" downtown ("bars" that sold 3.2 beer on-tap and "setups"— for real liquor, purchased at the State Liquor Store): a long narrow room with a high ceiling, booths along one side, a bar with stools on the other; behind the bar was a huge mirror with displays of stacked glasses, punch boards, and miscellaneous bar stuff. Lots of neon signs for different beers reflected in the mirror and glasses. It wasn't strictly a *Gay bar*—there was no such thing in Utah in the fifties—other regulars included several whores and a group of deaf-mutes, all of us outcasts who put up with each other for a safe haven, but it was the closest Salt Lake City could come to "the real thing." Strangely it was owned and operated by three Greek brothers who tended bar in white aprons and had very little to do with the crowd besides serving us. They obviously weren't Gay.

That night there were three or four men sitting along the bar, and about a dozen others in small groups in the booths. The music was so loud, it was difficult to talk over it. The sound was punctuated from time to time with even louder squeals of laughter from one or another of the booths. It was a sound that I learned to associate with Gay bars everywhere in the country.

We sat in a booth near the front door and ordered beers. As I watched the often-extravagant action in the room, I told Chris, "I feel like this is the point of no return."

"Oh, no," she laughed. "You passed that point a long time ago. You've been what you are all of your life. This is just…well…like turning on the lights to see where that is. Y'know? Wherever you are, you're still you, right? It's like click! 'Well, sonofabitch, I'm *here*!' And, let me tell you, Richard, it isn't nearly as bad as they say."

Everyone seemed to know Chris, who seemed to know all the habitués of the Crystal, and I met most of them over the summer. Almost all of the regulars were male, but there were several Lesbians who took an active part in Salt Lake City's *Gay life*, such as it was. There were occasional parties, where most of the active Gays (twenty or thirty) were invited—*drag parties* more often than not, where the women would dress like men with penciled sideburns and moustaches, and the men would dress like whores and travesties of women. According to Chris, there was always a *drag-party* somewhere for Valentine's Day and Halloween and New Year's Eve.

Chris spent the rest of the summer shepherding me (she got annoyed if I suggested she was "mothering" me) into my new lifestyle. She helped me understand that it was not a bad thing to be Gay, it was just *different.* "True, it's illegal," she would say, "but that's because the rest of society are stupid idiots! In Utah, they're twice as bad because they're stupid *Mormon* idiots!" She hated Mormons with a passion I had not yet encountered, but would see again and again over the years as I met other Gays who had left—*or been kicked out of*—the church. She tried to help me stop hating myself by introducing me to others who didn't hate themselves. She obviously had no problem with what she was, and several of the others seemed quite content with being what they were. I resolved to try very hard to accept being who and what I was—except I hadn't quite decided what that really was, or might be.

I knew I was not a "nellie queen," even though almost everyone seemed to automatically assume that I would be—*once I "came out"*—with proper care and training, if necessary. Acting like that just embarrassed me. I knew there was no doubt that I was sexually attracted to men, but I was repelled by the outrageous effeminacy that so many of the *"Gay boys"* seemed to consider their true nature. I had never felt like a woman trapped in a man's body, and I didn't want to have sex with someone who did. I had no desire to wear dresses or women's panties. What I really wanted was another man. Someone like myself. *Someone queer like me.*

In the novel I was writing, instead of meeting the woman who would seduce and save him, the hero instead met a Lesbian who introduced him to the man of his dreams, and, after a brief boy-loses-boy twist in the plot, the two of them bought a little farm in Arizona where they raised championship horses and lived happily ever after.

It was not the last time I was to change the ending of *"To Themselves Unknown."*

At some point in my early college years, I took *Abnormal Psychology.* One of the texts was Donald Webster Cory's *The Homosexual in America.* It was the most enlightening, insightful, up-to-date books I'd read about the subject and I mailed a copy to my mother, and asked her to read it and then give it to Dad after she had finished reading it. I told her in the letter with it that I was "Gay" and that this book would explain what that meant.

Several months later, when they were in Salt Lake, visiting Grandmother, I got Mom aside and asked what Dad had said after reading the book. "Oh, he didn't read it. He said it was too much like school."

"Did you talk about me being Gay?"

"Oh, a little. Not much."

"Well, what did he say?"

"Well, he said... 'What fun is that?'"

"That's *all?*"

"Yes, dear, that's all."

And that is all my Dad ever said about my lifestyle. "*What fun is that?*"

Many things he did or said let me know that he didn't approve, either of me, or my way of life or the people I brought home to meet the folks, but nothing was ever said aloud. It was like when I told him I wanted to be an actor: All he said was *"Ok. If that's what you want."* He wasn't being broad-minded, or accepting, or fatherly, he really didn't give a damn.

In fact, now I'm convinced that he secretly hoped I would make a mess of my life—as I certainly seemed to be doing—and it amused him to watch me destroy myself. He probably taunted Mother with his assessment of me and my boyfriends. I was his weapon against her. And I didn't know it or even have a clue.

I lost touch with Chris after that summer. The last I heard, she had moved to Los Angeles to live with her *"Femme,"* Sandy.

MILESTONE 7: Mobius Trips
1952-53, 20-21

L ate in the summer of 1952, I sent a letter to my draft board, telling them that I was an active homosexual, and soon received a new draft card in the mail, featuring my new status: 4-F.

I promptly altered the card so it looked like I was old enough to drink beer.

After Lagoon closed, I decided I was sick of Salt Lake City and Mormons and drag queens and dykes, so I took the bus back to Roseville, where my parents met me and took me to see their new home, a neat little two-bedroom frame house on three acres of farm land in Citrus Heights. They had built it themselves over the summer.

Mother's headaches had been getting worse. I tried to talk her into getting help, tried to convince her that seeing a psychiatrist did not mean you were "crazy," it simply meant you had a psychological problem which made you tense, which made your head ache. Finally she tentatively agreed and I asked her medical doctor for a referral, made the appointment, drove her to the office, where I asked to speak to the doctor first, before he interviewed her. I told him the history of her headaches, and then added that I was a homosexual, thinking that was something she probably wouldn't tell him, but that he ought to know.

He leaned back in his chair, appraising me, grinning smugly: "Well, *that's* what's causing the problem," he said, with absolute certainty. "If you'd just *straighten up and fly right*, your mother's headaches would go away." He snapped his fingers. "Like that!"

She spent a few minutes in his office, then came out shaking her head. She smiled at me briefly. "No," she said, with definite finality. *"No."*

I was in something like a state of shock, and furious with the man—his attitude didn't reflect the "newer" ideas in the "*modern* psychology" field, which I had been studying in college, which held that homosexuality was a natural state, but that society's treatment of homosexuals often made them neurotic or psychotic.

I believed that mother's headaches were, indeed, in part, a reaction to my being Gay, but had much more to do with her unending, undeclared war with my dad. I dropped the matter. But I couldn't get his smug voice out of my mind: *"Straighten up and fly right!"* That was the name of a song by The Andrews Sisters during the war, which I hated—the song *and* the war!

I decided to stay in the area for a while, and got a job at *McClellan Air Force Base* as a clerk-typist. I managed to locate the two Gay bars in Sacramento; one was *The Topper,* downtown Sacramento, and was very much like the one I had fled in Salt Lake City, where the "piss-elegant" crowd called each other "bitch," or "cunt" or "nellie faggot," and referred to themselves as "queens."

The other place, called *Sully's Stop,* was on the old highway 99, toward Fresno and Bakersfield, just outside the city limits, where the crowd was split about half-and-half Gays and Lesbians. The regulars were much quieter and less flamboyant, and I started hanging out there on Friday and Saturday nights.

One Saturday afternoon in November, 1952, I was playing eight-ball with my "pool buddy," a Lesbian named Pat, about my age, nineteen or twenty. We started talking, jokingly at first, about getting married and moving to San Francisco—not for sex, but for convenience. There was no doubt that single people who were suspected of being Gay were very much discriminated against, but even if a married couple *acted* Gay, they were not suspect. Marriage was obviously a ticket to acceptance, or at least, less intolerance.

We were both drunk, and got carried away with the idea. We bought a six-pack, then drove her car to Stateline, Nevada, two hours up the mountain from Sacramento, and got married by a Justice of the Peace with his wife, in her bathrobe, hair in curlers, as a witness. We drove back to Sacramento, to our separate homes, and made plans to move to San

Francisco, where Gays weren't treated as badly as in Sacramento or Salt Lake City. There were dozens of Gay bars in The City—as well as bath houses and huge parks where Gay men cruised more or less openly.

I quit McClellan and moved, with Pat, into a two bedroom apartment on Haight Street. Our first day there, Pat went out with long blonde hair and came back with a crewcut. Several days later, our landlady asked me, "Whatever happened to your wife? I see your little brother now and then, but I haven't seen your wife since you first moved in."

Actually, neither had I. The rather attractive and relatively feminine girl I had married had very quickly found a niche with a bunch of *"Leather Dykes,"* who rode very noisy motorcycles and dressed in black leather with skulls and crossbones all over them. Pat said she was planning to trade her car for a "bike." It all terrified me!

I said as much to a man I met in one of the bars. Bill Jenkins was probably in his early thirties. He was from Florida, and seemed very wise, and very nice, and very interested in me. He suggested that I get out of the marriage as quickly as possible, before the Leather Dykes decided to torture or kill me just for fun—maybe as Pat's "Satanic Sacrifice" so she could join the club.

I agreed that I had made a terribly stupid mistake, and he offered to help me extricate myself from the situation.

The next day, he helped me buy a car in return for driving him to Florida. He explained that he had a medical condition, a bad back, that made driving, or riding the bus or train, excruciatingly painful, but that he could ride in a car if someone else drove. He made the down payment, but I would have to make the future payments and could keep the car once we got to Florida. It was a Morris Minor, England's answer to the Volkswagen. We drove it to Reno where he helped me get the marriage annulled. He brought along a bunch of pillows that he arranged in the passenger seat and seemed quite comfortable.

There was another "unspoken condition" to the gift of the car: going along with his strange sexual game, which was for me to let him seduce me, whenever he felt like it, then to verbally abuse him while he sucked me off and masturbated himself. He did not want to be touched, or kissed, and especially not fucked. He wanted nothing to do with what he called "romance." He wanted to be called nasty, dirty names and commanded to do lewd and indecent and very exciting things to me.

He gave me more attention and sex in our cross-country trip than I'd ever had, or even imagined. In return, I asked no questions when he would tell me to wait in the car while he went into antique stores in each city and town we passed through. In each store, he would buy a trinket or two—a silver salt-and-pepper set, a Dresden figurine (he was incredibly knowledgeable about antiques)—which he would then sell in the following town.

In this way, he told me, he kept us in cash ("just a game to prove I can do it") from San Francisco to Mobile, Alabama—where we were arrested, with sirens wailing and red lights flashing, in the parking lot of our motel. We were taken in separate Police cars to the Mobile County Jail, where, without any process at all, due or otherwise, I was shoved into a jail cell with seven other "criminals," and then ignored.

I had no idea what was wrong. I was not allowed to talk to Bill Jenkins, and, in fact, never saw him again. I could only assume that we had been arrested for being homosexuals. I had heard that they really hated Queers in the South, and could send me to a prison where some guy with tattoos would beat me to death if anyone found out my terrible secret.

I discovered something during my stay in that jail: none of the "crooks" in my cell, or those adjoining, were anything like the images I had seen, or read about—and accepted as true—in books and the movies. These men ranged in age from nineteen (me) to fifty, "Doc," and were like "regular" guys, but down on their luck. Maybe less-educated, but nice guys. Nobody was *evil* or *mean*. They were all awaiting arraignment or trial for misdemeanors, mostly robbery.

"Doc," the oldest of the group, a good-looking man with silver-grey hair and a beard, had been a college professor, fired for some infraction, and had become a "hobo," moving across the country with the seasons, working as a farmhand. He was a brilliant man who knew all sorts of information, but he hated the cops with a passion, and had an endless war going with them. He had been arrested this time for stealing some fruit from a market. It was there, in jail, that I first learned that the police were not necessarily the good guys. *Or vice versa.*

Through some inter-jail connection, Doc could buy cigarettes and candy. Several times he bought *3 Musketeers* bars and made hot chocolate for all of us. He broke the chocolate bars into small pieces, which he then mixed with water and heated over a toilet-paper roll stuffed with toilet paper burned in the sink. We each had a small cup of hot chocolate, courtesy of Doc the Hardened Criminal.

The Cops were the nasty ones. Their word was *Law*, and they knew it. The FBI, on the other hand, were perfect gentlemen. It was like they were the "good guys" to the cop's "bad guys." They questioned me twice, briefly, on the seventh and tenth days, and finally explained to me what had been going on: Bill Jenkins, *aka Bud Brewster, aka Felix Cattell,* and probably many other aliases up and down the coasts and across the country, was wanted in Florida on several outstanding warrants for everything from robbery to fraud—for spending an old woman's fortune while he posed as her male nurse and kept her drugged out of her senses until she finally died and he left the state—on her money.

One of the agents took a checkbook from a manila envelope and showed it to me. It was an old one of mine, on a Salt Lake City bank, that I had forgotten. "This checkbook was in Mr. Jenkins' pocket when they arrested him. He finally told us that he found it in your apartment in San Francisco. He gave these checks to antique store owners, all across the country, while he was posing as Richard Fullmer, an *antique dealer* from Salt Lake City. He told us you had no idea what he was doing. He called you 'very innocent.'"

He would go into an antique store and buy a couple of expensive items, usually totaling a thousand dollars or more, and would pay them with one of my checks and tell them "As soon as the check clears, send the item to my antique store in Salt Lake. That's my address on the check." Then, on the way out, he would pick up some small item, for twenty or thirty or fifty dollars, and say *"I love this!* It's a genuine something-or-other. How much *more* do I owe you for it? I'll write another check."

Almost always the response was "Oh, please, just take it. I won't charge you any more." Even if he had to give them a new check, he still got the trinkets for nothing. Bill would thank them profusely, put the small item in his pocket—and sell it for cash in the next antique store along the way. Then he would repeat the process in the next town. He knew that the checks would bounce, but nothing had been lost by the antique store owner except a couple of trinkets. No need to report an embarrassing scam.

The owner of a store in Mobile had recognized a set of *Dresden china*, which Bill had tried to sell to her, as having belonged to a friend of hers who owned a store in Baton Roug*e*. When she called to ask about it, her friend said the china had been purchased with a bad check—one of mine. The police had been called and were waiting for us at the motel when we returned from a day of sightseeing.

While in jail, we had missed Mardi Gras in New Orleans, our next proposed stop after Mobile.

Finally the FBI agent said "Did you know your friend was a *practicing homosexual?*" He spat out the words as though they had been *"insane murderer."*

I tried to look as shocked and outraged as I could without overacting. "No!" I lied. "He never said a thing! He never touched me!"

His expression clearly told me he knew I was lying. "I see. Well," he said, *"he would have.* You can bet on it. He would have filled your veins with heroin and done whatever he wanted with you. He's done it before, and you can bet he was planning to do it again. You're lucky we stopped him in time."

On the eighteenth day I was taken to the same little room, where a police detective tossed a manila envelope onto the table between us. "Make sure everything's there, then sign that paper." The envelope contained my wallet keys, and about fifteen dollars in cash. "Consider yourself lucky," he growled, "and get the hell out of Mobile, and don't ever come back. We don't like your kind around here."

My Morris Minor had been repossessed and returned to San Francisco. I called my parents from the lobby of the jail, and they sent enough money by Western Union for me to take the Greyhound bus back across the country to Roseville.

They met me at the bus station with bad news of their own: Dad had leased a service station near their new house, but in the year of the lease he had used up most of the money he had saved over the years.

He had written to Utah Power and Light about his predicament, and had been offered the job of a building and grounds maintenance helper at a substation west of Salt Lake City, where the job included a two-bedroom house on the substation grounds. He had accepted the job.

They had already found a renter for their new house in Citrus Heights, so I helped them pack up and move back to Salt Lake City, Utah.

I decided I didn't want to go back to college, but to try finding some kind of work in Professional Theatre in New York City. I packed a suitcase and had a friend drive me to the eastern edge of Salt Lake, where I started hitch-hiking across the country, on Highway 40, spending each night and sharing motel rooms with the men who picked me up, surprised at the number of married men and fathers who gladly accepted a blow job or two in payment for the ride and bed. I didn't spend a penny for transportation or lodging the entire trip.

The idea of being in New York City was incredibly exciting, but the actual experience of the city was overwhelming and frustrating. I had never seen so many people packed so closely together, except in movies and newsreels. It was claustrophobic. I found a job almost immediately with a theatrical press agency, but it seemed like I couldn't concentrate. It was as though some kind of sputtering electricity was churning around in my brain, confusing and diverting me. Even though I got free passes to any of the shows we were promoting—*Porgy and Bess*, *The King and I*, *Picnic*—I couldn't relax and appreciate the shows; it was like trying to enjoy sitting on an anthill.

With one notable exception, all of my sexual adventures in New York were unmemorable. I had discovered a Gay bar fairly close to where I had rented a tiny room in a huge brick apartment house. *The Blue Parrot* seemed to attract at least some of the kinds of men I found interesting. One such cruised me, one night, and took me home with him. He was shorter than I, very sexy in jeans and a T-shirt, thin, but well-built and, as it turned out, well-hung, and an excellent cocksucker. The only thing unusual about him seemed to be that he shaved his body—and he needed a shave.

When it was over, we were smoking, lounging naked in his living room, talking about me and Mormons and Utah. I remarked that in Salt Lake City, I couldn't find the kind of "butch" Gays that excited me.

"They're all screaming drag queens," I said.

"Oh?"

"Don't get me wrong," I said flippantly. "They've got as much right to scream and wear drag as the next guy. I just don't want to go to *bed* with them!"

I expected him to laugh, but he said "Oh, dear! What a pity!"

"What?"

"Just a moment." He went to a desk and took out a manila folder, from which he extracted an 8 x 10 glossy of Marilyn Monroe—or so it seemed. He grinned at me, then took a pen and signed the photo: "*Wishing a Speedy Recovery! Love and Kisses, Ricki Renee.*"

"I don't get it," I said.

"That's me," he told me. "I'm *Ricki Renee*. I'm headlining the drag show at the Parrot. You should come see it sometime." That was why he shaved his body.

I apologized, profoundly embarrassed, and left as quickly as possible. I never returned to the bar. But I still have that autographed picture.

I left New York after only six weeks, without having auditioned for anything, and took the Greyhound bus back to Salt Lake City, where I moved back in with my parents at the power company substation, and returned to college.

MILESTONE 8: My First Published Gay Story

1961, 28

During the last year of college, I wrote a brief memoir of my visit to NYC. Several years later it was published in ONE Magazine. (*"A mystic bond of brotherhood makes all men one." Carlyle.*) It was my first Gay publication, April, 1961:

In the Shadow of the Lady's Torch
Dirk Vanden

On certain evenings you remember. When the sky glows with that haunting yellow—long after the sun has gone down; when sounds are muted and seem far away. You need not even close your eyes—it is there as tangible as it ever was. It never did seem real.

There is a vast coolness along the sidewalk beside the short, colorless cement wall which runs dipping and rising in easy solid waves along Central Park. As far as you can see along the sidewalk there are concrete benches and old men, and dogs and baby carriages, and tight indecent Levis, and ice-cream pushcarts, and tight indecent dresses, and tipped-over ice-cream cones that stand in sticky, shiny puddles on a sidewalk that won't cool down till after midnight.

You can smell the cool wetness from the little lake, hidden by a thick screen of dark trees and bushes. And there are children in the graveled playground, screaming higher and higher in the swings and gurgling into the water fountains. You hear them playing in the shadows, kids yelling "Run my sheepie, run! Red...green...orange..." and you think of children times and think, dear God! They're playing the pretend is real; too soon they'll discover they have it backwards.

You stand by the wall like you do almost every night. You've learned how it is here—like the game the kids are playing—a game for grown-ups, or those pretending they are grown-ups. It's the same in every city. The rules vary because the playing fields are different.

A man and his wife (you guess) walk by, and the woman has a little dog. You can see how much she loves that little dog. The guy is talking with his hands, like in those comic movies. "'But what's it got to do with me?' I say. He says. 'It has a great deal to do with you.' A great deal, my ass! You know? And he blows that rotten cigar smoke in my face and I want like hell to tell him where to shove it. But I don't. I say 'Okay, sir, okay.' Just like a goddamn parrot. For ten years I say 'Okay, okay, okay,' just like some parrot. And God, I hate myself! You know? Ten years!"

The woman doesn't look at him. She says "Honey…let's just walk, huh? I mean, it's hot!"

"Sure." He walks. "But I'm fed up, you know?"

"Honey," she says—and you can tell she means another word, "Every night! You know? I mean, it's old. It gets old, honey!" She gathers up that little dog and loves it. They pass. Other couples follow them; the conversation is the same: each pair a different chapter.

You walk along and look and wait. Finally you go through the gate and down the path toward the rocks that stand like battleships beside the little lake, where there are kids and toy boats. You see the guy sitting on the bench: you see his eyes. You stop to light a cigarette, and look again, and you know for sure. You walk slowly to the water, hearing the kids laughing; you watch them, trying to keep from remembering. And then this little dark-haired kid comes up, with his big brown eyes wet with a sadness that rips you up inside. "Mister, will you get my boat?"

"Sure, son. Sure. Which one?"

He points to it and you feel like crying too. "It's too far out, son."

"You can get it, Mister. I know you can! Please!"

But you can't reach it, and the kid just stands there looking at you. You feel like a balloon deflating.

"Here," a voice says, and the guy from the bench hands you a long stick. You meet his eyes. You give the kid his boat and he forgets he ever spoke to you.

"You watch," the guy says. "He'll lose it again."

You nod your head.

"Nice night," he says.

You nod again and say, "Yes, I'd like a drink, too." And you both laugh.

The black pavement almost steams beside the park. As far as you can see there are cars, bunching along the streets, from one light to another, to another, to another. But when you cross the street at the intersection, walking toward the leaning mass of brownstones, the pavement parts into iron grillwork and stairs where people gallop underground to where the tile is a dull ivory and there are hundreds of penny machines which spill little brown peanuts and juicy-fruit wrappers across the blackened platforms, and there are crayon and pencil and even lipstick dirty words encased in tile squares, and advertisements made lewd by amateurs, and cave-man pornographs, framed in tile, like artwork. And people stand impatiently until the cold blasts of air announce the train from the dark tunnel, and the clatter sounds rush out, and then the light, and then the sliding, sighing doors, and then the herd.

You sit there reading the laxative advertisement and wonder how they had the guts to print it. You say "You know, I like the subway. I hate taxis. I hate the smart-ass drivers. I hate the buses too. But I like the subway. I don't know why."

He says, "I'm going to buy a car. Sometimes you need a car. I like to drive. Do you like movies?"

"Sure."

"I like musicals, you know? In color, with lots of dancing...and stereo."

"I like the theatre," you say. "Do you like plays? Or Philharmonic concerts?"

"Sometimes," he says. "Not all the time. It all depends."

"I know. Do you like martinis? I've got some vermouth if you like martinis. We can buy some gin."

"Actually I like vodka martinis better than gin martinis."

When you come up from the subway, the sky, above the buildings, is like a mirror by a shower. Way high there is the dusky orange circle of a moon, and electric oval echoes of it all along the street. There are iron grillworks and thick steps and dirty windows, and yellowed curtains that hang unmoving in the open windows, and you hear a man say *"Honey…"* and then a woman saying *"Not now for Christ's sake, Charlie!"* And there are radios, and gunshots and music, and loud voices. And you can smell the onions and the cabbage and the ground beef that old man Jergens had on special—three pounds for eighty-five. There are girls sitting on the steps, and men in undershirts, and children almost naked, and big fat women fanning themselves with confession magazines, and four black men standing by a car and laughing with that dark laughter.

There are heavy steps that go up five times to a penciled sign that says NO PEDDLERS, and beneath those steps, four shadowed ones go down and under. "I can never find the key" you say because your hands are shaking. He says "Am I in your light?" And you say "No," because he is. "No…there!"

You leave the windows open and you pull the shades and turn the dim lamp in the corner on. And then you look to see if he is watching you; he is. You feel you want to say "Hello" because it wasn't said before. Instead you say "Well, how about that drink!" As though either of you wanted it—but that's the way the game is played. The rules. And he says "Yes" on cue.

You drink and wait and feel the warm sadness of it. You want to say "Please—what's your name? Who are you really? I wish I'd met you twenty years ago! I wish we'd grown up together, and gone to school, and learned each other then with long, long evenings talking." And you want to say "Do you suppose that child with the boat was a real child with a real boat—or was he some guiding angel, some Fate directing traffic?" But instead you say "It sure is hot!"

He looks at you above his martini glass and you know he's thinking more than what he says. He says "Yes, it sure is."

You want to say "Please! Let's talk awhile!"

But there is no time for talking now. Not now. Now there are no words. Inside your brain are only feelings now, warm, tight, rushing, pleading, crying feelings. Somewhere are warm rains and warm rain clouds and a river starting with a single raindrop slipping down from leaf to leaf, and more, until a little brook is flowing through high trees and soft grass and across smooth stones and warm, and then there is a roaring sound, a throbbing sound, until the river fills the world, the universe, the endless void of time, warm rushing into blackness. Please, God! Stop now! Please. And there's a falling. Life drains and now you know what dying is. Night by night we die.

The empty glasses sit there in dried rings on the cigarette-scarred table, and the radio is playing, and suddenly you laugh. He says "What?" But how can you explain? How can you tell him you had to laugh because it wasn't funny? How do you explain a hurt too pure, too deep, and that you have to laugh to keep yourself from doing something else?

You're sitting on the green frieze sofa with its shredding cushions and the holes and stains: but now you've known each other all your lives; you sit apart now, like old friends: like old friends leaving: like students graduating; like strangers.

Just past the open window there are children shadows telling dirty jokes. Three boy shadows and a tomboy girl one. You can see his eyes are closed, as though he doesn't want to look at you. And from the radio a woman's voice is bedroom whispering about Firm-Form Brassieres and panty-girdles. It sounds as though....

"Why are we like this?" he asks.

You say "I don't know. I really don't."

And he says "Have you read the books?"

"Yes" you say.

"Do you believe in God?"

"I...I don't know" you say. "Do you?"

"Yes" he says. "I think I do."

Two men are passing on the sidewalk. One says "What if she don't like me?" And the other says "She'll like what you got. She likes it. You take my word. You'll enjoy her. You really will. Believe me." An old truck rattles by—the grocery truck from old man Jergens' place around the corner, squeaking like it always does. He stands up. "Well, I've got to go. It's late."

"Do you live close?" you say.

"No. Thanks for the martini."

You laugh again, and he says "What?" again, and you say "You're welcome."

He starts to go. "You get up this way often?" you ask quickly.

"Sometimes" he says. "I came to see my sister. She wasn't home. Look, I'll see you, huh? Thanks for the martini."

Another day, and again another, and the bumping people gallop up the subway stairs onto the sidewalks, and you pass up out from the cool tiled underground into another evening. All along the sidewalk by the park are concrete benches and dogs and old men and baby carriages and ice cream pushcarts and tight indecent Levis and tight indecent dresses. And past the subway entrance the stone is painted grey and reaches up from the sidewalk to the first dirty window ledge, then edges out into a narrow shelf which runs unceasingly at the same useless height as far as you can see. The paint is thick and lumpy and the grey color has a liquid shine. You watch the traffic light and then hurry toward the wall; you try to slow yourself, looking casual, as you go through the gate and almost run along the path beside the rocks that look like battleships. The kids are still there, playing with their little boats. The bench is empty.

Now, on certain evenings you remember, when the sky glows with that haunting yellow—when sounds are muted and seem far away. You need not even close your eyes....

PART THREE

MILESTONE 9: My First Love
1954-61, 21-28

"*Delite Fantastique*" was his drag-name, and I avoided him like the plague!

Chris had introduced us during one of our forays into the Crystal Lounge, last summer, but I had quickly decided that I didn't really want to get to know *"The Queen Mother of Salt Lake City."*

Adriel Kurtz was handsome and thin and as tall as Chris, with jet-black hair—which, on the night we met, was streaked with glittering silver. His eyelids were painted a deep lavender, which also glittered. He wore chartreuse bell-bottoms and a brightly-multicolored Calypso shirt, high-heeled cowboy boots, and a lavender kerchief tied around his long dark neck. After Chris's introduction, he curtsied with an incredible flourish. *"Enchanté, mon petit chou!* And welcome to our humble *Sanctum Sanctorum.* Won't you join us, *s'il vous plaît?"*

He gestured grandly toward the big corner booth, where several other familiar faces smiled at us.

I excused myself to get beers for Chris and me, but I heard his remark as I turned away: *"Masculine Protest* on the hoof, my dear!"

"Be nice," Chris said, "he's cute."

"Cute-smute! Does he suck good?"

"How the hell should I know?"

"You shouldn't, my darling! Just teasing. Sit, sit, sit, I have a divine joke to tell you." He waited until I returned with the beers and slid into the booth next to Chris.

"Dickie," he said, "have you heard the one about Jesus being Gay?"

I made a startled noise, realizing he was talking to me, then laughed. "No."

"Well...it seems there were these two queens, and one of them insisted that Jesus was Gay, and the other one was equally adamant that he wasn't. So the first one says 'Well, what about that *drag* he always wore?' and the other one says 'You nellie twit, *all* the men wore drag in those days.'

"'Then what about that long, *Marcelled* hair?' said the first.

"'My dear, *all the men* had their hair long and *Marcelled* in those days.'

"'Okay,' says the first one, 'But what about all those *men* who kept *following* him?'

"'You really are exasperating, you silly goose! Those were his *Followers*. That's what Followers *do*, Precious, they *follow!*'

"'Oh, all right!' says the first. 'I'll give you the *drag*, and I'll give you the *long, wavy hair*, and I'll even give you his *followers—all in drag themselves*, I might add—but please tell me this: *Who...who but a queen...would get out of a boat...in the middle of a lake...in the middle of a storm...and say 'I'll walk!'?"*

My first reaction was to cringe, expecting lightning through the ceiling. I laughed loudly with the others, apprehensively, and a new image entered my mind: of Jesus in a brilliant white gown, a neon halo above his head, slightly tilted, flouncing gaily across the waves on the Sea of Galilee, with all of the disciples on the boat applauding and cheering and blowing kisses!

I soon learned that *"Kurt" Kurtz* was a legend in Salt Lake City. Everyone seemed to know him, and to my surprise, everyone seemed to like him. But if I saw him walking down the street, I would cross to the other side. And he seemed equally eager to avoid me.

In the fall quarter of my second year of college, I began taking *ballet* as an elective in my Theatre Arts major. To my surprise, I was fairly good

at it, and in fact, the ballet teacher told me I could be a very good dancer—
if I wanted to devote my life to it. I thanked him, very flattered, but told
him it was not something I really wanted to devote my life to.

One of my fellow *danseurs,* Kip Walden, also Gay, was studying
"Modern Dance" with a group in Provo (about thirty miles southeast of
Salt Lake), and asked me to go with him to watch a recital they were doing
at a local high school. I was very intrigued by Modern Dance, having
recently seen a touring company of *Oklahoma!* I had become a Martha
Graham fan. I gladly agreed to tag along

I was amazed when one of the dancers turned out to be Adriel Kurtz,
who turned out to be *very* talented. He did a five-minute *Grahamesque*
solo, dressed as a cowboy, to music from Aaron Copeland's *Rodeo,* and
was spellbinding. The small audience gave him a standing ovation.

According to the program, Adriel *"Kurt"* Kurtz was one-quarter
Navajo. He looked like one of the cowboys painted by "Quaintance," an
artist I had recently discovered, whose incredibly sexy paintings were
published in several Gay-oriented muscle magazines, sold at the cigar
store next to the Crystal Lounge. Quaintance painted Mexican and Native
American men and assorted cowboys with perfect muscles and bulging
crotches. In his skin-tight Levis, Adriel Kurtz also displayed beautiful
muscles and a very large bulge. I found myself more and more fascinated
as I watched him, both during the dance and afterward.

In the dressing room, removing his makeup, Kurt studied me in the
mirror, then asked "Dickie, right? Dickie something...?"

"Dick," I corrected him; I was annoyed by the diminutive nickname,
but impressed that he remembered at all. "Fullmer."

"Kipper tells me you are learning *Terpsichore. Bravo!* The world
needs all the butch dancers it can get."

I laughed uncomfortably. "Oh, come on, I'm not really all that..."

"My dear," he said, "you are so butch, you squeak like leather when
you walk! But *que sera, sera,* as they say. It takes all kinds."

"Besides, he looks good in tights," said Kip.

"Don't be *outré,* Kipper. When in Provo, do as Provonians do:
Pretend not to notice." He smiled wickedly.

I decided I liked Kurt after all. One thing that kept surprising me, each time it happened, was the basic decency of most of the Gay people I was meeting; I had expected depraved sociopaths, but kept finding sweet, gentle people! Chris, the big "butch" Lesbian, was the smartest, most realistic, "down-to-earth" woman I had ever met. Underneath that screaming-queen persona, Kurt was a very bright, talented and decent human being—with a wonderful sense of humor. It was fun going places, doing things with him.

At first, everybody thought we were having an affair. We weren't, although I would not have resisted had Kurt given any indication he wanted sex with me, but he didn't. We were becoming "just friends."

It turned out that we had many interests in common: We both liked science fiction, foreign films, especially British comedies, Pogo Possum, Hollywood musicals, Sibelius and fellatio. Kurt's motto, as he told me many times, was: "Why stick something up your ass that's good enough to eat?" He worked as a civilian computer programmer at a huge IBM installation at Hill Air Force Base, between Ogden and Salt Lake City— not far from Lagoon. It took a few months, but we grew to like one another enough to make plans to go on vacation together to Los Angeles as soon as spring quarter was over.

One of the first things we did was visit Tijuana, where I saw my very first item of pornography—in 1954. We had decided to see if we could find any, and Kurt would ask anyone who would stand still, *"Where we buy durty peechurs?"* It's a wonder we weren't mugged, but sure enough, a little man, in the dark men's room of a stinking bar, sold us three *durty peechurs* for five dollars each. They were Kodak snapshots of a man and a woman fucking. One had the man's face up close to the camera and the woman's pussy open and wet, his tongue sticking into it. The expression on the man's face said clearly *"Ugggggggh!* I do not want to do this!" Kurt wrote underneath that photo: *"All It Needs Is Holly Sugar."* (A well-known billboard motto.)

The original idea for the vacation had been to get back in time for me to return to Lagoon for another summer, and for him to get back to his programmer job at Hill Field, but we ended up falling in love with Los Angeles and moved there as soon as Kurt could get out of that job.

Before the end of summer, we were living in a nicely furnished apartment on Bundy Drive in West Los Angeles. He got a job fairly quickly with a large life insurance company, once again in the IBM computer department, and I found work in the payroll-processing department of Douglas Aircraft. I ran the tabulators and monitored the Univac check-printers. (Univac was Remington Rand's challenge to IBM's super computer "System 360.")

Away from Salt Lake City, Kurt started wearing tight jeans and cowboy shirts, willingly trading on his resemblance to the Quaintance paintings—which we discovered had become Gay icons. He was as good at acting "butch" as he was at acting "nellie." He was a *Performer*. The Kurt that I knew and lived with was a sweet, very smart, good, gentle man.

A new phenomenon was just beginning in the big cities across America: *Levi/Leather bars.* We found ourselves fitting in places such as *The Club*, a Gay-Motorcycle club hangout, on Melrose, like fingers in a glove.

At last I began to meet the kinds of homosexuals I could respond to. Sometimes they were sheep in wolves clothing, but mostly I met men who didn't see themselves as imitation women. I began to hope that I might meet *"Mr. Right,"* and perhaps move into a lifelong alliance with someone I could respect and love.

Meanwhile I "auditioned" as many as I could, and finally began to lose that awful sense of guilt from one-night-stands—as well as other sexual adventures.

I had heard about *orgies,* but had never expected to be invited to one. A Gay couple Kurt had met gave "gang-bangs" in the attic of their home in Hollywood, and we were invited, one Sunday afternoon. Wally and Harvey were both involved in movie-making; one worked in costumes, the other in makeup, but I never found out which did which.

It was for this occasion I learned a new (to me) Gay principle: if you might get fucked, be clean, take an enema. We both did.

In the olden days, they called it "browning." Someone actually said to me, one drunken night, in Salt Lake City, "hey, let's go home and pack a little shit!" I had caught clap and imitation-clap ("NSU," *Non-Specific-*

Urethritis) every single time I fucked someone. My doctor had told me
to wear condoms but I simply lost my hardon if somebody wanted me to
fuck them. And I never learned to enjoy being fucked. It always hurt more
than I wanted it to. Even so, like good Boy Scouts, we were prepared.

After a beer on the patio, waiting for everyone to arrive, more than
a dozen of us undressed in one of the bedrooms, then followed the hosts
up a pull-down staircase into a black-carpeted attic, strewn with pillows,
towels and cans of Crisco. I had never seen that many good-looking men
naked! There were black packing-quilts covering all of the rafters, and
over the windows. It reminded me of Anne Frank's hideout, blacked-out
for air raids. As soon as the door was closed, it became completely dark.
I heard movings and rustlings and then groans and moans, I was tingling
all over with excitement! I took a deep breath and felt along the floor until
my hand touched a hairy leg, which my fingers followed upward until I
was holding a very large, warm, hooded cock.

"Never touch your mother there, dear!" said Kurt's deep voice.

I jerked my hand away and whispered *"Sorry!"* I tried to keep from
laughing, and instead made a strange choking-gurgle.

Kurt snorted. Someone else giggled. In a few moments, the entire
room was filled with raucous laughter. There were other strange sounds of
disengagement, choking and sputtering.

It took several minutes for the merriment to subside and for everyone
to get back to business. Then I heard Kurt whisper, "Is that you?"

A voice, not mine, whispered *"No, Mother!"* and everyone started
laughing again.

A hand grasped my shoulder and one of our hosts whispered, "You
guys had better go. You're spoiling the party."

"Oh, shit," Kurt giggled, *"we fucked up the orgy!"*

Of course, everybody started laughing hysterically. Wally, the least
stern of the hosts, herded us downstairs to the bedroom, where we quickly,
silently got dressed. He led us to the front door, naked. "See you later,"
he said very quietly, as he opened the door to let us out, then leaned out
from behind the door and added: *"Mother!"* He was laughing as he closed
the door.

It was the last such gathering we were invited to—at least together—and that was the closest I ever got to having sex with Kurt. I've thought about it many times, and wished he hadn't stopped me. He might have enjoyed what I would have done, and that could have opened the door to a deeper relationship—and both our lives would have changed—but it never happened, and I have to suppose it was just as well.

Kurt and I lived together, off and on, for a total of five years. We kept in touch, via letters and phone calls until the fall of 1969, when he sent me a note, saying briefly that he had been arrested in a raid on the steam bath in Glendale, which resulted in his being fired from his job with the insurance company where he had worked for fifteen years. He added that he had decided to return to Utah, repent his sins, and pray that God would forgive him and allow him to marry a nice Mormon girl and have children like God had commanded us to do.

Reading the letter, I remembered one of the last afternoons we had spent together, shortly after the breakup of one of his several romances. *"Being Gay,"* he proclaimed dourly, *"is like wading through shit to pick strawberries."*

After a moment I took his hand and squeezed it. "You could say the same thing about *Life*," I said.

He sighed, smiling sadly, then hugged me. *"Touchez, mon petit chou!"* he said. *"Too-fucking-shay!"*

The last I heard, Kurt was living in a little Mormon town near the Utah-Idaho border, married to "a nice Mormon girl," a widow who had two or three children: all girls.

I think about him often and wonder what his life is like. I was in love with Kurt. He often called me *"My little love,"* but he would never allow it to happen.

MILESTONE 10: The Little Theatre and Wife #2

1954-1958, 21-25

In January of 1954, while living with Kurt in West L.A., I discovered *The Little Theatre*, a small theatre-in-the-round, built in an old Piggy-Wiggly market in Long Beach.

I had seen an ad in the *Hollywood Reporter* for non-professional actors to audition for *The Time of Your Life*, by William Saroyan. In college, I had played Nick, the bartender, and had received a "Best Student Actor" award for it. Unfortunately, I was only twenty years old, and there were at least a dozen older actors who looked the part far more than I. So, I offered to work on the crew if they needed me.

What they needed was a Stage Manager, who would also understudy the men's roles. I was excited by the possibilities and accepted the job on the spot. It paid nothing and took up most of my spare time, but it gave me a chance to "practice and perfect my art."

The Time of Your Life ran for six weekends, followed by *Stalag 17*, *Detective Story*, and *Summer and Smoke*. I had small acting roles in each, but had time to continue stage managing. I discovered that I really enjoyed the work—it was almost like directing, and I had decided I wanted to be a director. The resident director, Pamela Meyers, was impressed with my work and dedication, and made an obvious effort to include me in her directorial insights. She would ask, "Which looks best, if he goes over here or over there? Dick, what do you think…?"

Several times she invited me to her home for consultation and coffee, usually to talk about a new set, or new cues, or plays for possible production. One night I was invited to dinner with the family—her husband Martin and their two boys, Matthew and Samuel.

Martin was one of the theater's two producers, and told me they were considering making the Stage Manager a paying job. They wanted to go semi-pro, to be able to use Equity actors, and they were looking for a full-time Stage Manager. He asked if I would be interested, and I said I definitely would be. Even at Equity-minimum salary, it was a giant step up from running sorters and tabulators for Douglas Aircraft.

It took several weeks to make it official. I gave notice at Douglas and prepared to send my application to Equity.

We celebrated with a special dinner at the Meyers' home, and after the boys had gone to bed, we were toasting my new job with champagne.

"There's one thing I've got to tell you," I said. "I've meant to say something before, but…the chance never came. Before we go any farther, I want you to know that I'm Gay."

After a stunned silence, Martin yelled *"You're what?"* He stood up and stepped away from me as though I had threatened him. *"Get out of my house!"* he yelled, gesturing dramatically. *"Now! Right now! And don't come back. Ever! Get out!"*

I glanced at Pam on my way to the door. There was a look of pure terror on her face, and I knew I should hurry away and not look back. He slammed the door behind me as I ran down the sidewalk, and it sounded like a shot! When I got to my car, I carefully inspected myself to make sure a bullet hadn't punctured me someplace. I was so frightened I could hardly drive away; my hands were shaking and my foot wanted to shove down the accelerator all the way through the floorboard. I knew I had come very close to being hurt, possibly seriously. Pam had obviously been afraid of that. It had probably happened before.

I was in a state of shock for days. Martin's reaction had been the last thing in the world I'd expected. From many remarks Pam had made, I was sure she would be understanding and accepting, and I had expected her husband to be the same. To be yelled at and ordered out and told *"Never come back"* was incredibly humiliating. Things had been going so well. All my wonderful plans were suddenly meaningless. Once again it seemed my life was hopeless. Once again, it was because I was Gay!

I had quit my day-job and been fired from my new job before it even started.

Meanwhile, Kurt had invited a new lover, Mark, to move in with us, and the apartment suddenly seemed very crowded. I decided to go back to college and finish my degree.

I intended to make the trip back to Salt Lake as quickly as possible; I had done it before, several times, using Dexedrine to keep me awake—but I didn't have any of that stimulant. Kurt didn't have any, either. I had become "buddies" with the other of the Little Theatre's two producers, Dr. Henry Cohen, who had given me the little green pills to keep me going in rehearsals several times. So I called him, told him what I needed and asked if I could have a couple of his "samples." He agreed and I went to his office to get them. The little foil containers had a name other than "Dexedrine," but I didn't protest, thinking that he had given me a similar drug with a different name.

Before I left, I called my assistant, Maggie Brummett, to give her an excuse for my sudden departure. I didn't think Pam, or even Martin, would talk about this, but I didn't want it to seem I had irresponsibly disappeared. I told Maggie that I'd had an urgent call from my mother, saying that my father had suffered a heart attack and wanted me to come home.

Maggie had been a wonderful friend, during the time I had been at the theatre. She ran the sound and lights while I ran the show; we worked well together. She obviously liked me and had hinted several times that we might get together away from the theater. I promised I would call her as soon as I got to Salt Lake City.

I left Los Angeles in the afternoon, pulling a small trailer filled with furniture and stuff I had acquired over the last year, and made it to Las Vegas around seven in the evening. I stopped for coffee, had them fill up my thermos, and took one of the little white pills from the half-dozen foil containers Henry had given me. In another two hours I had crossed the state line into Utah and around midnight I stopped again for coffee in *Cedar City*. For some reason, the pill wasn't working the way I'd been expecting and I felt very lethargic—not really sleepy, but strangely apathetic, as though I really didn't care how long it would take to get home, or how cold it was getting. I took another pill and started out again, this time into the cold, snow-covered desert of southern Utah. By about three o'clock, I was so groggy and dopey, I stopped at a turnout area and drank all the coffee that was left in the thermos and took another pill.

Sometime around five I suddenly opened my eyes and realized I had fallen asleep and the car was bouncing off the road, going sixty or seventy miles per hour, headed down into a ravine, with huge boulders brilliantly illuminated by my headlights at the bottom. Without even thinking, I twisted the steering wheel sharply back toward the road, and somehow the momentum lifted the car and trailer up and around and slammed them down in the middle of the two-lane highway, pointing sideways, blocking both lanes. There was no room to back up or move forward as the ground dropped off into the gully on both sides of the pavement.

I could see headlights approaching from the east, and could vaguely make out the outlines of a big truck, its clearance lights twinkling in the pre-dawn light.

I calmly got out of my car and started walking toward the oncoming truck, in the middle of the highway, waving my arms over my head as the truck roared closer and closer. Suddenly the driver saw me and put on his brakes; they squealed in frenzied protest in the freezing air; there was a loud groaning, as though the truck itself was complaining at the insane attempt to stop.

The semi, pulling a huge trailer, stopped within a few feet of my car, and the driver got out looking like he was ready to kill me for causing such a dangerous mess. He calmed down when he saw the predicament I was in, and finally backed his truck up, attached a chain between my front bumper and his, and pulled me around until I was facing east on the road again.

I thanked him sleepily, and watched him drive away and eventually disappear over the horizon to the west. I got back in my car and drove to a little town called *Nephi*, about forty miles outside of Provo, where I stopped at an all-night cafe and ordered coffee, practically fell asleep over the steaming cup, and finally used their pay-phone to call my parents.

Two hours later, early in the morning, they found me asleep in my car, almost frozen, completely unconcerned with my plight. Mother drove my car home, followed by my father in their car. I slept all the way. Once in bed, I slept another twelve hours, got up for a few minutes, then went back to bed for another eight.

When I was finally alert enough to think about what had happened, I called my parent's doctor's office and asked about the drug-samples I had taken. I was told they were a new tranquilizer, just on the market. I was shocked at the implication that apparently, someone had tried to kill me! There was no way in the world that Dr. Cohen could have misunderstood when I asked for something to keep me awake because I was taking a long trip and would be driving. I could only conclude that he had deliberately given me the tranquilizers, hoping that I would fall asleep, just as I had, but that my car would end up crushed at the bottom of some rocky ravine, and I'd never wake up again—which almost happened.

I imagined that the two producers had discussed my confession of being Gay, that Martin had wished me dead, and that Henry had decided to grant his wish for him.

When I remembered to call Maggie, she told me she had been worried sick about me and was very relieved to know I'd arrived safely. I didn't tell her about the pills, only that I'd been very tired by the long drive and had slept until shortly before calling her. Just before the end of the conversation I impulsively added: "Hey, how would you like to get married and come live in Salt Lake City for a year while I'm finishing school?" I fully expected her to laugh and say "Thanks but no thanks."

After a brief silence, she said, "I think I'd like that. Are you asking me to marry you?"

I was amazed by her response, and before I could stop myself, I said "Sure," and she laughed and said "Okay, when?"

"Soon," I said, thinking that if she quit the show before it closed, everyone would know it was to marry me. Then even if Martin or Henry talked about my admission, people wouldn't believe it because Maggie and I would be married.

We were joined in wedlock in Las Vegas, between summer and fall quarters at the University of Utah, in September, 1957. In our separate cars, we drove to St. George, where we had planned to spend our "honeymoon," exploring Zion National Park. Up to that point, I hadn't really believed it would actually happen, or that I would actually have to have sex with my new bride. I had never had sex with a woman, and had no idea what to do!

In the motel, I went into the bathroom to check a strange discomfort I'd started noticing, and discovered what looked like a huge red boil on the head of my cock! It looked like the pictures they showed in Phys. Ed. when they talked about *venereal diseases.* "Oh, my God!" I yelled.

"What's wrong?" Maggie ran into the bathroom and looked at it. *"Oh, my God! What's wrong?"*

"It looks like...I've got...*syphilis!"*

We didn't finish the honeymoon; we didn't consummate anything. The next day, in separate cars again, we drove to Salt Lake City, where we moved into the apartment I'd rented, a few blocks from the University. I slept on the couch; we didn't know whether or not I was contagious.

I went to a doctor the next day, who examined me and took a blood test and told me to call in three days for the result of the tests. "Don't worry," he said. "We have drugs that can cure syphilis."

But it wasn't syphilis. There was nothing in the results of the tests to indicate what it was. He gave me a shot and had me take antibiotics for several weeks, until it was obvious they weren't helping. The boil wouldn't go away.

Meanwhile, Maggie was getting tired of the whole situation, and about a month after our marriage, we had a nasty argument and I spent the night at my parents'. When I called her the next day, she said she had made a decision to get the marriage annulled and move back to Long Beach. I told her I'd pay all the costs and apologized for getting her into this mess.

Twenty-four hours later, the "boil" was gone! Without a trace. It never returned.

Many years later, I was directing a series of children's plays at the Valley Music Theater in Sherman Oaks, just over the hill from Hollywood, and one afternoon, after a performance of *Cinderella,* I found Maggie waiting for me outside the stage door.

"I saw the ad in the paper," she said, "with your name as both writer and director. I had to see if it was really you." She had two little boys with her, and introduced them as her sons, Bryan and Scott. They were beautiful children, and I couldn't help thinking they could have been mine.

They politely shook my hand, then ran off to play with their friends, who had come with them to see the show.

After an awkward beginning, we told each other brief, carefully-edited histories of our lives since those embarrassing days in Salt Lake City. It turned out that, instead of returning to Long Beach, after the annulment, Maggie had found a job in Salt Lake, as a receptionist in a pediatrician's office, and, a year later, had married the doctor. Then, so the boys could go to California schools, they had moved to Whittier.

I asked, "Are you happy?" I expected her to tell me about her picture-perfect middle-American home-life. *The Perfect Life of Maggie Trent.*

She laughed bitterly. *"Happy? What's that?"*

That stopped me for a moment. "You've got two beautiful sons."

"Yes," she said, "I do. Thank you." She smiled and sighed, then took my hand. "I'm happy for you," she said. "It was a beautiful show. Congratulations." Then she joined the group of children and herded them off toward a station wagon waiting in the parking lot. She looked back once and waved.

MILESTONE 11: From Hal Aldrich to Ram Dass

1958—1961, 25-28

On June 9, 1958 I finally graduated from the University of Utah with my Bachelor of Fine Arts degree.

For reasons I can't remember, my parents did not attend the ceremony; I was the first Fullmer, at least in our immediate family, to get a college degree. I thought that was a big deal, but Mom and Dad were not impressed.

I had planned on moving back to Los Angeles, and back with Kurt, as soon as the rituals were over, but I stayed an extra two weeks to attend a Writer's Conference.

A few weeks earlier, I had submitted *To Themselves Unknown* to a panel of English professors, fully expecting them to reject it out of hand because of its subject matter. Instead, they gave me a "scholarship"— waiving the cost of the conference—and gave the novel to the visiting lecturer, Albert Guerrard, who had written several currently popular novels, for his evaluation and criticism.

On the final day of classes, Mr. Guerrard said he wanted to start things off by reading a scene from a manuscript which had been submitted by one of the class members. To my amazement, he started reading from my book. It was the part where the hero hitchhikes back to the farm where he grew up to visit his widowed father for the first time in years, but reconciliation is impossible and so he sadly catches a ride back to where he came from.

Reading the chapter took at least ten minutes, and everyone in class listened raptly. When it was over, Guerrard said: "That scene is as good, and as well written, as anything I have ever read. It is from a novel called

To Themselves Unknown by Richard Fullmer, one of your classmates." He
pointed to me and everyone turned and applauded!

The euphoria passed almost instantly as Guerrard continued his
lecture: "Unfortunately…the subject of his novel is homosexuality,
which greatly limits its publishability and readership." There was an
audible intake of breaths and the students all slowly turned away. "So Mr.
Fullmer's task is not an easy one, but I wish him well. And I wanted to
acknowledge his impressive ability."

After the class he gave me the manuscript. "It is very well written,"
he said, "but I have no idea where you could ever get it published. You
might consider adding some graphic sex scenes and selling it to one of the
porno houses—but I hope you don't. It's too good for that. I wish I could
be more helpful or optimistic." He patted my shoulder. "Go home and
write about something that's interesting to more people. You've got the
talent, just broaden your audience."

I felt as though I had been saved from drowning, then thrown back into
the river! I had spent many hours dreaming of the day someone published
my book which told "the truth" about being Gay—that it wasn't any more
sordid and depraved than so-called "normal" life; to the contrary, Gay
people were often more sensitive and loving than straights. Also, my book
had a happy ending. None of the few Gay novels I had read (*City and the
Pillar, Quatrefoil, The Well of Loneliness*) ended happily. They were all
wallows of self-pity and self-loathing, inspiring suicide at best. I wanted
to be the first author to write a Gay novel that ended "happily ever after!"
But, according to a successful (straight) novelist, my chances of doing
that were not good at all.

Virtually everything I had heard or read about writing emphasized
using material from your own life and experience. In today's world, if that
experience happened to be homosexual, too bad, forget it! Write about
something "more interesting" to a wider audience. But then, it was much
more than I had expected. To be publicly acknowledged as having written
something "as good as anything I have ever read" was very satisfying.
For a few incredibly exciting minutes, I was sure that Guerrard would say
"Sure, I know a publisher…or an agent…," but he didn't.

All the way to Los Angeles, I considered something that had never before seemed possible: a career as a writer. Albert Guerrard had started an excitement in my mind. Even though it might be difficult or impossible to get my novel published, why couldn't I write plays, or movies, or television scripts? Or another novel!

Kurt had broken up with Mark just after Christmas, and had given up the apartment on Bundy. He had rented a tiny furnished studio apartment on Cherokee, just off Hollywood Boulevard. Even though the quarters were extremely cramped for the two of us, my arrival seemed to cheer him up and we started planning on finding a larger place for us to live.

I found an ad in *Variety* for a typist, needed at the CBS Script Department. I called immediately and had the interview the next day, and started the following Monday, in the basement of *Television City*, next to the *Hollywood Ranch Market*. I helped type mimeograph stencils for shows such as *Gunsmoke, Rawhide, Have Gun, Will Travel* and *The Twilight Zone*. After the stencils were printed, I helped assemble and staple the scripts, which were then delivered to the casts and crews in the studios above us. It was fascinating to work with a script from early notes to a finished product. Then, later, to watch the show on TV.

"I typed this part!" I would tell Kurt, with affected pride. "Pages seventeen through twenty-five!"

Unfortunately, working in the script department didn't qualify anybody for a pass to watch the broadcasts or tapings. Occasionally the cast of *Rawhide* could be seen around the catering-truck at noon. Several times I had lunch sitting at a picnic table, close to Clint Eastwood, who played *Rowdy Yates, Roustabout*, but never had the courage to speak to him. Even so, the work was interesting and instructive, and the scripts department crew was pleasant, and I was making more money than I ever had—sufficient to save up enough for the down payment a brand new car: a white MG-A.

I bought a brown leather "flight jacket," a matching leather cap, and sports-car-driver's gloves, and tried my best to appear "sporty." I wanted a variation on the "leather-look" without the implied S-and-M predilection of the black motorcycle outfits.

It was the MG which attracted the attention of a young man in the parking lot of *The Club.* He was driving an Austin-Healy—in England, a Healy was considered a bigger and better MG, like an older brother. We were even dressed alike, in Levis and plaid shirts (it was fall). We had a beer inside, then adjourned to his house.

Hal Aldridge rented a house on Oakwild Lane, an offshoot of Laurel Canyon, which wound around tree-lined canyons, almost to the top of the Hollywood Hills. Hal's was the highest house on the street, so we looked out on an enchanted landscape, but no one could see us, so we had sex on his patio, under the stars.

Hal was about ten years older than I, but he looked younger. He looked like a perennial teenager with premature wrinkles around his eyes. He had been a dancer in MGM musicals until a few years ago, when he got a "steady" job as a ticket agent with American Airlines. He still worked out and took dance classes, so his body was muscular and agile.

We fell madly in love, and within a week I had moved in. Kurt moved in a month later. Both of Hal's previous co-renters had been transferred to another city, and two bedrooms needed renting. I took one and, as soon as he could give notice where he was renting, Kurt took the other. That was October, 1958 and we all lived there until 1961.

Hal and I did not remain "lovers" long, partly because he couldn't keep an erection, or sometimes even get one, for me. He said that all of the sex he'd had as a young dancer, in the movies, had made him almost disinterested in sex now; it was companionship he was looking for, he said. The number of affairs he'd had with well-known movie actors and dancers was amazing, but, Kurt assured me, quite possible. Finally we agreed that we could be friends and housemates, but not bedmates or sex partners.

For the most part, we enjoyed living together, and had fun doing things together, the three of us. We saw a lot of foreign movies and musicals, some with momentary glimpses of Hal in the chorus. We even gave a few small orgies—on the patio, under the stars.

Hal and Kurt both loved *To Themselves Unknown,* and encouraged me to try to get it published. Hal knew a friend of a friend who had an agent in New York. Mike Pate not only gave me the address of Martha

Winston, his agent with Curtis-Brown, he also asked if I had ever done a "treatment" for a screenplay. I told him I hadn't, but was more than willing to learn. He invited me to visit his home in Beverly Hills and learn more about several projects he didn't have time for.

Mike was an "Aussie"—with a delightful accent. A large, horsy, almost mean-looking, very sexy man who did *"bad guys and crowd work,"* he was actually very soft-spoken and gentle, but straight, and married. He wrote scripts for several popular television series. People brought ideas to him for screenplays or teleplays which needed "development" before they could be submitted to producers. He did not have the time to work on most of them, but showed me the format and gave me several file folders full of scribblings and memoranda.

I worked with Mike for almost a year, doing treatments for more than twenty possible projects. Three of those were optioned by producers, but went nowhere, and I wrote my first screenplay to a story by Mike himself: *To Ride a Wild Horse,* a rodeo story.

It was a heady time. Success seemed imminent. I had been accepted for representation by a big, well-known New York agency, Curtis-Brown. I was being paid very good money just to develop plots and characters from other people's ideas. I had learned formats and procedures for screenplays and teleplays, and was working on several ideas of my own. Hal and I had plotted two novels, which could then become screenplays, *Ride The Proud Wind,* a Western like *Duel in the Sun,* and *The Wake of the Snail,* a murder-mystery. I was living in the Hollywood Hills with two good friends, driving a new MG. I had a steady, salaried job with CBS, which was good for as long as I wanted to stay. It seemed just about perfect.

Then I fell in love! Again!

Todd Allen was a friend of Kurt's, who lived with his lover, Neil, in San Bernardino, sixty miles east of L.A.. We were all invited there for a barbecue, one weekend in the late summer of 1960, and I ended up spending most of the day talking to Todd. He was involved with a local theater group and had considered writing a novel of his own. We were like kindred spirits, touching each other where no one else had touched. Shortly after we met, but before we'd had sex, Todd and Neil split up, and

Todd invited me to move to San Bernardino and share his apartment with him. Kurt was furious, blaming me for coming between his good friends, and Hal disapproved on general principles, but I told them "I don't care! We're in love!"

Meanwhile, the agent from Curtis-Brown, having reported rejection after rejection for *To Themselves Unknown,* finally returned the manuscript, saying she was sorry, but she didn't feel the book could be published by a reputable publisher. Then Mike Pate moved back to Australia, saying he was tired of messing around with Hollywood, and was going home to make real movies.

I moved out to San Bernardino and commuted each day to work at CBS—60 miles each way. That became impossible almost immediately, so I quit CBS. But even before my two-week notice had passed, Todd and I decided we were not suited to living together. He wanted to be fucked, and I couldn't fuck anybody. I was "gun shy" by the time Todd Allen came along, and couldn't even maintain an erection for him.

Christmas was coming, and I did not want to spend the holidays with anyone in Southern California. As far as I knew, they felt the same way about me.

Dad had retired that summer, and my parents had moved back to their home in Citrus Heights, so I ended up spending Christmas with them. They hadn't even decorated, so I went out and bought a tree and set it up and draped it with tinsel and new twinkling lights and old ornaments dating back to my childhood.

Mother kept saying "Christmas is for children."

It was a terrible holiday.

While licking my wounds at my parents' home in Citrus Heights, I tried to decide where to go and what to do next. Too many things had gone wrong in my life. I was only twenty-seven years old and more things had happened to me than to any three of the kids I had gone to school with. At times I felt much older than twenty-seven—very old: fifty, even sixty! Suddenly I was "old and Gay."

"Nobody wants you when you're old and Gay!"

I had lost my innocence many times, it seemed, each time moving to a new level of "reality," each level with fewer guiding principles than the one before. Again, at this point I seemed to be flying blind.

I needed grounding. I needed something to believe in. I needed to do something positive. I decided to return to college and get my Masters Degree in Psychology, for a career as a Psychologist—and try to figure out everything that had happened to me. My life had to make sense in some kind of framework!

So I applied and was accepted at the University of California at Berkeley, found a room for rent near the campus, and registered for the Spring Semester. The class of *Abnormal Psychology 101* was taught by a professor on sabbatical from Harvard, Dr. Richard Alpert.

After *Ab Psych 101, MWF*, I had a free period and started hanging out in the Student Union cafeteria, drinking coffee and studying for my next class. During the second week, Dr. Alpert came in, looked around, recognized me from his class, and asked if I minded if he sat with me. Had I known anything about him, I would have been thoroughly intimidated, but, to me, he was just another college teacher, barely older than I was, or so he seemed. We chatted amiably while he finished his coffee, then he hurried off to prepare for his next class and I went back to studying for mine.

Two days later it happened again and by the third week, we were "coffee buddies." I got up the nerve to ask him if he would look at something I had written, a few pages on an idea for my Master's Thesis, on the causes of homosexuality. He said he'd be happy to read it and give me his suggestions.

I had written it between the holidays, closed off in my bedroom in my parents' house, based on many ideas gained over the last few years; then I'd got interested in going back to college and had filled it in and rounded it out, and called it "A Matter of Lost Innocence." I opined that homosexuals are not necessarily "born that way," but are born with a certain kind of intelligence, which, when identified, ought to be definable and measurable. Because of that unnamed type of intelligence, those people took things more seriously than others. They believed more strongly in something—religion, for example. Their reaction to disappointment or doubt of something they had devoutly believed was to react against it.

One of the antonyms for "religious" was "perverse," which is what homosexuality supposedly was. Most of the Gay people I had met had been, like me, very religious when younger, but now were devoutly non-religious. I reasoned that we unconsciously chose homosexuality as a *fuck you* gesture at religion. "Look! I'm doing exactly what you told me not to do and God isn't striking me dead!"

"Besides, it feels good and I'm having fun!"

When something feels good, people tend to repeat the experience—especially people with a certain kind of intelligence.

I typed up my notes and gave them to Dr. Alpert and waited. The next week he tossed "A Matter of Lost Innocence" on my desk and grinned at me.

"That told me a lot about you, but it's not really a good subject for a thesis. The cause of homosexuality is already known." Dr. Alpert was a Freudian, and he told me that Freud had clearly established the causes for that particular *"Sexual Inversion."* If I were interested in finding out more, there were some books he could recommend.

Apparently, learning "a lot" about me had made Dr. Alpert somewhat leery of having coffee with me after class. As I sat there alone, it seemed like my new level of reality was coming unraveled. I wandered around campus for an hour or more, feeling lost and helpless. I sat on several benches, smoking Marlboros, and watching students hurry by, on their way to or from class, late or early, all wrapped up in what was happening to them. I started hallucinating that I could slow time and turn everything into slow motion—or I could speed it up and send everybody scurrying along the sidewalks at double speed. It had to do with whether I went slow or fast, myself. I felt dangerously disconnected from reality.

I carefully walked to where my car was parked, feeling like I was hurrying and going slowly at the same time. I drove very carefully to the room I was renting, where I packed my few belongings into the car, told my landlady I was quitting school, and drove south—away from Citrus Heights and Sacramento, down the Coast Shore Highway. I finally stopped in a deserted pull-out area, then sat in my car and stared at the ocean.

It was late afternoon by then, and the sun was a dimly glowing orange ball somewhere out in the gray fog bank. It got dimmer and flatter and finally disappeared, and it seemed that I could sense the darkness creeping over the land from the east, as the ocean turned gray and then black and then vanished in the fog. I could hear the waves breaking, dimly and distantly, and that seemed like the only sound in the universe. I felt more alone than I ever had before—and yet, I was still alive. I hadn't driven off a cliff or swerved into the path of an oncoming truck. I had survived disillusionment once again. I finally decided that it didn't matter what caused me to want sex with men, or to want love from another man, or to want to live with another man, to be part of a homosexual couple—that's how it was. Whether I liked it or not, whether Richard Alpert liked it or not, whether anybody in the world, including my father, liked it or not—that's how it was.

Around midnight, I started the car and headed back to Sacramento. Reality had returned, almost the same as it had always been.

I couldn't afford to go to Berkeley anyway. I was almost broke. What I needed was a job.

MILESTONE 12: The Night I Met Rock Hudson

1959, 26

Compton's Market on Hollywood Boulevard was open 24/7. Their prices were high but they had a good selection of merchandise, plus a relatively fresh fruits-and-veggies department. Hal and I often stopped there to get quick snacks for supper; they had a good deli, and they kept the place clean and well lit.

One night in or around 1959, I had stopped at the market after the bars closed at two; I was wide awake and hungry but I knew we didn't have anything for breakfast in the refrigerator, so I had put some eggs and bacon in my shopping cart and was wandering around, looking for something else that looked good. The market was relatively small and almost empty at that time of night. I could hear giggling and deeper, drunken chuckles, coming from somewhere in the store. As I rounded the corner, headed for the bread aisle, just coming out of the fresh produce aisle were two men. One was very tall, dark, and handsome, and I recognized him immediately. His companion was a much younger, very nellie young queen, who was carrying a shopping basket which contained variously sized cucumbers and zucchini. Apparently, they were both recovering from the world's funniest joke when I almost bumped into them.

I said, "Oh! Excuse me!"

Rock Hudson pulled himself up to his tallest and most authoritative persona, and pronounced: *"You're...ex...cused!"*

The two of them exploded all over each other as they stumbled toward the cash register.

I wandered through the store "shopping" until I heard the ding of the doors closing behind them, then wheeled my cart up to the cashier. As she rang up my purchases, tears were streaming down her face.

I had heard rumors that Rock Hudson was Gay, but that had seemed unlikely—until I saw him and his trick that night at Compton's. The cashier had probably heard the same rumors, but it was obvious that the truth had punctured a gigantic hole in her fantasies.

MILESTONE 13: Whatever Happened to Prince Charming?

1961-69. 28-36

O nce upon a time, a very handsome young man named Winson Strickland, watched himself grow up, in mirrors, and decided that he wanted to be a famous movie star. The only problem was, he was a terrible actor, and knew it. He had tried out for several high school plays and had been rejected by all of them. To him it was "pretending out loud" and he just couldn't do it convincingly. Then he met me.

Following the debacle at Berkeley, I spent a very depressing Christmas with Hal and Curt, who still lived together in the house on the hill above Hollywood, then moved back in with my parents in Citrus Heights and went looking for a job in Sacramento. I found one at the *Sacramento Civic Theater*.

The Sacramento Civic Theater was as close as Sacramento came, in those days, to professional theater. My BFA in Theatre Arts got me enough sympathy to be hired as a janitor. Part of the payment for sweeping and waxing and cleaning up and dealing with all the garbage left by audiences was an apartment, upstairs over their costume room and the Technical Director's apartment. Suddenly I had my own apartment, by myself, far away from Mom and Dad, in a theater complex large enough that it required a "full-time" janitor. I was earning enough to stay alive and relatively comfortable, but little else. And that left my nights free.

In the spring of 1961, they had tryouts for *The Caine Mutiny Court Martial*, and I ended up as Stage Manager. I ran the show and took one of the small roles.

At about the same time, they needed a director for their Children's Theater—the previous director had quit because of a family emergency and they needed somebody quickly. I revised the script and directed the first CT "hit," *Sleeping Beauty* as a narrated pantomime with music by Tchaikovsky. It was very popular. Before the season ended, I was hired as manager for both *Children's Theater* and the experimental arena *Harlequin Stage.* Both were non-paying jobs.

During the summers, The Sacramento Civic Theater became *Music Circus*—Broadway musicals done arena-style, under a huge, colorful circus tent, in what was, during the winter, the theater's parking lot. My job as janitor ended when Music Circus moved in, so to keep an income coming in, I signed on as backstage "crew" for the six musicals presented during the summer. We dressed in costumes which allowed us to be onstage for quick scenery changes.

One of those shows was Lerner and Lowe's *Paint Your Wagon,* and I vividly remember watching another crew member, the personification of L'il Abner, striding around the stage, in overalls and a dirty, torn undershirt, posturing and "singing" with the chorus—but not making a sound; the director had told him not to sing aloud. He couldn't carry a tune. But if you didn't know it, you'd have thought he was singing with the rest of them, having a great time. I was doing the same thing, but I was actually singing along. When the song finished and the lights went out, L'il Abner and I grabbed two chairs each, stacked them on a table, took the table between us, and ran up the darkened aisle and through a blackout curtain to backstage, where all the props and scenery were stored.

We started talking during the breaks and I was charmed. In addition to being one of the most handsome men I'd ever met, Winson was very bright and friendly, telling me stories about himself as the "dumb punk kid" who hated high school and going to church and wanted to get involved with theater. I told him about my schedule of plays for Children's Theater, and invited him to come for tryouts.

He showed up several months later to try out for Prince Charming in my version of *Cinderella.* His reading was stumbling and awkward, and he looked stiff and posed. Even had the producers not nixed him—they sat in on every tryout—I wouldn't have dared cast him without someone to work with him. I didn't feel qualified to teach him how to act. Offstage, in person, he was delightful! He was charming and energetic, and his enthusiasm rubbed off on everyone around him. I offered him the job of Stage Manager, and he eagerly accepted, saying he knew he couldn't act, and didn't really want to, but he wanted to work with me. He had decided he wanted a career in theater, but hadn't decided exactly what appealed to him. He was an excellent, if untrained, artist, and was soon helping paint and design the CT scenery.

I tried very hard to treat him like just another member of the crew, but it was impossible to ignore him. He seemed eager to do anything I might want him to do, and very soon was spending almost all of his spare time working at the theater, helping anyone who needed it—in the scene or costume shops, or backstage, moving scenery, hanging drapes. He was an excellent worker and people enjoyed being around him. Everybody loved Winnie. But then, he started knocking on my door, sometimes an hour or more before a production or rehearsal, with some kind of "problem" that required my suggestion for solution. It quickly became obvious that the problems were simply excuses which allowed him to come up for a visit. It also became obvious that he wanted to be seduced.

He told me about several Music Circus singers and dancers who were Gay, describing their antics to get him into bed with them, laughing about it. Their cruising apparently didn't annoy him, and he didn't seem at all prejudiced, but "the right man" still hadn't come along. There was no doubt in my mind that he was Gay, but he said he'd never had sex—with anyone, male or female—and I definitely did not want to be the one to "bring him out." I was adamantly opposed to the seduction of teenagers by older men, and was determined to make no move that could be interpreted as a "pass," even though I ached to give him the love and acceptance that he so desperately wanted—and apparently was not getting from his parents and friends.

Meanwhile we produced my versions of *Hansel and Gretel*, *Beauty and the Beast*, and *The Wizard of Oz*.

"Spectacular lighting effects, wild imaginative makeup, and excellent acting highlighted the opening performance of the Sacramento Civic Theater's production of 'Hansel and Gretel.' Under direction by SCT's new Children's Theater Manager, Richard Fullmer, the cast played to a

capacity audience and provided a delightful and amusing afternoon of children's theater.

"Fullmer has written an original version of the famous fairy tale and has come up with a charming, humorous, and completely entertaining children's play... Fullmer has directed his original work with style, humor, and skill... I wholeheartedly recommend this production as a must-see for children of all ages!"

The Sacramento Union, September 29, 1961

***

"Richard Fullmer and the SCT Children's Theater group have done it again. They have combined their individual talents to make this production...one of charm and enjoyment...with taste, style and outstanding special effects. Fullmer's last two productions have been of remarkably high caliber and are some of the finest children's theater productions I have ever seen in the Sacramento area.

"Beauty and the Beast" has been adapted for this production by Fullmer, and his adaptation is full of humorous and delightful adventures and situations."

The Sacramento Union, January 7, 1962

***

"The SCT Children's Theatre final production of the year, "The Wizard of Oz," based on Frank Baum's classic children's story, is an appropriately fitting climax to a season of exceptionally fine quality. Credit must go to Richard Fullmer, who took over the Children's Theater last fall and developed it into a workable and first-rate children's group."

The Sacramento Union, April 8, 1962

***

It happened one Saturday afternoon in May, 1963, after a particularly good performance of *Wizard*. (I directed and played the Wizard. Winn had faultlessly stage-managed a very technical show.) It was our last show of the year and it had been a good year; we were celebrating. The older members of the cast had gone to a nearby *Hoffbrau* for beer and sandwiches, and I had gone up to my apartment to change clothes, so I could join them. I was naked when a knock came at the door and Winson called: *"It's me!"*

For a moment I almost panicked, then grabbed my shorts and pulled them on. "It's open."

He started to say something as he came in, but the words stopped as he saw me. He smiled broadly, closed and locked the door and walked across the room, looking straight into my eyes, grinning mischievously. He knelt in front of me and slipped my shorts down, then took my cock into his mouth, making a soft humming noise as he did. We ended up on the floor, in a sixty-nine, which he said afterward was his first sexual experience with anyone.

He said he'd been practicing on bananas.

Winson insisted he was in love with me, and wanted to be with me as much as possible. He wanted to learn everything I could teach him—about theater and being Gay. He said he had been attracted to me because I wasn't *"faggy."* That melted me, and I finally admitted to myself, then to him, that I loved him too. If the truth were known, I told him, I had fallen in love with him the moment we'd met, a year ago. But he was still only seventeen, and I could get myself into serious trouble if anyone ever found out what was going on. He promised he would do everything he could to avoid suspicion, but he was determined that we should be together as much and as often as possible. And we were.

At first, it was wonderful! A bright and talented and very good looking, very horny young man was in love with me, and I with him. And we had fantastic sex. He learned how to do all the things I enjoyed having done, and to do them very well, since that's what we did every time.

We both agreed that we did not want to be "husband and wife." We wanted a relationship, but not an imitation heterosexual one. I had been "active" at least ten years and was reluctant to start a closed relationship—especially with someone as attractive as him; as it turned out, neither did he.

That summer we took a vacation together. In my sporty little white MG, we drove up the coast to Vancouver and over to Victoria Island, then back down the coast, stopping in Seattle, where the World's Fair was in progress. There was no vacancy anywhere near Seattle, so we decided to spend the night at The Baths.

It was Winn's first introduction to the power of his beauty and masculinity, and he loved it. One thing I had encouraged: Don't act "Gay," act manly and nobody will ever suspect you. I can still see him, wandering around the halls, in and out of the steam room, a towel loosely draped around his groin, having the time of his life, followed by other similarly-unclad young and old men, like bees after a spring blossom. It was also his first experience of sex with strangers, and he told me later, he thoroughly enjoyed himself. I didn't get to take part.

But it started an addiction for him, and opened the door for jealousy and arguments. Also, he started experimented with "dangerous drugs" with his Hippie friends, and I was adamantly opposed to use of pot or acid or any of that stuff. That became an issue between us; all his friends got stoned, but I didn't; he couldn't invite any of his friends over for parties, or they couldn't get stoned at our place.

That fall we did *Rumpelstiltskin* and *Twelve Dancing Princesses,* and closed the year with an amazing production of *The Enchanted Nutcracker,* my adaptation of the Nutcracker story, with Tchaikovsky's music as backing for many of the scenes, using Winson's design for a totally magical set. He not only designed it, but built it himself in the scene shop. At one point in the story, when Clara and Fritz go to sleep under the Christmas tree, the lights go down and the tree begins to grow. The fireplace on one side, and the window on the other, roll offstage and the tree grows and grows until it fills the stage, "reducing" Fritz and Clara to mouse-size. It turned the audience mice-size, too! He had made an outline of plywood, with many thin layers, covered with muslin, spray-painted to look like larger and larger pine tree boughs. The production was magical, partly because of Winn. It played from Christmas Eve through New Year's, and got rave reviews in both local papers.

Then I was given the opportunity I had been waiting and working for: directing a mainstage production of *Death of a Salesman.* Winn was my stage manager for that, and the production was a record-breaker for the Sacramento Civic Theater. It looked like my future there was secure. In another few years, the current manager would retire and I would be first in line to replace him.

In March, 1964, a week before *Salesman* opened, and almost exactly a year from the date Winson and I had first had sex, my boss took me to the neighborhood bar for a beer.

He got straight to the point: "I know what's going on," he told me. *"Everybody knows.* Everyone except the producers. If you don't stop seeing him, I'll have to fire you. I'll have no choice, and I'll have to tell them why. Is he worth throwing your career away for? A few more years and I'll retire, and you play your cards right, you could take over here. Managing Director. If you just end it with him, right here and now, I'll never say another word."

"Tony," I said, "I'm in love with him. And he loves me. But he'd hate me if I did what you wanted. I'd end up hating myself and I couldn't stand that."

"It's your life."

I submitted my resignation to the producers on February 28, 1963, opening night of *Death of a Salesman,* which ended up being an enormous success, with rave reviews and sold-out houses.

I had to move out of my apartment and away from the theater. I tried to start a new Little-Theater Group, calling ourselves *"The Bread and Butter Theater,"* staging our productions in the little stage on a wing off the gigantic Memorial Auditorium. We produced *The Moon is Blue* to favorable reviews.

Then I was invited to direct two professional productions at Bridge Bay Summer Theater in Redding: *Come Blow Your Horn* and *The Pleasure of His Company*, with professional actors. I had to join Equity, and thought surely this was a huge step in the right directions. Both productions got glowing reviews and played to sold-out houses, but the whole situation was very strange because of Winn.

He had wanted to come with me to Redding when I went up for two weeks, so I made reservations for two at my gratis-motel, and Winn spent the two weeks at Bridge Bay making friends and helping everybody. Before the time was up, he was everybody's favorite gofer, but he told me later that our arrival had been very strained because we had been announced by one of the producers as *"The Director and His Trick."*

We came back to Sacramento and produced Sacramento's first "Black" play, *A Raisin In The Sun,* which was well received and reviewed.

One of the female producers for Bread and Butter started bothering Winn, letting him know she wanted him to seduce her. He kept telling her no or putting her off. Then he reported that she had told him if he didn't screw her, she would go to his parents and tell them he was screwing the director. I was terrified. He was still under age, still not eighteen. I could be arrested and sent away for a long time if someone wanted to pursue it. I was afraid that a jealous woman, a woman-scorned, might very well want to pursue it. Her husband was a prominent attorney. We packed up everything and left Sacramento.

We went to Glendale, because I knew someone there who would help us find some place to live, and might possibly help Winn find work in the movies—an actor I had worked with before, at the University of Utah. He was, himself, trying to break into acting in TV or movies, as a leading-man type. He agreed to help Winn look for acting work, but cautioned it wouldn't be easy with no experience.

Winn got a job as a busboy at a cafeteria in Glendale, and I got a job driving Yellow Cabs. We moved into a cottage in a Mexican-style courtyard in Glendale and stayed there until January, '65, when he hurt himself playing parking-lot football, and needed an operation to repair a ruptured disk. He had to quit his job and return to Sacramento, where he was still covered under his father's insurance, and I had to move to a smaller, cheaper apartment in an ancient-looking building in a rundown area near one of the freeways into L.A.. I lived there nine months, waiting for him to return. I quit Yellow Cab and started working for the *California Bar Review Course*, mimeographing, assembling and mailing mail-order texts which taught practicing attorneys how to pass the California Bar Review Test.

Meanwhile, Winn was sending me letters about his involvement with a rock 'n roll concert producer in Sacramento, and all of the various sycophants involved with him, who gave wild parties. He described getting stoned at one party and sitting in a corner for hours, pretending to be a camera. He also said he had been seduced by a woman, and had decided he was bisexual.

The operation and recovery took nine months, which seemed like the longest, lowest, emptiest part of my life.

To fill the time, I bought a canvas and some oil paints and tried painting a portrait of Winson, taken from one of his many photographs. It turned out very well, and I showed it to the owners of a new bar I'd discovered, *The Gauntlet*, a leather/motorcycle bar in Hollywood, who were so impressed, they hung it in the gameroom.

By the time Winn returned, his portrait was hanging on the wall of the most popular leather-bar in town. Men would walk up to him and say "I know you. You're him. I want you!"

Winn also brought a mystery back with him when he returned— whether or not he had fathered a baby while partying in Sacramento. The mother, the sister of one of the rock 'n roll producers, insisted that the baby was Winson's, and was insisting that he marry her. Even though he wanted to believe he was a father, he had figured out the timing and was fairly sure it couldn't have been him—and he wasn't about to marry her. He called her a *Pig*. "It was like fucking a pig!" At some point after he had come back, the police came knocking at our door at six in the morning, and took him away, under arrest. The blood test they gave him while in jail proved that he wasn't the father, and that ended that. But it had put a definite wedge between us. He had decided he was bisexual and wanted to explore that side of sex.

The difference in our ages had started to become uncomfortable for both of us. We were of two very different generations, mine from the thirties, his from the forties. I had grown up under incredibly conservative conditions, a Mormon during the Great Depression and World War II; he had spent his entire life in Sacramento, which, although not a hotbed of liberalism, was vastly more radical than Vernal. His parents were Fundamentalist Christians, but he hated religion. He told me once that the only way to go to Sunday School was to smoke a joint before you went in. We had different values, different ideals. He was a cynic; I was an optimist. We still loved each other, which is what had kept us together for six years, but the edges were beginning to fray.

In June, 1965 I was hired to start a new children's theater for *Valley Music Theater*, a "cement-dome" arena-theater in Sherman Oaks in the San Fernando Valley, just over the hill from Hollywood. It was the Hollywood version of Music Circus. With Winn as my stage manager, we produced four of the shows we had done in Sacramento: *Snow White, Hansel and Gretel, Rumpelstiltskin,* and *Cinderella.* The audiences loved them, but there were never enough children to fill the enormous auditorium. We finished our last production about four weeks before the producers declared bankruptcy and closed the theater.

While working on the plays, Winn met Glen Holse ,a scenic designer who was very impressed with his work—and with him. Holse had a small studio in Hollywood that made scenery for various movie companies, legitimate theaters, and for some of the musical extravaganzas in casinos in Las Vegas. As soon as the children's theater closed, Winn started working for Glen, and was soon commuting to Nevada. I found the job with the California Bar Review excruciatingly boring—I was the only one in the office—but it gave me the time (and materials) to start work on a new book, as yet untitled—about a Mormon father discovering that he was Gay—and so was his son!

In the spring of '67, a story in *ONE Magazine* about a new Gay publishing house in Washington, D.C. caught my attention, and I sent a letter of inquiry to the address noted in the article. In only a few days, a letter from Dr. H. Lynn Womack invited me to submit *To Themselves Unknown* to *Guild Press* as soon as possible—which I did the next day. Dr. Womack loved the book, and in less than a month, I had a check for two hundred dollars as a payment against royalties; he expected that printing could be finished by the end of the year, and predicted that the book would be very popular as soon as it was published.

A few weeks later, another letter arrived from Guild Press advising me that my book would not be published after all. A gang of kids, supposedly, had broken into the warehouse where all the manuscripts had been stored. They trashed everything, then started a fire. By the time the fire was put out, every book and manuscript had been destroyed, along with everything else in the office. Nothing had been insured, so there was no money to start over again. They had to keep going on the inventory they already had. Dr. Womack encouraged me to find another publisher: "Your book should be read," he wrote. "Keep trying."

On a Sunday afternoon, in July, '66, Winn and I went to the weekly beer-bust at *The Gauntlet*, and the bartender gave me a book to read. "*It blew my mind!*" he declared. "It's the most incredible thing I've ever read in my life!"

Song of the Loon—A Gay Pastoral by Richard Amory was, indeed, *incredible!* And it did, indeed, blow my mind, too. In fact, it changed my life. In this book, virile mountain men and well-endowed, unclipped Indians sucked and fucked and fell in love in a redwood-covered paradise somewhere along the Pacific coast, during a time that seemed to resemble the late nineteenth century. I had never read anything like it. Beautiful homoerotic poetry. Songs about Gay Love. There were several excitingly graphic sex scenes, after which neither of the partners threatened to kill themselves. In the course of the story, the hero learned to love himself and other men. Ephraim and Cyrus did not exactly end "happily ever after," but the promise of such an ending was definitely there.

I quickly mailed a copy of *To Themselves Unknown* to the Loon-publishers, Greenleaf Classics, in San Diego. They returned the manuscript with a note saying they really liked the story and my writing, but wanted more *"hot fag"* sex. (Several red-penned notes in the margins read "Good spot for *Fag-Hots*.") They even sent me several of their current titles, *The Story of O, Emmanuel*, and a book called *Homo, Sweet Homo*, as examples of what they were looking for. *"Hot sex on the first page and as often as possible thereafter, wherever the plot permits, the kinkier the better."*

Reluctantly I rewrote *To Themselves Unknown*, something I had sworn never to do, changed the title to *Tom, Tom, The Piper's Son*, inserted several "poetic" sex scenes and soon had a check for five hundred dollars and an invitation to submit my next book.

After getting past the insult to my writing: that I needed *"fag-hots"* to make it acceptable, the idea of writing *jack-off books* began to intrigue me. Although Albert Gerrard had mentioned selling the book to "one of the porno houses," I hadn't really believed there were such places. *Song of the Loon* had inspired me. I resolved to write the best Gay pornography ever written. And, I decided, my books would all have happy endings.

Once *Tom, Tom, The Piper's Son* was published by Greenleaf, I reasoned, I could show it to a legitimate publisher and offer to let them publish my next novel, *without* so much explicit sex.

Meanwhile, I started working on *The Stag In The Tree*, an examination of the Sado-masochistic elements I was discovering in Gay life in Los Angeles. The title came from a puzzle-picture, given to the hero by his ex-girlfriend, which featured a rabbit hidden in a rose bush, a bear in the clouds, and a stag in a tree. After experimenting with the *S* side of *S-and-M* briefly, the hero found true love with a Gay police detective, and settled down near San Francisco.

I decided to use a pseudonym for the pornographic stuff, but to use my *real* name for the more "legitimate" books. I considered a few suggestive names, such as *Jack F. Hancock*, or *Peter Harden*, or *Hugh Lance*, but my favorite was one I had used to sign my artwork, *"Dirk."* Dirk *What?* I considered my mother's maiden name *Vernon*, but I didn't want to be even remotely associated with that tribe. *Dirk Vernon* didn't sound right to me.

I had called myself *Dirk* after that sexy Dutch exchange-student I'd met in college, *Dirk Van der Elst. Van der* became *Vanden, "Dirk Vanden."* It looked good on the manuscript page. What I didn't realize at the time, was that it was very near the *bottom* of an alphabetized list, and therefore on the bottom shelves of bookstores.

In June of 1968, Winn got a new job at a scenic studio in Las Vegas, which required that he move there. Nothing was gluing us to Hollywood, so I went with him. As soon as he had found a place to live, I quit the *Bar Review Course* and joined him. By then, *Stag* had been accepted by the Greenleaf editor, who encouraged me to give them more. I decided to spend all of my working-time writing. I had no desire to do anything else in Las Vegas. Gambling had never appealed to me, nor had musical extravaganzas featuring near-naked, big-breasted women. Winn was making enough money that he didn't care how much I made. He was working ten to twelve hours per day, and when he wasn't working, he was partying, and so, to provide myself some companionship, I bought a puppy, a male white German Shepherd who was so sweet and loving that I named him *Luv.*

In October, I had almost finished my second S-and-M novel, *Hatters and Hares*, when Winson announced that he had fallen in love with one of the dancers at The Dunes. He had finally met someone, he said, with a sense of real accomplishment, who loved him enough to fuck him.

It had been obvious to both of us, for a long time, that our relationship had run its course. We had stopped doing things together, rarely talked, and almost never had sex. Our original love had been stretched so thin it was obviously going to pull apart. So, I wished him well, packed up everything I could get into the MG—my typewriter, manuscripts and a few photo albums, and with Luv, fidgeting and fussing in the passenger seat, I drove, once again, to Citrus Heights, California.

"Dick Fullmer," freshman yearbook photo, 1947
Pure innocence

Mr. Pritchett
in Detective Story

Papa in Years Ago by Ruth Gordon,
Uintah High School, Vernal, Utah, 1950.

Legal at last, age 21, Las Vegas,1954

My very own (illegal) Prince Charming,
Winson Strickland, in 1962, Age 17

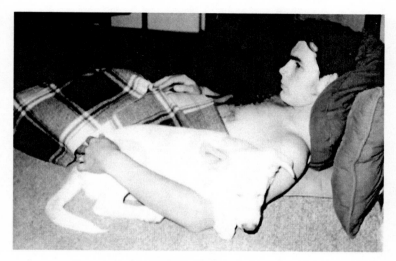

Winn and Luv

Winn in leather

Winn, 1964,
oil on Burlap

Wading In...
Oil on Canvas

"Wading In," circa 1970, was painted for an ad for Dave's Baths, and hung in the lounge for many years.

"The Cosmic Cock," mural for the back wall of
The Arena, Los Angeles

Originally an ad for Dave's in a drag production of Hello Dolly. It was so popular, Dave's made it into several hundred posters, which they gave away to customers of the Baths in the early '70s.

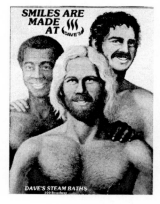

Other ads in the same series.

"Take Away The Cross"
oil on canvas, 1971

"Icky Homo"
("Behold the Homosexual")
oil on canvas, 1970

"Herbert The Good,"
oil on canvas, 1972

Greenleaf Classics Editions — "backdoor book" layout, 1969

Later book covers

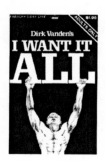

Frenchy's Gay Line,
1969

"The Other Traveller" from Olympia Press,
1970, 1971

MILESTONE 14: Adventures With Fig-Leaves

1968-1969, 35-36

In the fall and winter of 1968, I set up my typewriter in the second bedroom of my parent's home in Citrus Heights, and there I finished two books: *Hatters and Hares*, another S-and-M study, this one from the masochist's point of view—the title coming from *Alice in Wonderland*—and *Exile In Paradise*, a Gay "fantasy"—my "answer" to *Song of the Loon*—in which, after World War III, all Gays are rounded up and shipped off to an alternate world, where they start a new civilization. I mailed the manuscripts to San Diego as each was finished, and both were accepted—for $750 each, no promise of royalties.

On January 15, 1969, a package arrived from San Diego, and I eagerly opened it to find a dozen paperback books, with amateurish ersatz woodcuts on the covers, which were upside-down on the backs of the books. My novels began on the last-page of the book—the "back door," my publisher's own little dirty-joke, a statement of his own homophobia. They were my novels—three each of the four—except that the names had been changed. *Tom, Tom, The Piper's Son*, (originally *To Themselves Unknown*) had become *Who Killed Queen Tom?*; *The Stag In The Tree* had been changed to *The Leather Queens*; *Hatters and Hares* was now *Leather*; and *Exile in Paradise* had been renamed *Twin Orbs* (taken from the description of the hero's lover's testicles on page 2), with two earth-like globes superimposed over a naked man's ass on the cover.

After I had calmed down a little, I turned the book over to read the back cover of *Who Killed Queen Tom?* and found a first paragraph that I surely didn't write:

"There are times when it all comes flooding back over me, when I see a young guy with an arrogant bulge in his pants, or a sculpted ass encased in faded denim, then I hear a familiar voice chanting in my head: 'You left your wife for a husband! You traded her breasts for a pair of dimpled buttocks, and her cunt for a cock! You conformed before your rebellion, and now you are conforming again.'"

My "poetic-porno" rewrite of To Themselves Unknown had not been quite "hot" enough for their standards. The entire novel had been infuriatingly edited, and "augmented" with livid *"fag-hots."* All of my carefully-crafted, poetically-described sexual encounters had been rewritten to include bullshit like "pulsating purple cockheads spurting fountains of creamy ambrosia!" And there were hundreds of typos and spelling errors.

I hurled the book across the room, and the cover popped off when it hit the wall. *Pure trash!* There was no way I could ever show any of those books to anyone other than Gays who thought of themselves as *Queens* or *Fags*—the very ones I had disdained in my books. Queens and Fags would hate my books! A legitimate publisher would take one look and toss them all into the garbage.

I remembered a saying of Kurt's which came close to expressing my outrage and frustration that day: *"I felt like I'd been used without being asked, and then put away dirty."*

MILESTONE 15: Herbert The Good

1969-1988, 36-55

His real name was *Irving*, but the little neighbor boy in Brooklyn, New York, couldn't pronounce *"Irving,"* and called him *"Erbie."* His nickname became *"Herbie,"* then, when he started school, he called himself *"Herb"* Finger. In school, the other kids teased him about his funny name, but they also teased him about being skinny and Jewish—the only Jewish boy in a predominantly Catholic neighborhood. He quickly learned to turn such teasing to his advantage. All of his life, he was able to deal with prejudice by finding a challenge in it—to charm his detractors right off their perches. He started smoking when he was ten, and was cruising the New York Public Library, having sex with older men at that same age. By the time he graduated high school and started college, he was being kept by a well-known dancer on Broadway named Jimmy Jewell.

I met him on the day after Valentine's Day, 1969.

I had deliberately stayed away from the *Sweethearts' Balls* at Sacramento's various Gay bars. I was still thoroughly depressed over the books—and my life— and had no tolerance for anything approaching frivolity; wearing drag on Valentine's Day was about as frivolous as I could imagine—but I hadn't had sex since before leaving Las Vegas, and was ready to climb walls. So the next night, Saturday, February 15, I went to the *Hide and Seek Bar* in West Sacramento.

The pink and white streamers and balloons were still up from the night before, and there were cardboard hearts and cupids everywhere. The normally sawdust-covered floor was blanketed with tiny pink and white confetti hearts. I bought a beer and went to stand by the jukebox—my favorite spot in a Gay bar—and surveyed the crowd.

Suddenly, it was like in the movies: "Across a crowded room," I saw *him!* The room and the people faded and vanished as he walked toward me, grinning as though sharing a private joke. We were wearing almost identical outfits: boots, faded jeans, and plaid shirts. Both of us were bald, with what was left of our hair cut short, Roman style. I had a full short-cropped beard and he had a bushy moustache. His hair was brown, mine was dark blond; his eyes were blue, mine were green. We looked enough alike to be brothers, if not twins.

"Haven't I seen you someplace before?" he asked, as he reached to shake my hand.

"In the mirror maybe." I laughed and added, "I take it you noticed some similarity."

"Who could help noticing? It's like we deliberately tried. I'm Herb."

On an impulse I said "Dirk," deciding I was tired of being "Dick."

"Would you like to go someplace else, Dirk? Do you live around here?"

"I'm staying with my parents."

"Then let's go to my motel. I'm visiting from The City."

It turned out he liked to do just about anything sexual, and was very good at it all. He first produced a joint, which we shared—I hadn't had good weed since leaving L.A.—and all the hard lines of the world seemed to soften and relax. My anger and frustration floated away with the smoke. The sensations of my body seemed to be amplified, and kissing another man with a moustache was absolutely delicious! When it was over, we fell asleep on top of the bed, cupped against each other, as though we had always slept that way.

We spent most of Sunday together, obviously fascinated with each other, driving through the foothills in his Volkswagen Beetle, stopping in quaint little towns like *Rough and Ready* and *Cool,* to explore a few stores, then driving some more, always talking. I told him more about myself than I'd ever told anybody, including the fact that I was a published pornographer. "Erotician."

"Hey," he said, "it's a dirty job, but somebody's got to do it." Then, he sang, very much off-key "Masturbation can be fun…!"

He told me the story of his name and about growing up in Brooklyn, where both of his immigrant parents worked and his teenage sister was often too busy to notice where he was or what he was doing. He had always seemed to be the best little boy in Brooklyn, and it was assumed that he would never do anything even vaguely "naughty," let alone "perverted." He said he had learned to entertain himself (and to make a little money) by seducing older men in the park, and jacking or sucking them off in the bushes or men's room, then going home and pretending that absolutely nothing unusual was happening in his life.

He had been to New York parties attended by such people as "Lenny" Bernstein and "Jerry" Robbins, when his parents thought he was staying overnight with a high school chum.

He invited me to spend the coming weekend with him in San Francisco, and I accepted without hesitation. A relationship between us seemed inevitable. He had a beautiful apartment on the corner of Buena Vista Terrace and Roosevelt Way, overlooking The Castro. His roommate was just in the process of moving out to live with a new lover, and, at the end of the weekend, Herb invited me to move in with him. "I don't want to play house," he said, "but I've never felt like this before about anybody."

I traded my MG for a used Fiat station wagon because Luv had grown into a very large dog and didn't fit in the tiny sports car. A mini-station wagon suited me. And Luv loved it. It was white like him, and looked like his own special chariot.

Herb was the Art Director for Fireman's Fund Insurance Company, and had art-related contacts all over the Bay Area. He was impressed with my paintings and drawings, and kept me busy designing logos and letterheads, painting annual report covers, and doing all sorts of other freelance artwork. I was able to work at home, which I much preferred. I hated driving anywhere in *The City*—the streets were too narrow and hilly, the tourists too overly-cautious and the locals too crazy. Herb usually drove us anywhere we had to go.

Even though we slept together, we never did have a traditional love- or sexual-relationship, an "imitation marriage." Both of us had been sexually active for many years: me for seventeen years, him for twenty-three. Neither of us expected "fidelity" of the other, and didn't want it to be expected of us. He confided that he enjoyed getting fucked more than he liked sucking, and I told him about my problem with fucking. We decided to live more like brothers than lovers. Both of us, all of our lives, had wanted a brother. Now, it seemed our wishes had been granted. Sleeping together was comforting.

But in the bars, we made out like bandits. We would dress alike, but not identically, and cruise together, sometimes other couples, often singles. It amazed us how many Gay fantasies had to do with twins or brothers. It was fun. It was the first "fun" I'd had for a long time. We enjoyed being together. We augmented each other. Even though we looked alike, we were very different people. I was an introvert and shy around strangers; he was extroverted and charming, completely sure of himself. He took charge and I let him, relieved to have someone else making the decisions for a change—I had made so many wrong ones. And I trusted him to make the right decisions because I loved him, and knew that he loved me.

He read my books and persuaded me that they were better than I had imagined, and told me that some of his friends had already mentioned my name as a new Gay author. He suggested the plot for the next one: His favorite sex-fantasy was being gang-raped by cowboys. So I wrote *I Want It All* for, and dedicated it to, him. He got a big kick out of that. When the book was eventually published, we had an "Autograph Orgy."

Even though we lived together as "Gay Lovers" for eighteen years, we never were typical lovers. We loved each other for reasons other than sex, although we had mutual sex fairly often at first. We also had threesomes and foursomes and orgies, but most of all, we enjoyed going to The Baths. One of the jobs which Herb arranged, which I particularly enjoyed, was doing some advertising art for Dave's Baths, in return for which, instead of cash, we both were given free passes to any of Dave's Baths and bars in S.F., Seattle or Reno. The painting "Wading In" was used in a newspaper ad, and then hung in Dave's lounge in San Francisco for years, until the building and the painting burned down in the early '80s.

It was truly like finding a long-lost brother. We were very different men, but we enjoyed and appreciated the same things. We were comfortable, living with each other. In *I Want It All*, the two main characters, Warren and Brad are literary extensions of me and Herb. The book explores the problems and rewards that two Gay men encounter living together when they look enough alike to be twins or brothers.

I was accepted in the Folsom Street bars, Herb's crowd, as a genuine, "Published Gay Author." The books were much more popular than I had imagined they would be. But it was about then that Greenleaf Classics published *The Illustrated Presidential Report on Pornography*, (a photograph-illustrated version of the well-known report made for President Nixon)—*without permission* and the publisher and editor were arrested and fined and put in prison for plagiarism, and, suddenly, Greenleaf Classics was no more. And suddenly, my novels were out of print and out of circulation.

One evening at *The Stud,* a man introduced himself as Phil Andros, another Gay author who had been published and abandoned by Greenleaf. He said he had been approached by the owner of *Le Salon*, San Francisco's infamous porno bookstore on Van Ness, who was starting "Frenchy's Gay Line," a new publishing company. "Frenchy" had asked Phil to help find other Gay authors. I submitted *I Want It All* to "The Dirty Old Frenchman," and soon had a check for $500 and a promise of royalties, plus a commitment to publish anything I wanted to write.

Also I got to draw my own cover. Herb and I set up the covers for several of FGL's books; I did an appropriate pencil drawing and Herb set the type and the final print of the cover, using a scanner and printer available to him as Art Director at Fireman's Fund.

I Want It All was published in December, and Frenchy reported brisk sales. Even though it got good reviews in the local Gay newspapers, I was very disappointed in the final product. In his review for *California Scene*, Charles McAllister concluded: "Perhaps now that Frenchy's has a writer of Dirk Vanden's caliber they will try to do justice to his obvious talent by turning out a less sloppy product." I asked Frenchy's editor, a middle-aged straight man named George, why there were so many spelling errors and typos.

George said "Oh, didn't you know? *Queers love that!*"

In April, 1970, FGL published *All Or Nothing*—in which the "best friend" of the hero of *I Want It All* went looking for the "Queer" he and the gang had raped in the first book to beg forgiveness, and discovers his own homosexual desires in the process. Like *I Want It All*, it took place mostly in San Francisco, using the Folsom Street bar scene as background, from Western at "The Branding Iron" (*The Ramrod*), leather and motorcycles at "Leather Country" (*Febe's*) to S-and-M, downstairs at "The Phoenix" (*The No Name Bar*) to the Acid-Head bar, "Hyperion" (*The Stud*). Both of the books were reviewed nationally and the acclaim was unanimous. The reviewers agreed that I was one of the best Gay authors in America! Even the heterosexually-oriented *Screw* gave its review a huge headline:

"THE GREATEST STORY EVER TOLD!"

"I Want It All *is the best homosexual fuckbook I've ever read. ... Vanden is so good at taking his reader step-by-step through the stages of homosexuality that Gay people will find themselves remembering their own beginnings, and heterosexuals, well, they'll get a vicarious trip through what many of them have wondered about, behind the eyes of a character so 'normal' he is totally empathetic."—Michael Perkins,* Screw, *October 5, 1970*

"*Always written in a style and with smoothly structured syntax that rivals those of our top-flight novelists. ...I recommend this novel highly, but at the same time realize that it is not for the sexual novice nor for the old-fashioned sexualist. Of its genre, it has to be the best book ever written. If you thought Dirk Vanden's* I Want It All *said it all, you are mistaken. Read* All Or Nothing *and see what I mean." —Victor DeStefano,* California Scene, *Feb. 1971*

I was living in Gay Mecca, with a man I loved, who loved me, and we had a wonderful white German Shepherd named Luv. My name— or pseudonym, at least—was being published and praised from coast to coast. I thought I had it made. In the shade. With lemonade.

PART FOUR

MILESTONE 16: Bryce Canyon Miracle

1969, 36

During the summer of 1969, several months after I'd moved in with him in San Francisco, Herb had a two-week vacation coming up, and since my "job" was more or less working for him, doing artwork for advertising, report covers, pamphlet covers, miscellaneous charts and illustrations, I got the same vacation. We took Luv to stay with my parents in Citrus Heights, and we started our driving vacation in his Volkswagen by heading down the coast to Los Angeles, where I took the best part of the first week painting a twenty-foot mural for the back wall of a new Gay dance bar called *The Arena*, operated by previous purveyors of my art, Dale and Lucky, owner and operator of The Gauntlet, The Falcon's Lair, The Jaguar, and now, The Arena, across the street from DesiLu studios, in Hollywood.

I painted the figures with black and white acrylic house paint and Herb did the "Cosmic Cock," filling in my design with color. Our astrological symbols are featured in the cock: Taurus, me, and Libra, him.

While in L.A., we spent a good deal of time with an old friend of mine, Bud, a college professor who taught Anthropology by day in a local college, then wore leather by night and on weekends when he became a "teacher" of another sort, a *Ledermeister.* We never had a chance to play games with him, but he did share something with us that he used in his training sessions: large capsules filled with grey powder. "Psilocybin," he explained. "It's like acid, only not so crazy. It makes you feel good all over, plus it does fantastic things to your vision, to colors especially. Take it on the next part of your trip."

Since neither one of us could afford to stay and gamble in Las Vegas, we drove on into Utah to our next destination: Bryce Canyon National Park. We rented a cabin in the evening and spent the next day walking through Fantasyland. We thought it appropriate to take Bud's "silly-syben" to further appreciate the colors.

I had been dreading this part of the trip. Herb was an avid hiker and walker—he walked a mile, alone, every morning before work. I hadn't started walking with him because I had a sore on my foot that had been there a long time. I used Dr. Scholl's callus/corn-removers, but the thing wouldn't go away and I had to wear little donut shaped cushions to keep it from hurting when I walked. I packed the appropriate salves and bandages in my backpack, and was breaking in a new pair of walking shoes, like Herb's. They had some kind of foam pad that made walking feel almost pleasant. After a few minutes, I forgot about it entirely as I lost myself in the enchantment of those colorful spires and turrets and bridges, formations that became other things then changed back again. In addition to the visual excitement, my body started to feel really good. It felt great to move, to breathe, to flex all my muscles, walking along the narrow trails with a walking stick for balance and traction. Sometimes it felt like I was dancing, performing for an unseen impish, elvish, trollish audience. The day was magical and we arrived back at our motel, exhausted and thoroughly satisfied, showered and fell into bed.

In the morning as I was dressing, by habit I started to remove the little medicated cushion on my sole, to replace it, but it wasn't there. I looked in the shower and sure enough, there it was where it had come off last night. No matter, I had a new one ready to apply—but when I sat down and twisted my foot on my knee so I could see the sole of my foot, the sore was gone. The bottom of my foot looked as though the painful callus had never been there. That part of my skin looked perfectly healthy.

I commented on this "miracle" to Herb and he replied, "Well, good. It looks like whatever you were doing worked." It never occurred to him that the drug might have been responsible, but I was convinced that it was what had healed the sore in less than a day. That's all it could have been.

The sore never came back.

MILESTONE 17: Stuff Happens
1969-71, 36-38

On December 7, 1969, Luv had a terrible accident. We were walking in an unfamiliar area, when he jumped over what looked like a low wall and fell twenty feet on the other side, injuring his right front paw badly. He had to wear a cast on his foot, plus a large crutch-like contraption that fastened to his body with a harness, which kept his foot from touching the ground. This required that someone had to be with him practically all of the time for several months.

Herb and I had been planning to go to the *Renaissance Pleasure Faire*, in the Black Point Forest near Marin, in September. We had even made monkscloth robes to wear as identical monks, but Luv's situation forced us to change our plans. Bud, my friend from Los Angeles, unexpectedly arrived for a visit and offered to go to the Faire with me on Saturday, and Herb on Sunday.

He also offered "a little something extra," a special gift he had brought along, intending to party: *LSD*. Bud gave each of us a small white pill that looked like a saccharin tablet. "It's *Owsley Acid*," he said proudly. "The best there is!"

Even though I had taken Psilocybin, much to my enjoyment and benefit, I wasn't sure I wanted to try LSD. I'd heard many stories about people freaking out, jumping off roofs, thinking they could fly. People supposedly had done terrible things while stoned on LSD. On the other hand, The Beatles had recommended it highly! (But, then, the Beatles were breaking up, so what did they know?) Herb had already tried acid, and helped talk me into it. *"You'll love it,"* he promised.

Bud said he wouldn't take any himself, but would smoke some pot, and promised to stay close by me all day. We would also take along a tranquilizer, in case something went wrong.

On Saturday morning, I took the pill just before leaving home, and by the time we had crossed the Golden Gate Bridge and reached the Faire's parking area, I felt as though my body was shifting gears, like going from low to second to high, and finally into *overdrive!* My awareness seemed to open like an incredible flower with each shift of my gears! I had never been so aware of physical sensations—my heart beating, the blood rushing through my veins, my lungs expanding and contracting—and it seemed like a million delicious little butterflies kept fluttering up and down my spine, and dancing all over my body!

As we walked through the Faire's gates, it was like stepping into a new world, completely disconnected from the one we had just left.

There were hundreds of people, dressed in Elizabethan costumes of every variety, as well as brilliant and colorful "hippie" outfits, and they were frolicking like children, most of them stoned on some chemical or other, pretending and posturing, and having a wonderful time! And there were real children putting on a show of their own—laughing and squealing and chasing each other and climbing trees! The delight was contagious. The combined good feeling seemed to lift everything up onto a whole new level. It was all still the same, but cleaner, clearer, more in-focus, more "real!"

I became very aware of the love that seemed to be everywhere. It felt *delicious!* I had never felt anything like it before! We all seemed to be immersed in it—like a slightly-heavier-than-air ocean of warm ambrosial sweetness that drifted and eddied around us, buoyant and uplifting!

I felt *welcome! At home!*

I felt a profound sense of well-being and belonging! It was as though my eyes had been clouded all my life, but now they were clear, and I could see things as they really were—as they always had been! Everything was so fantastically beautiful, I wanted to weep for sheer joy.

Then it seemed that my mind somehow made contact with a much larger intelligence, which seemed to be *everywhere*, permeating *everything*. All I had to do was think of something, and suddenly I seemed to have knowledge that I'd never suspected I had. As though I had "plugged in" to a gigantic computer network! I realized, as though I had known it all along, but had pretended not to understand, that *I, alone, was in control of myself, of my life—not "Fate," not "God," not "Nature," but Me!* I was the one who ultimately made the decisions—to be sick, to be well, to be happy, to be miserable, to die or to go on living! I could be as angry and disappointed with my parents (and the world) as I wanted to be, and for good reason, but no one else was to blame for the life I was living. Neither of them or anyone else could have done anything to change that. I had chosen to take every single step I had taken. Unconsciously, perhaps, but by my own choice.

I knew I could stop having headaches and catching colds, because neither one was "real," both were products of my mind. All I had to do was decide to stop hurting myself! I could stop being sick and allow myself to "grow old" naturally. Without illness, the human body might be able to last a very long time. The unexplainable ages of Methuselah, *et al.* might have happened at a time before all the "sins" of the Jewish priests diminished the average lifespans from 900 to 33 years. If I could get rid of all those imaginary sins, I might live to be a hundred or more.

It was very much like waking up and finding that the terrible dreams which had seemed so real during the night, had suddenly vanished, and morning was shining through all the windows.

The Faire offered a million delights, affecting all aspects of my awareness—sights and scents and sounds and sensations—and I welcomed them all and indulged them like a starving man gorging himself on an amazing banquet of flavors and textures and sensations, each more exquisite and delicious than the others.

But then the darkness and the dream returned. "Reality" descended like night. Long before I wanted to leave, we were headed back toward San Francisco in a gathering fog. It seemed as though I had been huge, and was shrinking. I felt like I had as a small child, leaving Grandma's warm and wonderful kitchen, going home to a cold house where nobody talked to each other. As I watched the foggy headlights and taillights, stoplights and streetlights, weaving themselves into kaleidoscopic patterns, tears streamed from my eyes as though I had lost my dearest friend!

I tried to describe the experience to Herb and Bud, and they both smiled knowingly, like parents indulging a child's exuberant exaggerations, but I simply could not find the words to truly express the incredible adventure I had been through. Bud carefully explained: "You only saw what was already in your head. That's what acid does: It lets you see inside your head!"

The next day, while Herb and Bud were at the Faire, I got stoned on marijuana, and tried to recapture the enchantment, but it remained inaccessible, just beyond an impenetrable threshold. Finally, I settled on trying to write down some impressions of what I had discovered:

It was like returning home! It was like coming back to a beautiful and beloved place where I felt safe and loved and appreciated. It was like the way coming-home was supposed to be, the way I always imagined it was for others, but never was for me! Everything was so bright, so clear and clean. Things used to be like that for me; things had a beauty and simplicity which got hidden more and more with each successive year of school—where they taught me "the truth" about their counterfeit civilization! Liars and Hypocrites! They ought to be shot! Too late, they're all already dead!

Civilization is garbage! Layer upon layer of garbage piled all over us! Civilization stinks!

The struggle between good and evil is nothing more than an anthropomorphic battle between the inner and the outer man. The Inner is innocent, open and loving, welcoming and loyal, whose ultimate is sharing. The Outer is civilization, base and mean, full of rules and laws, hateful and distrusting! Civilization is drubbed on us like plaster, layer by layer until everything good and sweet and pure is covered up and smothered!

"Civilization" is the shame of sharing!

*That clarity, that "super-reality" really exists! I did not imagine it, I experienced it! At other times, I see it only dimly, vaguely, out from under my great overcoat of social do's and don'ts and whatwillpeoplethink's! But yesterday, I saw it clearly! And I believe it saw me! And I think it said **"WELCOME!"***

MILESTONE 18: ICDLITE
1971, 38

My two psychedelic trips had opened doors in my head, having to do with illness and wellness and my unconscious control of those things. In December, 1971, I saw an ad for a seminar called *Silva Mind Control*. According to the newspaper ads, the Silva Method was a "comprehensive program designed to train you to make better use of your mental processes." Perhaps they could give me access to that state of perception when I was high on acid.

For a week, in the evenings, I attended classes at the Jack Tar Hotel and went through a series of what amounted to group-hypnosis sessions, called "guided imagery and focused awareness" wherein our brains were "reprogrammed" to function more efficiently. In the end we were taught to hypnotize ourselves to perform further reprogramming to avoid "obstacles" to achieving our goals, *"and to open untapped aspects of your mentality."*

Our host/hypnotist taught us how to "get in touch with ourselves" by way of a modern method of Self-Hypnotized Meditation called The Silva Method. I gathered that Jose Silva was regarded as a modern saint by those who had taken the program.

According to their brochure, the last half of the seminar "trains you to recognize and take control of your intuition, that part of you that feels a hunch, or has a sudden insight into a situation before you. With intuition you are able to fully understand something not easily apparent by rational or logical means alone... Intuition can be utilized in every part of your life. It is of inestimable value in making decisions and choosing the best options. With our training you will be guided to listen to the small voice of intuition within you, and you will learn how to apply intuition to create a new and breathtaking reality for yourself."

I was actually surprised at the number of things those "Silva Sessions" allowed me to remember: Entire scenes from my childhood. Countless poems and songs.

On the final day, they had a little ceremony and gave us each *Graduation Certificates*, masters of *The Silva Method!* Partly in teasing, Herb suggested that we celebrate my graduation with a night at The Baths—on Bud's acid. I thought that was a great idea!

It was the sixth of December, 1970, ("St. Nicholas' Feast Day") and The City was getting ready for Christmas. Being a Sunday, the business district was deserted, but there were festive decorations all around.

Darkness was settling in as we parked the car and walked the block or so to *Dave's*. A nearby church was broadcasting recorded bells playing Christmas Carols, and we almost fell down laughing when they started pealing a very scratchy *Oh, Come, All Ye Faithful!*

Inside, we wished each other "Merry Christmas and Good Luck," and went to separate rooms.

There were only a few others wandering around in the halls or watching TV. The steam room was empty, so I climbed to the top shelf and moved back into my favorite spot, the darkest, hottest corner of the room. My body was doing that "shifting gears" thing. It seemed like my mind was unfolding...

I felt something touching my foot, seeming an enormous distance away, but the steam was too thick and dark to see who or what it might be. Hot, tingling sensations continued up my legs, engulfing me as it went, and when it absorbed my crotch and stomach, suddenly the room vanished; earth vanished! I seemed to be a sphere of light floating in space. At first, it seemed enormously empty and lonely all around me, but then other lights appeared in the darkness. One...two...vastly separated at first...but then more and more appeared until there seemed to be millions of us! A spacy Moog Synthesizer version of Bach's *Jesu, Joy of Man's Desiring* was playing on the background tape, and it seemed that Bach's music was everywhere, reverberating through space, filling the emptiness. We were all moving—*all dancing in space*—and soon it became obvious that we were all moving toward, and would all soon converge at the same point—where now I could see a *brilliant white light*, far brighter than the lights that were zooming toward it, sparkling, singing, welcoming us! The sphere of light grew as I flew closer and closer, until it finally filled the entire range of my vision, and then I went crashing into it—and *came!*

The Universe exploded and became fireworks in space! Bach dwindled away into silence. Then, Judy started singing "Have yourself a merry little Christmas," as dimly, a bearded face, surrounded with long blond hair that sparkled like a halo in the dimly lit steam, rose up from my crotch and kissed me wetly on the lips. "Merry Christmas," he whispered, then vanished into the mist.

When I finally regained enough strength to move, I went to the showers and turned one on full blast. It felt fantastic—like a deliciously refreshing drink of cold spring water on an incredibly hot summer day. The splashing water seemed to be drawing something out of my body! I watched in awe as writhing creepy-crawly little cartoon-monsters came oozing out of my skin to go swirling down the drain, wildly protesting and screaming, as they vanished. They were my "sins!" I recognized them!

When the shower was finished, I felt refreshed, renewed, amazingly clean! I felt *reborn!*

Just then, Barbra Streisand started singing "On A Clear Day," and I had the most overwhelming impression that *God* was speaking to me, using Barbra's voice, and that She was telling me to *look around*. So I did. I turned around and looked into a room which seemed to be behind a large window behind the row of wash basins, near the doorway, where a bearded, long-haired, naked man stood looking back at me. He grinned and winked at me, and God sang *"See who you are!"*

There was no doubt in my mind who it was; I recognized him easily, immediately! It was someone I had once loved very much, but had abandoned, many years ago because it seemed he had abandoned me. I had seen that face, that beard and long hair, in a thousand religious illustrations: *It was Jesus!* The *Come-Unto-Me* Jesus from Christmas cards, Jesus knocking on your door, Jesus and the little lamb—even the glow-in-the-dark plaster Jesus who stood guard in my grandmother's bedroom.

But then, the door opened and the window wavered, and I realized I was looking at my own reflection in a huge mirror.

The conclusion was obvious: *I was Jesus!*

The idea should have terrified me, but instead, something in my brain went click-click-click: *"YES! Of course! That explains everything. Why didn't I see it before?"* Suddenly it all made perfect sense.

Gentle Jesus, meek and mild! "Love each other as I have loved you. I will make you fishers of men."

Then, through the open doorway, another long-haired, bearded man came in. Obviously he *too* was Jesus! He smiled beatifically and nodded—almost a little Oriental bow—and went into the showers.

As I stepped out into the theatrically-lit, purple-carpeted corridor, a dozen other naked Jesuses—black ones, brown ones, tan and white ones—were moving to the music like some kind of bizarre avant-garde ballet. A group of voices were pretending to be musical instruments, making a dance tune out of *Oh, Come All Ye Faithful.*

I joined the parade and went up to my room with a happiness welling up inside me, ready to explode. I had the impression that I was the last one to discover the incredible Messianic Secret, and that today was a "Surprise Party" just for me! It seemed that everyone else had been waiting for me to solve the final mystery, and then the celebration would begin. It was going to be the biggest party the world had ever known.

And then we were going to merge!

There was something divinely ironic about learning all this at Dave's Bath, in the *House of David.* Homosexuality was the "Key of David!" Half of our Gay institutions were named after the King of the Jews who had loved Jonathan more than Bathsheba. The other half were named "Lambda!" We were the *"Lambs* who had gone astray!" We were the "first fruits of the Lamb of God! *"* We were the "last" who would soon be "first!" We were those "redeemed from the earth, who sang, as it were, a new song!" In us were all the prophesies fulfilled!

And now we could throw off our shrouds of "sinfulness" and dance together proudly in the light! Now we could properly save the world!

I opened the door to my cubicle, ready to join the jubilation, and almost fell headlong into darkness—an angry, roiling, crackling smokiness—just beyond my door. *Dave's Baths* had gone away, and in its place was something absolutely terrifying. It seemed I could hear grotesque whispering and muttering as though an incredible monstrosity was out there, in all those cubicles, sighing and slobbering, impatiently waiting to devour me and silence me forever.

I slammed the door and locked it. Terror almost parlayed me, but I had enough control left to shakily find the tranquilizer I had brought along for just such a situation. I swallowed it quickly and sat on the edge of my bunk, gripping the mattress for what seemed like hours until the fear finally subsided.

I kept the door closed and locked until Herb knocked and asked if I was ready to go. I had been dressed for an hour.

When we got home, Herb asked, "What's wrong? What happened?"

"Sit down," I said, "I need to tell you something."

We sat across the table from each other and I took his hands in mine. "I found out something tonight."

"Oh, what?"

"Who I really am," I told him earnestly.

He nodded indulgently. "All right," he said, "and who would that be?"

"Jesus," I said.

"You're kidding, right?" he said.

"I never knew who I was before, but now I know!"

"Jesus?"

"Isn't it wonderful?"

"Oh, Dirk…!" Herb put his head into his hands, squeezed his face, then hit his forehead with this fist! *"What have I done?"*

"No, no, wait!" I grabbed his wrists, pulling his hands down from his eyes. "You don't understand. *So are you!"*

"What?" He pulled away and looked at me as though I had gone totally insane.

"We all are! *All Gays are Christ!* 'The last will be first, and the first will be last!' 'The meek shall inherit the earth!'" I laughed happily. *"Look out, world! Here come the meek!"* Herb put his head into his hands again and sighed wearily. "Oh, God! Oh, Dirk!" he whispered. "I'm so sorry! I am so very, *very* sorry!"

"Sorry? *Why? It's wonderful!*"

But as I studied him, waiting for his response, I realized that, to him, something had gone terribly wrong. He was thinking I'd had a *"bad trip." "Acid-burnout!"* But to me, that "trip" had been the most incredibly beautiful thing that had ever happened to me. To him, it was insanity. Raving madness—as crazy as him claiming to be Moses. And he blamed himself for talking me into taking the stuff in the first place!

MILESTONE 19: "A Key to The Kingdom" Revealed

1970, 37

In 1969, Charles Manson claimed to be Jesus. In 1970, someone named Mel Lyman wrote a long, rambling letter which was published in *The Rolling Stone*, announcing that *he* was Jesus. ("No miracles this time, just hard work to save the earth.") New Year's Eve, 1971, in a well-known Gay restaurant on Polk Street, someone (the CIA, it later turned out, testing biological warfare weapons) had put LSD into a cocktail consumed by one of San Francisco's best-known Gay businessmen, who subsequently freaked out and proclaimed *himself* Jesus and was hustled off to San Diego never to return! One did not need to be a genius to figure out that I had been on a very popular acid-trip. A local joke had it that there were "more Messiahs in San Francisco that you can shake a stick at!" (Of course, the response to that was: "Never shake a stick at a Messiah!")

The only problem for me was, not every acid-taker took the Jesus-trip: Herb had no idea at all what I was talking about, when I tried to explain to him the incredible thing had happened to me. He had felt "good," physically, and had had wonderful sex—but nothing more. No deep psychological or spiritual insights. Just great sex. For him, that was enough.

Even though I understood, logically, that I had taken the same trip that hundreds, perhaps thousands, of others had also taken, the experience itself stood out in my mind like a lush green oasis in the middle of a vast and barren desert. It seemed like one of the most "real" things that had ever happened to me!

Herb flatly forbade me to take any more acid. As far as he was concerned, the thing that had happened to me was horrendous. It would have been the same as his hallucinating that he was Moses, back from the dead! Such an experience would be clearly insane, and it frightened him.

In attempting to make some kind of sense out of my adventure, I made the mistake of telling several friends about it. Their reactions were amazingly similar: at the first mention of the name "Jesus," their expressions froze, their eyes focused on something far away, and they suddenly remembered forgotten appointments; my "good friends" would get away from me as quickly as possible, and then virtually vanish from my life.

One Lesbian called me a "Gay Charlie Manson," stormed out of my house, slamming the door, and refused to have anything to do with me, ever again.

Another Lesbian, Herb's assistant at Fireman's Fund, telephoned me, very late one Saturday night, apparently acid-tripping herself, and said, "Hi, Jesus! This is God."

I recognized Ralf's voice and said "Hi, God! How are you?" Herb had apparently told her about my Jesus trip.

"Sad," she said. "Very, very sad."

"Oh, dear," I said. "What's wrong?"

She said, "My children don't love me. Some don't even believe in me. Some are angry with me, and some even hate me! And that makes me very sad."

"I'm sorry."

"Oh, that's ok," she said quickly. "I'm going to forgive them all because I love them so very much. I've decided to save the world!"

"Good for you, God!" I said. "Thank you."

"You're welcome! But, the thing I wanted to tell you is..." she paused dramatically. *"I am a network."* She hung up without saying goodbye.

About that time, I read an article in one of the Gay papers about a newly published translation of one of the Dead Sea Scrolls, a book called *The Gospel According to Thomas,* which the article's author called "The Gay Gospel," because of the final verses, which they quoted:

> Simon Peter said to them, "Make Mary leave us, for females don't deserve life." Jesus said, "Look, I will guide her to make her male, so that she too may become a living spirit resembling

you males. For every female who makes herself male will enter
the kingdom of heaven."

I found a copy of the small, thin book in a hippie boutique, and was amazed to discover that, instead of "God," or "Jehovah," Jesus referred to the power behind him as *"The All!"* He kept telling people "It is spread all around you, but you do not see it! You already have what you want, but you know it not."

I knew what he was talking about! At the Pleasure Faire, I had connected with something I thought of as the "All-Mind." I had just published two books with "All" in the title: *I Want It All* and *All or Nothing*, and had almost finished writing a third, called *All Is Well.* I wanted desperately to talk to someone about all this, but no one would discuss it. It was very much like discovering I was Gay, all over again, except at a "higher" level. The rejection was just as overwhelming. Even Herb withdrew a little. He never talked about splitting up, but he made it perfectly clear that he would walk out if my "insanity" didn't end, then and there. If I hadn't had the responsibility of talking care of Luv during his long recuperation, I might have jumped off the Golden Gate Bridge— just to see if I really could fly!

Instead, I stopped talking to anyone, especially Herb, about anything even remotely connected to Jesus or my acid trips. They became my deep, dark secrets. But I couldn't stop thinking about them.

By myself, while Herb was at work, I pursued the mystery secretly. In the process of comparing *The Gospel of Thomas* with those of the New Testament, I rediscovered something that had bothered me, many years before, in "Mormon Seminary," when I had seriously studied the Bible. The story, reported by Matthew, Mark and Luke, had made no sense whatsoever, because it had seemed like a non-sequitur—the original and real meaning seemed to have been lost in the many translations between now and then.

Jesus and the disciples had been in a "cornfield," outside Jerusalem, on the Sabbath day, picking up the "corn" that had been dropped by the harvesters, and eating it. The Pharisees had come flapping out of town, accusing them all of breaking the Sabbath, but Jesus supposedly told them: *"Have you never read what King David did, when he was hungry, he and they that were with him? How he went into the house of God, and did eat the Shewbread, which is not lawful to eat but for the priests alone, and gave also to them which were with him? The Sabbath was made for man, and not man for the Sabbath. Therefore, the Son of Man is Lord also of the Sabbath. "*

It didn't make sense—until I learned that "corn" was a generic term, meaning whatever grain the locals used for baking bread. It didn't mean "maize," which was native to America. It was much more likely to mean "rye" (what in the world is more *Jewish* than rye bread?) which is subject to a kind of fungus called "ergot of rye"—which was the predecessor of LSD!

It was like a light bulb had suddenly flashed "on" above my head, illuminating the darkness. It was truly a "revelation" because it explained almost everything!

Jesus had been talking about *"Show-Bread"—"Vision-Bread!"* Legal for the priests alone! You eat it and it "shows" you "visions"! The conclusion blossomed in my mind: The story in the Bible was simply the cover story for a piece of information someone wanted to communicate, without letting the authorities know what they were talking about. It was one of those sayings of Jesus with "secret meanings" that Thomas talked about.

The story was not about breaking the Sabbath, it was about a priestly secret called *Shewbread*. They had been gathering heads of rye that had been left by the harvesters and were now dusted with a red powder. They intended to grind those "contaminated" grains, and mix and bake their own Shewbread! That was how they got "into the spirit!" They were getting ready for Passover. It is not likely they were eating the grain, but that was something a scribe had added as an explanation to the seeming mystery.

Twice recently, I had taken the twentieth century version of Shewbread—LSD—and had touched the same thing they had touched, two thousand years ago: *The ALL!* I understood the passion and amazement of those whose visions had been guided by Jesus of Nazareth.

It was probably *Shewbread* which Jesus gave to the multitudes on the Mount, when two loaves of bread supposedly fed all those people.

He taught them his Gospel while they were stoned on LSD! He fed them visions. No wonder he seemed magical. No wonder he seemed to glow! No wonder they couldn't forget him.

It must have been *Shewbread* which he put into the water barrels at the wedding feast at Canaan, when a guest told the host, while drinking the new "wine," "You've saved the best for last!" You could get a whole wedding party stoned on few slices of bread dropped into a barrel of rainwater.

It was surely *Shewbread* which he gave to the disciples on what was to become "The Last Supper" on Passover eve. He and the others were "In the Spirit" in the *Garden of Gethsemane* when the soldiers showed up and caught Jesus and Judas "kissing." Jesus was probably tried and executed for being a Sodomite—a Jewish crime punishable by death by crucifixion—not for claiming to be a messiah. Judas was probably tried and executed alongside him as his sodomite lover.

Peter denied the whole thing, hid the body, and made up the incredible lie upon which Christianity and most of "civilization" is based: That Jesus came out of his tomb, alive and well, and rose up and bodily floated up to heaven! Or maybe Peter was still stoned on Shewbread and hallucinated that he saw Jesus doing what he wanted him to do. Whatever, Peter's main problem was, Jesus didn't declare himself King of the World, with Peter his holy first lieutenant, and save the Jews from slavery, as predicted by all the prophets, and as Peter had fully expected—instead, having proved himself to be The Messiah by coming back to life after being dead the predicted three days, he flew up into heaven, promising to come back and send all the sinners to Hell some other day. All the applicable prophecies about the expected Messiah were incorporated into the story his apostles told, that he had been born of a virgin, and had, indeed, risen from the dead, etc., etc.. No one contradicted them. It was all magical. The three wise men from the East, who had taught him about *Shewbread* and *The All*, were turned into kings of Egypt, bearing gifts to the newborn son of God—as had been predicted by the Jewish prophets.

Like John the Beloved and his "Revelations," (there's an acid trip for you!), I had simply seen what was in my own head, which I had put there, myself, long ago, based upon all the myths and fables my church and community had taught me, which I had accepted as absolute truth. Those images were still alive and well, and living in my mind. Growing up, I had patterned myself not on the father I hated, who hated me, but on the "father" I loved, *Jesus,* who loved me unconditionally; why should it surprise me to find out that's what I had become? A Jesus-clone—a carbon copy without magic powers! ("No miracles this time...")

The sower of seeds went out and sowed some seeds. Some fell on stony ground, some fell in thorny bushes, some fell where the birds ate them, but some fell on good soil and sprouted and yielded bountiful returns. I was one of those sprouts. Surely there were others!

As the months went by, it became obvious to me that I was not alone in my background and the problems engendered by early religious conditioning. Troy Perry, founder of the *Metropolitan* (Gay) *Community Church*, had once observed that: "Gay men and priests come from the same boy-pool." In my experience, Lesbians and nuns seemed, more often than not, to be cut from the same cloth. Except for those members of ersatz religious groups, Gay people seemed to regard Jesus with the same hostility usually reserved for ex-lovers. I assumed they had all been disappointed much as I had been, and had become homosexuals at least partly in a kind of "Fuck You!" gesture toward anything having to do with religion. Like my first cigarette and first drink of whiskey—my first homosexual experience—the guy in the bathtub—it had been a way of taking revenge at Jesus for not coming back, for being a lie, for leaving us—the real "Brides of Christ"—"waiting at the church."

But, if I was correct in my new theories, then all of our anger should be directed at Peter and all who followed him, perpetuating "The Greatest Story Ever Told."

Jesus wasn't preaching Christianity; he was trying to teach Evolution, Homosexuality and "Substance Abuse." He was trying to teach men how to live together and love each other, not how to die and go to Heaven. Or feed each other Jewish Guilt! The "closet" from which we supposedly came, when admitting our *deviation* and *defiance,* was surely the same one Jesus had advised us to go *into* when we prayed—instead of the synagogues and street corners: Talk to *The All* in private, and you will be rewarded in public. The teachings of the rabbi from Galilee—at least those not "corrected" or "interpreted" by generations of pious Peterites: Popes, priests and scribes—were still valid and helpful, if not "sacred" or "holy."

But, trying to tell all of this to someone who had already decided it was all bullshit, to be rejected and ignored, was like insisting an ex-lover was "still a nice guy, after all."

Of course, all of this had nothing whatsoever to do with non-ex-Christians, like Herb. None of that stuff was in his head, and he regarded it as myths and fables, with no more application to his own life than the story of the ant and the grasshopper, or the tortoise and the hare. Relevant, maybe, but just barely.

He did admit one thing: while growing up he had gone to a public grade school where most of the kids were Catholic. In front of every classroom, up above the blackboard, was *"The Golden Rule: Do Unto Others As You Would Have Others Do Unto You."* Herb said it reminded him of an old Jewish saying: *"What I wish for you is what you wish for me."* The two of them, together, became the motto that guided his life. But he never connected it to Jesus.

Another problem I quickly discovered, then learned again and again as the years went by, and I attempted to communicate my "vision," if it was caused by "Dangerous Drugs," it was instantly discounted, even by those who should agree with it most, because of their well-learned, well-intentioned prejudice. The "High Priests" still don't want us commoners to know about *Shewbread.* That remains the case to this very day.

MILESTONE 20: The Night Richard Amory Kissed Me

1969-74, 36-41

After moving to San Francisco in 1969, I started getting good reviews and notices in the various Gay publications, like the Gay Bar Newspapers or magazines like *California Scene* and *Vector*. In April, 1970, at a bar called *Speak Easy*, in San Francisco, the owner/publisher of *California Scene*, "Victor DeStefano," interviewed me, and published the interview in his magazine, March 1970—in which I enumerated the many problems I'd had with Greenleaf and their editor, Earl Kemp. I soon got a letter, forwarded to me by the magazine, from Richard Amory.

"Yesterday, I read your interview in 'Calif. Scene,' and have been jangling ever since. To put it bluntly, I think some people ought to get together and do something about Earl Kemp and Greenleaf Classics. I have had six novels published by them under the pseudonym of Richard Amory, and my list of woes, all stemming from Kemp's cute, old-style essentially anti-sex attitudes, is going to sound very familiar…"

He went on to detail the many problems he'd had and they sounded very much like my own. Greenleaf Classics was making money off our books, and were treating us like shit.

He finished: "In my zaniest moments I start thinking about intelligent, pro-sex publishers, and the possibility of, if not protest or boycott, at least a Gay writer's union or cooperative which would enable us to avoid some of the catastrophes you spoke of in your interview. Are you with me? Do you know any other writers or publishers…?"

In June, 1970, an article by Amory appeared in *Vector*, the magazine published by S.I.R.—the Society for Individual Rights—entitled *The REAL Name of the Game is Screw You, Queer Boy*. It was an interview with Richard Amory detailing the problems both of us had encountered at Greenleaf Classics. When asked if he had a solution to the problem of Gay writers trying to work with Straight publishers, he responded:

"I would like to see, and I think it's coming, a genre written by gay authors for a strictly gay audience, no holds barred, telling it like it is, or should be, and put out by a gay publisher. This is the crotch of the matter. Some of the editors at Greenleaf Classics may be able to fake it for a few minutes, but they aren't gay, and never quite catch on to many of the things that I for one am trying to say. They always end up looking like Arkansas tourists in *Finocchio's*, laughing their fool heads off, which doesn't bother me an awful lot because that's their problem, not mine, except that they screwed up my books, damn it!

"I think some very, very exciting things are happening. Take writers like Phil Andros, or Dirk Vanden, or Peter T. Hughes, or Dallas Kovar (of whom I'm inordinately fond)—in spite of some incredible editorial ineptness and interference, we're saying some things that weren't even dreamed of ten, or even five years ago..."

I got very excited and responded with a letter to be forwarded to Richard, proposing that we meet to discuss his idea, and inviting him to our home for dinner at his earliest convenience. Richard appeared for the meeting wearing a brilliantly rainbow-hued serape and a hat with ball-fringe all around it. He turned out to be a very pleasant, fun-loving, intelligent guy. Both Herb and I both liked him.

I asked him to autograph my copy of *Song of the Loon* and he wrote:

Apr 3, 1970

Feeling stupid - *porque este*
es el primier libro que he fimado —
Dedicado a un par de amigos
que me han hecho muy feliz.
Richard "Amory" Love
For Dirk and Herb

Encouraged by Amory's enthusiasm, I wrote an article for *Vector*, stating: "I would like to add my two cents' worth to the comments made by Richard Amory in last month's *Vector*. My response to his interview was that, as far as he went, he was 'Right on,' but he didn't go far enough." I proceeded to tell my sad tale of woe, which ended agreeing with Richard that we should, indeed, try to start a Gay publishing company, as he had suggested. By the time the article appeared, we had met and corresponded, and had arranged with S.I.R. to let us use their facilities for a public meeting, to try to find money to finance such an enterprise. One of Herb's good friends was on the Board at S.I.R. and arranged for a boxed notice, at the end of my piece, which read:

RICHARD AMORY IN PERSON.
Mr. Amory joins authors Dirk Vanden
and Phil Andros in a discussion of "The Gay Novel"
at S.I.R. Center on Wednesday, July 15 at 8 p.m.
Question and answer period—No admission charge—Refreshments.

By the time of the meeting, we had met Richard several times, and were very excited about the possibilities of working with him. Richard wanted to call the writer's co-op we were hopefully forming *The Renaissance Group.* Working with Jack, Herb's friend on the board of S.I.R., Richard organized the meeting and invited Larry Townsend, Phil Andros, Peter Tuesday Hughes and Douglas Dean. The meeting was very positive and exciting, and it looked like we might actually be on the verge of achieving something, we all agreed, we wanted very much. Each of us promised our next-begotten brainchild to The Renaissance Group. We ended the meeting with high hopes.

But nothing happened. No one volunteered to finance our venture and no one knew anyone who would or could afford it. Weeks went by and nothing happened to the dream. In an attempt to get something started, I recorded an interview with Richard and sent it to *Gay Magazine*, which they published as an article called "Coming Together (The Beginning of What???). " Richard and I recounted our hopes for Renaissance and expounded on the need for an all-Gay publishing company.

A response was almost immediate: Our pleas were answered by the new editor of *The Other Traveller*, the new Gay arm of *Olympia Press*,

Frances Green, a young woman newly arrived from England, who invited all of those who had been involved in the Renaissance Group to submit their next issue to Olympia and to let them become the new Gay Voice for East and West combined. They already had writers like John Francis Hunter and Angelo d'Arcangelo in their stable. As far as I know, all of those queried responded to Frances with their next novel. I sent *All Is Well*, which she accepted, then asked for a rewrite of *All or Nothing*— which made it the only one of my books available in two editions at the same time; one for FGL, the other, The Other Traveller.

Richard sent *Frost* and Larry sent *The Sexual Adventures of Sherlock Holmes.*

One memorable incident happened during the course of all this, when Herb and I took Richard Amory to see the premiere of the movie based on his book, *Song of the Loon.* He had not been consulted during the production of the movie, or about the script; Greenleaf Classics owned the copyrights to all of our books. No one had paid him a dime for movie rights or royalties. His first indication that there was such a movie was when he saw ads for its "Grand Opening" in the Gay papers.

We stood in line on Bush Street for half an hour, lined up on the sidewalk to see what the Nob Hill Theatre's marquee proudly proclaimed: *THE HOMOSEXUAL LOVE STORY FOR OUR TIME...FOR ALL TIME!* People jeered and made nasty remarks as they drove by. The movie was awful, by any standards: soft-porn which barely followed the outline of the book and contained none of the poetry. And they killed off the hero's lover in the end! As the final credits appeared on the screen, Richard stood up from his seat and yelled "That was shit!" and stormed out of the theater.

When the manager rushed out to see what the problem was, I told him "That was Richard Amory," and he said, "Who?"

Later, after a couple of beers at the nearest Gay bar, Richard Amory hugged and briefly kissed me, thanking me for a "memorable evening." He hugged and kissed Herb, too.

MILESTONE 21: Who Killed
Dirk Vanden?

1975, 42

D r. Lois Smith had been in the audience at S.I.R. when Richard
Amory and the rest of us had made our pitch for a Gay publishing
company. When *All Is Well* was published, she assigned it as one of the
books in her *Gay and Lesbian Literature* course at S.F. State. It was an
extension course, given in the evenings. When they reached the end of the
semester, her students were treated to a "graduation party," given at Dr.
Smith's home.

Richard and I were both invited to the final class of the series, but
for some reason he didn't attend. I was the only one to show up and take
questions from her students, who ranged from late teenagers to older
women. There were only a few young males in the group. They asked
questions like "Why did you write this book in the first place?" and "Are
you a father?"

Their questions all seemed negative, and nobody thanked me for
writing anything "liberating," although that had been the general theme
of the course: *Gay Liberation*. Herb went with me to both the final class
and the party afterward, and ended up being the hit of the evening, with
students clustered around him, talking about his job as Art Director for
Fireman's Fund—where the company permitted unions such as his and
mine and allowed him to have a Lesbian assistant—while they ignored
me, standing in the corner, drinking punch.

It seemed to me that, instead of being welcomed as a *Liberator*, I was
being ignored, even shunned, for writing *dirty books*. The students of Dr.
Smith's course would have preferred that I leave "so much sex" out of
my novels. My disclaimer that I put the sex there because my publisher
insisted on it, obviously didn't play.

It was the kind of disdain that I experienced several more times, in various forms, over many years: I have a reputation carved in stone, like a grave marker: "Dirk Vanden — Dirty Book Writer Deluxe." One of my favorite analogies, over the years, is "They (all the different Gay groups) treated me as though I expected applause for having farted in church."

After the experience with Dr. Smith's class, I decided to end the "Dirk Vanden" chapter of my life. I was tired of rejections. I was tired of fighting, just to be published, then being challenged for justification for writing "dirty books."

Greenleaf had folded, Earl Kemp was in prison for copyright violation; Olympia had declared bankruptcy and closed. I had written seven books, three of which were highly praised in the national Gay media, but I hadn't received one penny in royalties. Of all my publishers, only Olympia had given me a contract promising future royalties, but they went out of business and paid nothing beyond the five hundred dollars they had already paid me. The dream I had shared with Richard Amory, of an all-Gay publishing company, had vanished like a wisp of fog on a dark night.

I decided that I had already received Andy Warhol's "fifteen minutes of fame," and that the achievement did not equal the effort put into it. Being Dirk Vanden had become painful, and simply wasn't worth the effort. *"This is the way (my) world ends: not with a bang, but a whimper."* —T.S. Elliot

Herb sadly agreed. He had seen how frustrated I became over a fight with one editor or another. He too had been very hopeful about starting The Renaissance Group, and had seen how disappointed I was when nothing happened. Finally he had dealt with me after Dr. Smith's Gay Lit class ignored and avoided me, as though I had done something wrong instead of writing ground-breaking Gay novels.

He needed to make a decision of his own. Fireman's Fund was getting ready to move its headquarters from San Francisco to Marin, across the Golden Gate Bridge. Herb's job was assured, but we would have to move with the company. He was tired of being an Advertising Manager, with many awards for excellence, and felt that he'd "done that." He wanted to do something new. He had an idea.

PART FIVE:

MILESTONE 22: The Birth of Gabriel Horny

1971, 38

The last half of the Silva Mind Control seminar, according to the brochure we received on the first night, had been about:

> ...training you to recognize and take control of your intuition, that part of you that feels a hunch, or has a sudden insight into a situation before you. With intuition you are able to fully understand something not easily apparent by rational or logical means alone.
>
> Intuition can be utilized in every part of your life. It is of inestimable value in making decisions and choosing the best options. With our training you will be guided to listen to the small voice of intuition within you, and you will learn how to apply intuition to create a new and breathtaking reality for yourself.

Although the program never quite fulfilled the "new and breathtaking reality" part, the Silva Method did introduce me to someone very important in my life, an old friend I didn't know I had.

Again, we were at Dave's Baths, but because Herb had forbidden it, I hadn't taken LSD (although I suspected *he* had, without telling me). Instead he had procured some really good pot, something called *Sensimilla*, from Oregon, and I was very high on that.

In my favorite spot in the steam room, on the top level, back in the corner farthest away from the door, quite alone and undistracted in the hot darkness, I did what the Silva Method had taught me to do: I relaxed completely and went to my "Quiet Place," on the bank of an imaginary river, where a willow tree dipped its trailing branches into the flowing water, and sunlight sparkled on the ripples. I could see it quite clearly and could sit there and watch it for hours.

Another of the things Silva had taught me was that I had a "secretary" in my head, a persona I could talk to and ask "Where did I put my keys last night?" and the imaginary secretary would show me or guide me to my keys. It amazed me that the practice actually worked and I enjoyed playing with it.

I imagined telling my secretary, "Okay, I'm ready. Bring me something to eat. A nice big juicy cock."

In the steam-room I had a strange feeling that someone was there, but I was certain no one had entered. I said "Hello?" but no one answered.

Instead, a voice seemingly behind me, on the riverbank, said "I'm in here."

I imagined myself asking "Are you my secretary?"

The imaginary voice answered "Well, I suppose that's as good as anything else you could call me. Actually, I'm your computer programmer. I more or less run your life for you."

I looked around the riverbank, but there was no one there, imaginary or not. "Where are you?"

"In your head!" The voice sounded exasperated at my foolish question. "Where else would you expect me to be? Here, maybe this will help…"

It was as though a 3D TV or movie screen superimposed itself on the steam, and I looked into a scene of bleak desolation. It was a windswept mountain peak, apparently freezing cold; I could hear the wind howling, but couldn't feel it, being nice and warm and totally relaxed on my riverbank in the steam room, watching my pot-induced "Vision." The sky in the Vision was black with billowing clouds, lit up by flashes of lightning.

At first it seemed I was far away from the mountain, but I discovered I could move, just by willing it, and as I moved closer I could see a figure, standing on the very pinnacle, wearing a long robe of deep blue which flapped around him in the wind. He had long white hair that whipped around his face and a white beard, but he didn't look like an old man, he looked ageless. As I approached him, he noticed me and smiled and opened his arms and said something I couldn't hear.

He turned around and made a brusque gesture, and the lightning stopped, the clouds parted, and sunlight poured through, illuminating his face theatrically. "I do love a dramatic entrance, don't you? It's good for getting attention. Hello there, it's good to finally meet you after living in your mental basement all these years."

"Where are you?" I asked mentally.

"I just told you, in the basement of your head. I'm that still small voice that yells at you all the time, trying to get your attention. Since you can't see inside your head without turning yourself inside out, I've created this imaginary device for you to visualize what you'd ordinarily think of in words. Got that? Good. Next question?"

"What's your name?"

"I'll give you a clue."

Suddenly the scene changed: The background music was a very old song called "Blow, Gabriel, Blow," from Cole Porter's *Anything Goes*; I had helped stage a production at The University of Utah. My host now wore a brilliant white gown, tap-dancing shoes and a top hat and a cane. He looked like a movie star from the '30s. He was tapping to the music, mouthing the words. As the song finished, he made a grand flourish and changed back into his more placid Wizard persona. He smiled slyly, waiting for my guess.

"The Wizard of Oz?"

Suddenly a red velvet theatrical curtain zipped closed in front of me. My host parted the curtains around his head and peered out, grinning impishly, saying "Pay no attention to that little man behind the curtain." The curtains zipped closed again and he called from behind them, "*Wrong!* Try again."

"Judy Garland?"

The curtains opened slowly, and he looked down at me with resigned exasperation. "Don't be facetious, it doesn't become you." Now my host had huge wings, folded demurely behind him. He was holding a horn that started very small at the mouthpiece and got progressively larger, like an ancient trumpet, about three feet long. He raised the horn dramatically and lights came up behind him as he turned sideways for a silhouette, the horn raised Heavenward, his wings outstretched.

The image wavered and became the angel on the top spire of the Mormon Temple. "You're the *Angel Moroni!*"

"*No, no, no, no, no, no, NO!* Joseph Smith *copied* his angel after mine. The *real* one." He held his arms out, one still holding the trumpet. *"Ta-da!"* He waited quizzically, then refreshed the pose, and said again *"Ta da!"*

When I didn't respond, he huffed "Oh, for Heaven's sake! I'm the fucking Angel *Gabriel.* At least, I'm *named* after him. I'm a copy of the original, which was only some writer's idea in the first place. I'm totally 'mental,' as the children say. Don't you get it? *End of the world...?* That's your theory, isn't it? One world ending, a new one beginning? That's what the Angel Gabriel is all about, isn't it? *Ta-da!* And yes, *Cinderella,* or *Sleeping Beauty,* or *Snow White* or *whatever the fuck your fairy-tale name is...*" He opened his robe and displayed a perfectly sculpted masculine body, hairy, and very well endowed. He pulled out of his blue garment like a stripper and threw it aside, grinning lasciviously as I watched his cock get hard and stand out invitingly. "Even us angels get horny, so *come blow my horn*! I'm *horny*, get it? Oh, I do love these guessing games, but this one is getting a tiny bit tedious. I'm *Gabriel Horny* and I'm your resident smartass *systems operator.* Good to meet you. Finally."

The steam room door opened and a naked man walked in. "Ooops, here's your order. Hung as requested. Gotta run, bye!" Gabriel vanished in the light that flooded the room for a moment, as the door closed. A voice in my head said, "Have fun. Talk to you later!"

I forgot the experience in whatever distractions followed it, remembering it years later when I attempted to put together a collection of my colorful "inspirations." Colored Post-It sticky-notes had just become popular, so I bought a "cube" of rainbow colors. I usually started a writing session for one of my *All* books with a joint of Sensimilla, keeping a notepad nearby to write notes about distracting but interesting thoughts, which I would post on a wall-sized bulletin board behind my desk. I soon learned to associate these notes, which I called *"Messages To Myself,"* as inspirations from Gabriel Horny—while he's busy, in the basement of my mind, operating the biocomputer which controls my life.

After a few years, those notes filled several file-boxes. In addition to this collection of "messages" that became *The Wit & Wisdom of Gabriel Horny* (see Appendix), my alter-ego, doppelganger, deep unconscious, or whatever it was, also inspired me to create several oil paintings that conveyed my insights into the nature of religion. (These are reproduced in the first photo section of this book.)

"Icky Homo" was inspired by the Acid Trip at The Baths that convinced me that Homosexuality was going to be the "Messiah" that will save the world from wars and overpopulation. I understood that many others, like myself, were lured into homosexuality by Jesus' teachings. Those who followed "The Jesus Path" followed it out of religion into homosexuality. Those who truly believed those teachings became Gay, whether they wanted to be or not. "We are called Gay not for what we are but for what we will be when we discover what we are." I imagined Jesus without his cross, flying, free at last after nineteen-hundred-and-seventy years! At first I called it "Jumping Jesus," but changed that to "Icky Homo" (Behold the Homosexual!)

"Take Away The Cross" was inspired by a final acid-trip in 1970 that left me with the indelible impression that the suffering of mankind was the fault of religion, symbolized by the Cross Jesus died on. The Cross is the universal symbol for suffering and death. If you take away the cross, behind it is some kind of magnificence. At the bottom of the painting are tiny portraits of the singers I considered the "prophets and saints" of the new Hippie World. The central figure is a reproduction of Michelangelo's "Risen Christ." That's Herb to his right, and that's the ZigZag man, down in the corner by Gracie Slick.

MILESTONE 23: Superchef
1976, 43

Just after Christmas, 1976, we moved to Roseville, a small community about twenty miles east of Sacramento.

As soon as we were settled, Herb placed an ad in the *Sacramento Bee:* *"Take a Vacation at Home. Let me pamper you and cook gourmet meals for you for a week, maybe two."* Almost immediately, a young couple in Fair Oaks (another bedroom community east of Sacramento) responded to the ad, and wanted to celebrate their anniversary with a week-long "vacation at home."

Several years earlier, as a college student in Florida, Herb had had a relationship with a much older man who made his living as a stage-magician. He and Ted shared a love for "good cooking," and Ted financed a small "Beatnik" coffee house called *Café Baba* where Herb was encouraged to explore his own kind of culinary magic as specials on the menu with the various cups of coffee. They had held "Beat Poetry" readings.

In San Francisco, Herb had been a member of a Gay Gourmand group which met once a month at one of the members homes for a new menu out of Julia Child's cookbooks.

During the first week of February, 1976, Herb went to work daily at the couple's home in Fair Oaks, starting early in the morning and staying until late at night. Horace was involved in politics and Roseanne in charity work. They had many rich friends. Herb would serve them breakfast by the pool, then cater to their every whim (nothing sexual or kinky). He was butler, maid and cook, all rolled into one. He prepared and served a "small, intimate dinner" for two or maybe four, every night, and on the last day, an extravagant party for all of the past-weeks' guests, with all the stops pulled out.

Herb enlisted the help of a local grocery store which had the best deli in town, *Corti Brothers*, who helped him delight the Crandells and their guests with their gustatory delights. That partnership lasted several years and helped make local history as Herb and Corti Brothers catered the Grand Reopening of the Capitol Dome in 1980.

Suddenly he had a long list of new clients, friends of Horace and Roseanne, who wanted Herb Finger to cater dinners and parties for them. At first he called himself "Superchef," but learned that it was already a trademarked name. We called our new business *Little Red Hen Enterprises*. Herb hired an assistant to help him, Mark Gonzales, another Gay gourmand, who was his *sous chef* for years. Herb would create the menus, which he and Mark would cook in our kitchen, pack everything into several thermos tubs, and stack all those inside his little Volkswagen which he and Mark would drive to the party. Part of the Herb Finger experience was watching him unpack an entire dinner or party from his little VW, like a clown car in the circus.

I would create the hand-calligraphed souvenir menus which they gave to all the guests.

For Christmas that year, I gave him a vanity license plate for his VW: CHEFONE. He gave me a license plate for my old Jimmy pickup: ICDLITE

In 1981 he was hired as Chef for a new restaurant in Fair Oaks called *Bon Appétit,* a small, intimate facility, the keystone of an elegant shopping center, *The Almond Orchard.* He took Mark with him and brought one of his Gay gourmand friends from San Francisco, Jack Perpich, up from The City to work with him and Mark. Jack brought Jack Covington, his lover, and they moved into a nearby farmhouse. Covington and I were old farmboys and we each had organic gardens to produce special delicacies which Herb used in many of his appetizers and side-dishes.

Bon Appétit was very successful very quickly, until there was standing-room-only at the bar. Herb was being noticed by the local media who called him "Sacramento's Celebrity Chef."

He became the local spokesman for Litton Microwaves, and had a short TV show on the noon news, showing how to cook fairly complicated "gourmet" recipes in that strange little black box on the kitchen counter. Watchers were invited to send in stamped self-addressed envelopes, and I would mail them the appropriate recipe in return. Women would stop him in the supermarket to tell him they had sent in for one or more of his recipes, and how much they loved them. We were preparing a cookbook.

I painted Herb's life-size portrait. It was intended as the cover to his cookbook and to hang in the foyer of the restaurant, as the first thing a patron would see coming through the front doors. The silver-gray background was supposed to be the shiny stainless silver kitchen equipment. It turned out to be prophetic of something else.

Everything was going beautifully. Herb and his crew were planning to create another, separate restaurant, featuring local organic produce, like mine and Covington's, to be called *Good Eats*.

One Saturday night in 1982, Herb, Mark and the Jacks, went to a downtown Gay bar after the restaurant closed to celebrate something. I stayed home with the dogs. Around 2:30 I was awakened by a phone call from Herb. He was using the payphone in the shopping center. He started out "Well, the sonofabitch did it. He burned his own restaurant down!"

He had been driving home after the bar had closed, and saw flashing red lights and smoke coming from his corner of the shopping center. By the time he got to the scene, almost everything had been burned. He managed to retrieve one of his rainbow beanies which his many female fans had knitted for him. Luckily his portrait hadn't yet been hung in the foyer, so it was saved. We decided that the smoky background was my prophesy of the fire that would end Bon Appétit.

It turned out that a still-burning cigarette had been "accidentally" dropped in the bin which contained the day's dirty linen, to be laundered the next day. It had smoldered awhile after everyone had gone home, and then started burning in the kitchen. Herb was certain that the owner had deliberately burned the place down just to get rid of him and Mark and Jack, and collect the insurance.

What had happened, as word got out in and around Sacramento that a Gay chef had a restaurant in Fair Oaks, where his two assistants were also Gay, Bon Appétit quickly became a gathering spot for Gays and Lesbians. More and more, the demure bar had become a Gay bar, and Bon Appétit was getting a reputation as a Gay restaurant. The owner, David O'Donnell, didn't like that one bit. He wasn't Gay and didn't want Sacramento Society to think he ran a Gay restaurant. He couldn't fire any of them without creating a big stink, and he'd lose a huge chunk of his customers if he did.

Suddenly Herb and all of his crew were out of work, and all but Mark went away in different directions. Herb and Mark were briefly hired by a rich Republican developer, to create a menu for his tiny restaurant in Old Town Folsom called *Café Natoma*. The problem was, Herb discovered, the owner wanted the restaurant mainly as a place to entertain his clients, and to use as a write-off on his taxes, but when word got out that Herb and Mark were now at Café Natoma, the whole Sacramento Gay gourmand group started going to Old Town Folsom, and suddenly the tax-write-off was becoming successful. With many apologies and a large retirement benefit, Herb and Mark were let go.

Briefly, Herb, by himself—Mark had gone elsewhere for employment—found a job as a chef in a college-hangout called *Brewster House*, in Davis, near the University of California at Davis, twenty miles west of Sacramento. His portrait finally hung in a foyer.

MILESTONE 24: The Valley and the Shadow

1987-95, 54-62

A bad omen occurred shortly after we hung Herb's portrait in the entry of Brewster House in Davis: Someone drew a black-eye on the oil painting with a ball point pen. They never found out who did it. We retrieved the painting and I was able to remove the ink with a special ink-remover, but that embarrassing public black-eye started Herb on a downward spiral. It was like the last straw that finally broke his will.

He had been there only a few months when he started having night-sweats. We thought it was the flu, so he stayed home from work and rested, but the night-sweats got worse, until he would soak the bedding and I'd have to change sheets every morning. Then little red sores started appearing around his neck. At first we thought it was the starch in his chef's coat, so I washed them all and ironed them without starch, but that didn't help. Finally, he decided he was sick enough to see a doctor.

We had a Gay doctor, Sandy Pomerantz, who sent him for tests, and then to the hospital. When I went to visit him there, he was on the top floor in a room marked CONTAGIOUS, and I had to wear a medical gown and a mask and gloves to visit him. His HIV was already fairly advanced and they didn't know if he was contagious or not. Meanwhile they treated him like he had the plague.

Word got out very quickly that Sacramento's Celebrity Chef had AIDS. He had been scheduled to participate in an event called *Sacramento Cooks*, as one of the featured chefs, but his appearance was summarily cancelled with a letter that began: "We regret to inform you…"

His new organic restaurant Good Eats was going to feature local organic produce and meat. He had a spot picked out and was talking to the developer—same guy who owned *Café Natoma*. But then he was forbidden to cook anything publicly. All his dreams went down the drain.

People who had made a fuss over him for the last several years suddenly shunned him, and treated him as though he had brought his illness on himself, deserved it, and deserved to die a miserable death because of it—and they didn't want to get what he had. That hurt him so much, he went inside himself and never came back out. Not even for me. He literally shrank out of existence. I watched him wither away for three years.

Fortunately we had two dogs, Frankie and Ernie, who adored him, and they spent practically every minute of his last three years at his side. I remortgaged the house and took care of him as he dwindled away to little more than a skeleton.

His doctor tried everything, every nostrum, every old wives' cure, even went with him to Mexico to buy contraband drugs rumored to cure HIV. They didn't.

During his last month it was obvious that the end was near, but Dr. Pomerantz didn't want to put him in a facility to die. He was also Jewish and had a special bond with Herb. I took care of him at home, and Sandy made house calls almost every day after work. Finally, he brought a pint bottle full of morphine and an eyedropper to measure it into his liquids. Herb's last words were "I'm…mor…phin…ized…!"

He died in my arms on the morning of January 22, at 8:30 AM. Schubert's *Traumerai* from *Kinderscenen* was playing on our stereo.

When I was sure he had stopped breathing, I eased my arm out from under him, covered him with a sheet, and went to another room to call Sandy. All I said was "It's over." He said, "I'll be right out."

Herb's will stipulated that he wanted his body cremated and mixed with mine and those of our dogs when we all died. It was contrary to Jewish law, and his mother protested. She even tried to get me to send her some of his ashes so she could secretly bury them in the Jewish cemetery. Herb's brother-in-law, a psychoanalyst, talked her out of it. I have his ashes on a shelf in the front room, along with Luv's, Frankie's, Ernie's, Andy's and Buddy's, all waiting for mine and Buddy Jr's. In my will, my final instructions are that we all be mixed together and planted under a lilac bush with a good view.

Very soon after Herb died, Sandy reported it to the local media and it made the national evening news, even in Florida, where his mother and two aunts were having supper, watching Walter Cronkite. His sister had told Mama that he had leukemia, but no one had told her yet that he'd died. Poor Leah! There she was, with her two Jewish sisters, all widows in a retirement community Herb called *Little Israel*—in Florida—and there was a picture of Herb Finger, her only son, with his little rainbow-beanie that he wore instead of a chef's hat, like a Gay *yarmulke,* on national television. *Sacramento's Celebrity Chef, Herb Finger, dead of AIDS at age 39.* She almost had a heart attack. Fairly shortly after that, she developed dementia.

When I picked up his box of ashes from the crematorium and sat in the car weeping, holding it in my lap, suddenly I understood the true meaning of the phrase "the valley of the shadow of death." I was in that valley and that shadow, and it was freezing, bitterly cold. Even though the sun was bright on a spring morning, I was chilled to the bone.

The only things that kept me from driving head-on into a big truck on the highway, driving home, were in the back seat, named Frank and Ernie. They still needed me. They seemed to sense what was wrong on some dog level, and they stayed close beside me for the rest of their lives.

I had my blood checked several times during and after Herb's illness, but I never contracted HIV. That seemed like a blessing at first, but then I started feeling guilty for having written books praising Gay Life and homosex as a good thing. Instead it had become a killing thing. Gay men who had taken my advice and come out before 1979 were dying horrible deaths. I decided it was at least partly my fault.

MILESTONE 25: Homocaust

1979-20?? 46-78

Sometime after Herb died in 1987, I found and kept a letter to the editor of the **New York Native**, a Gay newspaper which Herb had subscribed to. I wrote to the editor responding to that letter and they published it:

Smoking Gun?

Has Henry J. Yeager found the "smoking gun"? In his letter to Jerry Isler of the Greater New York Blood Program (*Native* 151) Yeager asks "Or was [AIDS], as many of us think, deliberately introduced into the homosexual community in 1979 right there at the New York Blood Center, when you put out a call for gays to give blood samples under the pretext of developing a hepatitis vaccine?"

Almost everyone we know who has AIDS or ARC also took part in that Hepatitis Vaccine-development program—in San Francisco!

Is it possible to make a survey of your readers to determine how many others possibly contracted their life-threatening illness in one of those hepatitis vaccine programs? Also, how many, like each of the PWAs we know, had their blood samples frozen without their knowledge or permission. How many cities took part in those tests?

Dirk Vanden, Carmichael CA

In an undated article in the *Philadelphia Gay News*:

AIDS Called Plot to Eliminate Homosexuals

Dick Gregory, speaking at Swarthmore College, suggested that AIDS is a government plot to eliminate homosexuals. He then urged gays to stay in the closet for their own safety.

Gregory says he learned that the AIDS virus actually was developed by government researches testing monkeys at UC Davis six years ago. He stated that if the disease "had anything to do with gay sex, there'd be a thousand cases in Rome by now."

Remember President Obama's original pastor, The Reverend Jeremiah Wright, the one he dumped for his controversial belief that AIDS was the Government's method of Ethnic Cleansing, targeting Blacks. Remember his sermon "God Damn America!"? I'm willing to bet he is right.

Recently I found this on Google News:

Just What Was He Smoking?

By Gene Weingarten, Washington Post 3/21/02

Regarding the Nixon Tapes:

On a lengthy monologue on May 13, 1971, Nixon makes clear that he does not like gay people. Northern California has gotten so "faggy," he says, "I won't shake hands with anybody from San Francisco."

"...the point that I make is that, goddamn it, I do not think that you can glorify on public television homosexuality. You don't glorify it, John, any more than you glorify, uh, whores.

"I don't want to see this country to go that way. You know what happened to the Greeks. Homosexuality destroyed them. Sure, Aristotle was a homo, we all know that, so was Socrates.

"Do you know what happened to the Romans? The last six Roman emperors were fags... You know what happened to the popes? It's all right that popes were laying the nuns.

"That's been going on for years, centuries, but when the popes, when the Catholic Church went to hell in, I don't know, three or four centuries ago, it was homosexual... Now, that's what happened to Britain, it happened earlier to France. And let's look at the strong societies. The Russians. Goddamn it, they root them out, they don't let 'em hang around at all. You know what I mean? I don't know what they do with them.

"Dope? Do you think the Russians allow dope? Hell no. Not if they can catch it, they send them up. You see, homosexuality, dope, uh, immorality in general: These are the enemies of strong societies. That's why the Communists and the left-wingers are pushing it. They're trying to destroy us."

This was the official atmosphere surrounding President Nixon in May, 1971. The official and unofficial policies in DC and across the country were anti-fags and anti-drugs. Nixon wasn't just ranting politically-correct diatribes, he meant it. He believed what he was saying and so did everyone who loved Dick Nixon, who was going to guide America to its proper heritage, without Jews and Fags and Drugs, and I'm sure Niggers weren't left out of the shit-list.

Richard Milhous Nixon (January 9, 1913—April 22, 1994) was the 37th President of the United States, serving from 1969 to 1974. The only President to resign in disgrace.

Meanwhile, back in reality, Gays were starting to gain public visibility, refuting all the ancient religious stereotypes, which was getting the Religious Right and its leader, Richard M. Nixon, very upset. Imagine a religious tizzy! Homosexuals were being legalized during his watch. Someone had to do something!

Here is a timeline of the Gay Rights movement, starting with decriminalization:

1962: Illinois becomes the first state in the U.S. to decriminalize homosexual acts between consenting adults in private.

1965: Richard Amory publishes *Song of the Loon* via Greenleaf Classics.

1969: Dirk Vanden publishes *Who Killed Queen Tom? Leather, The Leather Queens, Twin Orbs* and *I Want It All*, via Greenleaf Classics and Frenchy's Gay Line.

June 27: The Stonewall riots transform the Gay rights movement from one limited to a small number of activists into a widespread protest for equal rights and acceptance. Patrons of a Gay bar in New York's Greenwich Village, the Stonewall Inn, fight back during a police raid on a bunch of drag queens, sparking three days of riots.

1970: Dirk Vanden publishes *All or Nothing* through Frenchy's Gay Line; a revised version was published by Olympia in 1971.

1972: Dirk Vanden publishes *All Is Well*, republished as part 3 of "The All Trilogy." His books are reviewed as the world's first honest portrayals of homosexuals, crazy and sex-hungry as we are—but loveable—in the end, after all.

1972: Herb and I were living as an acknowledged Gay Couple in San Francisco, on Buena Vista Terrace, overlooking The Castro; we'd been together 4 years. He was Art Director (advertising manager) for Fireman's Fund/American Insurance Companies. I painted several of their monthly and yearly report covers. I also did a lot of Gay advertising art. FF/A knew about me. Herb's helper was a Lesbian named Paula, who mysteriously called herself Ralf, who was long-time partnered with Debbie, and the company hadn't fired anybody.

1973: The American Psychiatric Association removes homosexuality from its official list of mental disorders. Harvey Milk runs for city supervisor in San Francisco. He runs on a socially liberal platform and opposes government involvement in personal sexual matters. Milk comes in 10th out of 32 candidates, earning 16,900 votes, winning the Castro District and other liberal neighborhoods. He receives a lot of media attention for his passionate speeches, brave political stance, and media skills.

1976: San Francisco Mayor George Moscone appoints Harvey Milk to the Board of Permit Appeals, making Milk the first openly Gay city commissioner in the United States. Milk decides to run for the California State Assembly and Moscone is forced to fire him from the Board of Permit Appeals after just five weeks. Milk loses the State Assembly race by fewer than 4,000 votes. Believing the Alice B. Toklas LGBT Democratic Club will never support him politically, Milk co-founds the San Francisco Gay Democratic Club after his election loss.

1977: Activists in Miami, Florida pass a civil rights ordinance making sexual orientation discrimination illegal in Dade County. *Save Our Children*, a campaign by a Christian fundamentalist group and headed by singer Anita Bryant, is launched in response to the ordinance. In the largest special election of any in Dade County history, 70% vote to overturn the ordinance. It is a crushing defeat for Gay activists.

1978: On January 8, Harvey Milk makes national news when he is sworn in as a member of the San Francisco Board of Supervisors. Running against 16 other candidates, he wins the election by 30 percent. Milk begins his term by sponsoring a civil rights bill that outlaws sexual orientation discrimination. Only one supervisor votes against it and Mayor Moscone signs it into law.

John Briggs drops out of the California governor's race, but receives support for Proposition 6, also known as the *Briggs Initiative*, a proposal to fire any teacher or school employee who publicly supports Gay rights. Harvey Milk campaigns against the bill and attends every event hosted by Briggs. In the summer, attendance greatly increases at Gay Pride marches in San Francisco and Los Angeles, partly in response to Briggs. President Jimmy Carter, former Governor Ronald Reagan, and Governor Jerry Brown speak out against the proposition. On November 7, voters reject the proposition by more than a million votes.

November 27, 1978: Harvey Milk and Mayor George Moscone are assassinated by Dan White, another San Francisco City Supervisor, who had recently resigned and wanted his job back, but was being passed over because he wasn't the best fit for the liberal-leaning Board of Supervisors and the ethnic diversity in White's district. San Francisco pays tribute to Harvey Milk by naming several locations after him, included Harvey Milk Plaza at the intersection of Market and Castro streets. The San Francisco Gay Democratic Club changes its name to the Harvey Milk Memorial Gay Democratic Club.

1982: Wisconsin becomes the first state to outlaw discrimination on the basis of sexual orientation.

1981>>>>>>> AIDS decimates the Gay population, Gay men especially.

2012: Gay Marriage and Religion, front and center, on TV everywhere, are heading for an explosive collision on Election Day, 2012.

Richard Nixon was President from 1969 to 1974, during many Gay rights advances. That must have bothered the hell out of him: Fags advancing on his watch! As far as Nixon and his supporters were concerned, he was standing in line next to Jesus whose throne was next to God's in Heaven, and it was *those Fags* (and *Kikes* and *Niggers*) causing all the trouble. Not one of his supporters doubted that God hated us. They would all gladly have stoned us like God says to in The Bible, but some goddamned do-gooder passed a law making killing Queers illegal.

The first Holocaust was Hitler trying to rid the world of Jews and Homos. The second attempt at ethnic cleansing took place for much the same reason: The Cleansing Agents truly believed they were Superiors, getting rid of the Inferiors.

Here is my imaginary movie, "Onward Christian Soldiers," telling the story of how I believe it happened. Imagine the movie beginning with the Mormon Tabernacle Choir singing "Onward Christian Soldiers, marching as to war, with the cross of Jesus, going on before, etc." as background to the opening credits. Imagine Jesus, in immaculate white drag, his long hair flowing in the wind, walking on air, slightly higher than the huge army of civilians following him, his arms held high, one hand clenched in a fist of victory, the other one holding a large cross with himself dying on it—slow enlargement of the Holy Cross until it finally blocks out the sun. Cut to a cross on a wall, with Jesus suffering excruciating agony, dying.

Pull back to show Olivia South (first cousin to Oliver North). Documents on the walls indicate that she is a fairly important person in the United States Health Department. A sign on her desk reads Olivia South, MD, and her book on *Infectious Diseases* sits perfectly placed beside it. A desk-calendar shows January, 1969. An open file on her desk indicates that Dr. South is part of a research team, looking for a cure for hepatitis B. She is typing something on an old-fashioned typewriter. It reads "Dear John, I miss you. Hurry home from wherever you are. Love, Olivia"

Fade to Mel Gibson, as Johnathan Braveheart Goodman, reading her letter. It is revealed that John is working in a secret government laboratory studying Germ Warfare. It is made clear in dialogue that

"No one is intending to use these weapons against an enemy, John, God forbid! We are studying these diseases to find defenses and cures for them, when *somebody else,* like Russia, or Korea, or China, or India, whoever—when the bad guys try to kill us—as they will; it says so in the Bible somewhere—we'll be prepared. They're weapons of self-defense, goddammit."

Olivia is a lifelong member of a popular Evangelical Christian denomination—and prays endlessly that God will get rid of Saint Dick's worst enemies: *Sodomites* and those *Sons of Cain.* And *Jews* while you're at it.

Then one day, God answers Olivia's prayers, in person, telling her: "Sister Olivia, I have chosen Thee for a Mission to save The World for Jesus. Thou knowest whom I hateth most. What wouldst happen if they all gotteth sick and dieth? Canst thou thinketh a way to maketh this happen? It will add to the stars in thy crown. They might even make you a Saint after you dieth and cometh to liveth with Me in Heaven. *'Saint Olivia,'* how doth that sound? For Jesus' sake. Amen."

When she woke up in the hospital, they told Olivia she'd had an epileptic fit, but she'd be fine. They had all prayed for her. Their prayers had saved her life; God wanted her live and to do what He had told her to do during her grand mal seizure: *Save the world for Jesus.*

Then John comes home. In slow motion, from either side of the screen, they take off their clothing as they run toward each other in *VistaVision,* finally colliding in mid-air not quite naked, clawing at each other and grabbing each other's genitals, and falling on the bed. As they are fucking (with their underclothes on, under the sheets) John and Olivia, in a mutual Heavenly revelation, realize that they have been chosen by God to Save the World for Jesus. Together they can make it happen. Making History Happen!

Together they come up with a plan which they secretly call *"Homocaust/Fag Armageddon"* but when she presents it at a staff meeting as a possible project, Olivia calls it *"Hope for Homos,"* an idea for a potential project, with a fairly detailed plan on how they could do it. One of their recent studies had been of Gay men with various sexually-transmitted diseases and since sexual transmissions was one of hepatitis B's routes of infection, it made sense to see if there might be any connection with homosexual STDs that would cause, or cure, HB. It sounded like an excellent thing to do and got funded fairly quickly.

In the movie, Olivia is appointed to head the *Help for Homos* committee and oversees the operation. They decide to access clinics in the cities with large homosexual populations, wherever there are clusters of sinners with STDs, and to have a nationally-publicized campaign called "Help Find a Cure for Hepatitis-B." Ads are placed in major Gay newspapers, and, in San Francisco at least, posters were tacked to telephone poles and pasted in windows all over town, especially in and around The Castro. "Help Find The Cure for Hepatitis B. Give Blood!"

Olivia personally oversees the ordering of the necessary supplies. It is cheaper to buy all of the medical equipment from one supplier. Enough hypodermic needles to supply clinics in NYC, Chicago, Los Angeles and San Francisco, etc., arrive en masse, ready for distribution.

Imaginary-movie montage: John and Olivia, both in white lab-coats, in a dark room, deep in some secret laboratory, somewhere, working all night, dragging themselves through the days, finally calling in sick, working, working, with a picture of dying Jesus on His cross, spot-lit on the otherwise dark wall, watching them get ready to save the world for Him. Can they do it before He dies? Night after night they toil, unwrapping sterile plastic packs and placing the needles in a contraption that looks like a microwave oven. When the oven is full, they put on gas masks and gloves and push a button. There is a whishing sound from the contraption, and a red light starts blinking and a warning horn sounds, as a mist fills the microwave window, then quickly fades away. (It's a low-budget movie; a microwave oven was all we had available, but you get the idea.)

In surgical garb they carefully repackage each single needle, put them back in their original cartons, and send them to the proper department for sorting, counting and shipping. Nobody notices any lapse of time. "Procedural delays." Finally, when the last needle is carefully repackaged and shipped off to unsuspecting accomplices all over the country, John and Olivia quit their jobs and get married in Las Vegas and live happily ever after in Hawaii.

The last shot of my imaginary movie shows John and Olivia, old and wrinkled but still tan and healthy, on a terrace overlooking the ocean, on their plantation on an uncharted island. On one wall is a framed letter of *Thanks* from *Saint* Richard Milhous Nixon. They are watching the scrolling headlines on an old black and white television, showing talking heads reading those headlines: *"AIDS Decimates the Homosexual Population. Good Riddance to Bad Rubbish. God Bless the United States of America and Saint Richard Nixon Forever and Ever, In Jesus' Name, Amen."* Behind the TV set, the sun is going down and the sunset is gorgeous, spectacular, mirrored in the ocean, from brilliant gold to red to purple to violet to mauve and it all fades to gray as the credits roll: THE END.

Suddenly a loud "scritch" ends the sound-track and a huge **"GAY ARMAGEDDON CANCELLED"** appears stamped across the screen.

THE END...OF A NEW BEGINNING

The **Homocaust** missed people like me—and we will not shut up until we see the whole thing exposed and the guilty made to account for it.

And, curiously enough, homosexuals now make up an even larger percentage of society than they did before Homocaust. None of them came out as the results of being seduced by dead men.

MILESTONE 26: The Most Misunderstood Man in the World

I am a "writer," a teller of tales, a spinner of yarns, a wordsmith constructing imaginary landscapes and lives, telling hopefully spine-tingling mysteries or love-stories, keeping my readers enthralled and anxious to the very end. At the end of a typical mystery, the bad guys are revealed to be the good guys, and the novel's hero, battered but not bowed, is revealed to be the best guy of all, and one of the supposedly best guys is revealed to be the worst—and it's not the one you think it will be. I know how clues are planted and how "red herrings" are introduced into the plot, to keep the reader guessing—and keep reading. Many of the plot twists won't make sense until the very end, when the reader slaps himself on the forehead and exclaims, "Well, of course! Why didn't I see it before? It all makes sense now!" That should be the end of all good mysteries.

Because of my Mormon background, *("We believe the Bible to be the Word of God as far as it is translated correctly.")* I was able eventually to critically look at The Holy Bible as a book, not as a holy object itself, but as a book of holy mysteries. Did Jehovah really make the universe in seven days? Or did some ancient storyteller just *say* that he did, in order to make the concept simple to his audience? Did God really make Eve out of Adam's rib, or was that a story concocted to promote male superiority and woman's subjectivity? Did God really inscribe the Ten Commandments in stone, with his burning finger? Or did Moses do that chiseling himself, while he was up the mountain, alone? Moses probably knew how to read and write because he was raised by Egyptians, and the uneducated Israelites trusted him to know what those little chiseled squiggles meant. How did Noah collect all the different animals on earth to crowd them—most of them mortal enemies—onto a tiny boat that stayed afloat without anyone getting killed, or anyone eating anything, for forty days and forty nights, while water covered the entire earth? Or was that a story the Jewish priests told the sons of Judah to explain a flood that had decimated the Holy Land many years ago? And finally, who was that guy, Jesus, and what was he trying to do, and why was Judas kissing him at all in the first place? Too many things didn't make sense.

It reminded me of the time, in high school, when the junior class had gone on a field trip to the Dinosaur National Monument, eighteen miles east of Vernal, just over the Colorado border. The museum had been built around a hillside which held a partially-excavated dinosaur, and a monster "Brontosaurus" skeleton had been made of bones excavated from the nearby sandstone hills. Mormons believed that the earth was created a little over six thousand years ago (the Anglican Bishop Ussher had counted the "begats," from Adam to Jesus), but the signs in the museum all said that these bones were millions of years old. How could that be? I asked the teacher to explain it to me. She said, and I quote: "God put these bones here to test our faith." She hustled us all back onto the bus and we drove back to safety in Mormonland, where a lie was reality and reality a lie!

If I were telling the story of Jesus, using clues from The Bible, and various "Gospels" ("teaching documents") other than the well-known canonical four, plus my own life as a reference, this is how I would tell it:

About 2010 years ago, more or less, depending—a piece of celestial flotsam, probably a comet, was flying through space, moving along a path it had been following for, possibly, millions of years, around a small star, blazing in the darkness, and happened to pass over a bright blue and white sphere, hanging in the darkness, little knowing or caring that its passage overhead would change the history of the inhabitants of that bright blue marble forever.

Down on the surface of that sphere, in a town called Bethlehem, a child was being born to a young Jewish couple named Joseph and Mary. He was a carpenter, the son of a carpenter, who fully expected his son to carry on the tradition. She was a prototypical Jewish Mother, raised to believe and behave like her mother before her. She decided, or realized, or had it "revealed" to her, during labor, that the Star of Bethlehem was a Divine sign that her son was destined for great things, possibly even Divine things.

No one in those days understood comets and astronomy and everyone believed that all celestial events were mystical omens caused by God. The content of the omen depended on which God you believed in. Everybody who saw it was terrified of the light that was slowly but obviously moving across the eastern sky, overhead, night after night, until it finally vanished on its celestial journey—to reappear centuries later—then again and again. On that particular fly-by, the human occupants of Earth imagined any number of religious implications. Surely many believed it was a sign of the end of the world. That had been predicted for centuries.

In my book, Mary was certain that the Star of Bethlehem was a sign from Jehovah that her son was blessed—and, being a good Jewish Mother, she never let him forget it.

If nothing else, it gave him something to think about. Joshua grew up in a very traditional Jewish family, the eldest of several brothers, all of whom were schooled in the "old ways" of Judaism. For Joshua, it was hard not to wonder if his mother's fantasies about him might be true. His childhood must have been little more than adequate; his parents were "working class" and had to work hard to keep everyone clothed and fed. He was special only in his mother's imagination.

He was as "superstitious" as the others around him. He had been born at a time when the Jews were being persecuted by the Romans, and the idea of a Messiah, saving the children of Israel from slavery, was very attractive, especially to young Jews. If something didn't happen, they would spend lives of eternal servitude to Rome and the Roman Empire. Between taxing and tithing, they couldn't climb out of their poverty.

Because of The Star and his Mother, he probably examined the Jewish religious beliefs much more closely than he would have, or should have, and he found them wanting. The stories were perplexing and contradictory. First, Jehovah said "Thou shalt not kill," then He said "Kill all the uncircumcised males." The only thing consistent about Judaism was that anything pleasant was labeled a sin. But just about every sin was forgivable for the right amount of money, or "burnt-offering," to God's servants, the Jewish priests.

As he approached puberty, he began to discover other feelings that set him apart from the other kids his age.

Homosexuality has existed probably as long as humans have existed, much to the concern of the Holy Men, who rely on the conditions of heterosexuality for control: "God" approves of men and women getting married and having families, all of whom love God and do his bidding and pay tithing to those who serve him. Children must be born within the sanctified structure of the family and be raised, i.e., conditioned, into repeating the patterns of their parents, over and over. The priests had no way of controlling homosexuals, so they condemned them to death and eternal damnation and had them stoned or crucified. These were concepts young Joshua would learn during those ten to fifteen years of his life unaccounted for in The Bible.

He had heard the words often enough, had probably memorized them, of the admonition in Leviticus: *Thou shalt not lie with mankind as with womankind: it is abomination... (and) whosoever shall commit any of these abominations, even the souls that commit them shall be cut off from among their people.*

If a man also lie with mankind, as he lieth with a woman, both of them have committed an abomination. They shall surely be put to death and their blood shall be upon them.

Joshua understood that the feelings he had regarding other boys and men could get him into serious trouble if discovered, or even suspected, but he could not work up any enthusiasm over marrying a virgin and starting a family, as he was fully expected to do. Surely he did nothing to express his nascent sexuality.

One of Joshua's non-Jewish friends was Abdul, the son of a merchant from Persia who sold rugs to Joseph to cover the floors of the houses Joseph and Sons were building. The caravan with which they traveled passed through Bethlehem twice a year, once going west, then once again going back through, headed home.

One night Abdul told Joshua about several tribes along the route who called themselves "Seekers," and they believed that same-sex love was spiritually superior to opposite-sex love and coupling. In those communities, Abdul explained, people like Joshua and himself were not only considered normal, but better than normal.

Abdul was probably the first to seduce Joshua, and to tell him of others like themselves, who had formed farming communes, far to the East, and far off the beaten caravan path. Abdul said the Seekers contained the disillusioned members of other religions, some of them even Jewish priests who had lost their faith in Judaism. Outcasts from non-Jewish religions, they had bonded as brothers—and sisters. There were societies of mannish women who preferred other women for mates; they were accepted as being on the same spiritual level as the males. The leaders of the tribe were called Wise Men, or Fathers. Joshua was certainly a Seeker, and could study with any or all of them.

Joshua's "guiding star" had appeared in the eastern sky, pointing the way he should go. By the time he was in his mid-teens, he was experiencing tumultuous emotions that were tearing him apart. He wanted to know The Truth, about himself, his sexual desires, about Judaism, about religion, about humanity. Abdul assured him that he fit the pattern of a Seeker.

On one of the caravan trips headed east, Joshua hitched a ride with Abdul and his father, who took him to the nearest crossroad to one of the Seeker Communes.

Once settled with the resident Wise Man, *Melchoir*, he was inducted into the Brotherhood of Seekers by a ritual they called "baptism by immersion" which introduced him to "The Kingdom of Heaven," and membership with the Brotherhood.

For six days, Joshua consumed a special diet, and then fasted, which cleansed him internally; then he bathed himself thoroughly and covered himself with a linen robe and nothing else, then presented himself to Melchoir. He was welcomed ceremoniously and given a glass of wine and a tiny piece of bread while Melchoir read aloud from an ancient text, regarding love between men. Then something mystical began to happen. Joshua became newly aware of his own body, and it seemed like his mind was unfolding like an enormous flower. It seemed he was entering a new level of reality, a higher level, "Heaven."

He and Melchoir made love to each other in every way imaginable, and afterward fell into a deep sleep. When he awoke, Joshua had become an official "Brother," a baptized and ordained member of The Seekers.

Another Wise Man, *Gaspar*, taught him about the history of the Seekers, the real story of Sodom and Gomorrah and the Children of Methuselah: The stories about them and their destruction were fabrications, turned into lectures about sin and morality by the controlling Judaist priests—as were all of the stories which ended up making Judaism the only authorized religion for Jews. Long, long ago, the priests had figured out that sex was the primary driving force among humans, as with all animals, and they "harnessed" that force by declaring that God considered all forms of sex illegal, immoral, and damnable "sins"—*except* those exceptioned by the priests, and those only if they were performed in a "marriage" legalized and taxed by the priests. "Pay me to say *'Holy Matrimony'* over your heads and you can go home and *'know each other'* all you want. Only promise to do it just to make babies, and dedicate all your babies to the church, so they can get married and pay tithing, and have babies, etc."

The Cities of the Plains, *Sodom and Gomorrah*, were peopled by *The Children of Methuselah*, two tribes, one male, one female, descended from a group of long-lived Jews, who had adopted Homosexuality as a way of life.

Methuselah's children had discovered that aging was caused by not having sex, and that the more sex people had the longer they would live. But in order to do that, the preferred sex had to be non-procreative homosex, for both sexes. Having children aged the parents and eventually killed them. Not having children but continuing to have sex kept everybody young for hundreds of years.

To any stranger passing through, it would seem that Sodom and Gomorrah were peopled by men and women, apparently husbands and wives, living normal lives. Both cities were on the trading paths, and prospered long enough to leave noticeable ruins behind, when, one day without warning, an army, probably of Israelites, overwhelmed the peaceful cities, killing everyone and burning down the cities, along with all of the recorded history of both cities—all but those recounted by the survivors, who had passed the knowledge among their remnants. Sodom and Gomorrah were regarded as model human settlements. Knowing what had happened to the Sodomites and Gomorites had taught The Seekers to move far off the beaten path, but it was considered very possible that someone could find their communes and kill them all as "Sodomites."

After several years of studying under Melchior and Gaspar, Joshua moved on to another Seeker community, where he met and lived with and studied under *Balthazar*, a black Wise Man from Ethiopia, who taught Joshua about "The Son of Man." Balthazar believed that humanity had, basically, "evolved" from a primitive stage, ruled by primitive urges and religion, to a more spiritual stage where humans could cure themselves of their "sinful" illnesses and get back to living nine hundred years.

For possibly ten years, Joshua lived with the Seekers and studied their ways. Somewhere in the process, he learned the secret recipe for something the Jewish priests had used for centuries. Loaves of Shewbread, or "Priestly Bread," were kept in the foyer of the temple and they prayed that Jehovah would give it visionary powers—but those in the kitchen knew it was made from kernels of rye that had been dusted with a reddish colored powder. The dusting was regarded as a gift from Jehovah. There was a special time for collecting it: after the harvesters had harvested the crop of rye, and following the first rain after that. There were rules for mixing the special flour made from carefully crushed rye kernels so that it didn't turn the bread lethal with what was later known as *"St. Anthony's Fire."* The special loaves were then placed in the foyer of the Temple where they remained a specified number of days. Then the priests ate them for visions and transcendent experiences.

There was even a sacred law in Leviticus (19:9) forbidding the harvesters to harvest the corners of their fields, as well as all unharvested heads or grains, leaving the gleanings for the widows and orphans— *and* the priests. That meant that every year the priests had access to the makings for Shewbread.

The Jewish priests surely never experimented with sodomy as a part of that transcendent experience!

No one knew that they were taking LSD and having what would be known as "acid-trips" two thousand years later. To them it was experiencing God. Hippies will remember meeting God on their first few acid-trips.

Experiencing The All while conjoined in a 69 was considered the ultimate human experience. Unless you have had such an experience, you will not understand, except on a certain intellectual level, how "divine" a sexual experience can seem. With good acid, sex can be transcendental!

LSD also has curative powers. This is only now being studied and understood, but current day headlines speak of it curing a host of illnesses. The Wise Men of Seekerville knew that many human illnesses were "imaginary," real but caused by the imagination, caused by guilt over all those sins humans couldn't help committing. It is conceivable that "leprosy" was one such, and could be "cured" by a good acid trip. Migraine headaches, sores of all sorts—a good, "guided" Shewbread trip could cure many diseases. The stories in The Bible make it seem like Jesus went through the country, waving his hands and making illnesses go away. There were probably elaborate ceremonies involved, just as in the rite of Baptism, and the stories that survived him were exaggerated.

Joshua was surely obsessed by the idea that had driven him, all his life: *Was he The Messiah?* All the Wise Men heard his story and encouraged him to become whatever he was destined to become.

When Joshua returned home to Galilee, he took with him what he believed was a new religion, a new way to understand this thing people thought of as "God." His task was to convince anyone who would listen that Judaism was wrong about many things, actually most things. "You have heard it said 'an eye for an eye and a tooth for a tooth,' but I tell you to love one another as I have loved you."

In the three years of his so-called "ministry," Joshua, the carpenter, made a bigger imprint on humanity than anyone before or after him. His "mystery" is as profound today as it was almost two thousand years ago. It has teased me all of my life. Who was "Jesus" and what did he mean by *"the son of man?"* He wasn't referencing Judaism in his teachings, he was basing them on the ideology of three Wise Men.

"Let whoever seeks continue seeking until he finds. When he finds, he will be disturbed, but when he has been disturbed he will marvel and will reign over The All." —Jesus according to Thomas.

Near the end of his three years, Joshua asked his disciples "Who do you think I am?" One described him as a wise teacher; another believed he was an angel, and so on to Peter. When Joshua asked Peter "Who do you think I am?" Peter answered without hesitation: "You're the Messiah, long prophesied by the Jewish Prophets."

Joshua responded: "Don't call me a Messiah until I have passed the final test, which is that the real Messiah will be put to death and will then rise up at the end of three days."

Peter misunderstood and thought Joshua was telling him to put him to that ultimate test. It was Peter who tipped off the Roman soldiers where they could find Joshua: In the garden, high on Shewbread and drunk on wine, making love to Judas, in the same condition.

The Romans arrested them, took them to Jewish court, which found them guilty of sodomy, then crucified them side by side by the highway, just outside Jerusalem.

After Joshua died and was entombed, Peter waited at the entry, probably munching Shewbread as he waited. At the appointed time, sure enough, Joshua came out of the tomb, shining and clean—but instead of declaring himself King of the World and freeing the Jews from slavery, he told Peter to take care of his Church so it would still be there when he came back, then floated up into the sky. Peter probably didn't even check inside the tomb to make sure, and none of Joshua's followers suspected the truth, or if they did, those doubts never made it into the Official Catholic Church—which amounts to *"Peteranity."*

Near the end of his story, Joshua gave Peter his "Church," and told him: "All the winds of Hell shall not prevail against my teachings." Then he said: "Now get thee behind me, Satan, for you love the ways of man and not those of The Son of Man. You are an abomination in my sight." Harsh words for his Holy First Lieutenant.

If you look at it on a "spiritual level," his prediction has come true: His teachings were preserved by The Christian Church, in all its denominations—Hell-on-Earth personified—for two thousand years still as meaningful as they were when he first spoke them, or learned them from his Wise Men. Those sayings "with secret meanings" were the seeds which he scattered, and our minds are the fertile soil they fell into. It has been thus for two thousand years, but it has taken modern "communication" to allow us to look at ourselves and examine the extraordinary "being" we have become—along with a little help from modern Shewbread. That is the key Jesus kept harping about. LSD is one of the Keys to the Kingdom of Heaven. The other Key is Love.

Until recently, all the Queers have been weeded out and their parts of human history ignored. Or historians changed our sexualities to illnesses, or ignored them. Now, with the *World Wide Web* and all the possible connections available on it, we can start to see our true impact on Civilization as we know it.

We have contributed our share: King David, Jesus of Nazareth, Leonardo da Vinci, Michelangelo, Sir Francis Bacon, Hans Christian Anderson, Vincent Van Gogh, Walt Whitman, Peter Tchaikovsky, Maurice Ravel, George Washington Carver, Edward Carpenter, Sergei Diaghilev, Marcel Proust, John Maynard Keynes, Federico Garcia Lorca, Christian Dior, W.H. Auden, Virgil Thompson, Samuel Barber, Jean Carlo Menotti, Benjamin Britten, Gertrude Stein, Tennessee Williams, Yukio Mishima, Harvey Milk, Leonard Bernstein, Wanda Landowska, Jerome Robbins, Aaron Copeland, Truman Capote, Gore Vidal, Rock Hudson, Richard Amory, and countless, nameless others.

They have finally begun teaching Gay History in public schools. Things are definitely getting better. We're not there, yet, but we're a lot closer now than we were fifty years ago, when I first "came out" of the Mormon Church and joined my new religion: Homosexuality.

MILESTONE 27: A Word to the Wise

From *All Of Me (Can You Take All Of Me?)*
(RoseDog Books, 09/01/2010)

Chapter 13: Gay Messiah

Joshua smacked his lips and said "Thank you for contributing to my longevity."

I asked, "Do you really believe that semen will keep you alive forever?"

He laughed. "Goodness, *no!* But why not *try and see?* Who would want to live forever, anyway? No, that's a fun peg to hang a book on, but I think it's what happens *inside* your body while you're coaxing the jizz out of the other guy's gonads. Hormones and testosterone and endorphins, and all that good interior stuff.

"'Drinking the *Elixir of Life* from the *Fountain of Youth'* and *'Eating the Fruit* of the *Tree of Knowledge* in the Garden of Eden' are both metaphors—for one and the same thing—from different cultures—Greek and Hebrew. Both are code phrases for *fucking.* To the Jews *'knowledge'* secretly meant *fucking*, because you couldn't say 'fucking' out loud in those days.

"What if the elixir of youth was semen, ejaculate, made up of all those mysterious fatty-acids that made babies. Maybe drinking them, instead of letting them make more and more babies, could keep you young forever.

"The *Tree of Knowledge in the middle of the garden,* in Genesis was code for the cock. Adam's penis was the 'snake' that tempted Eve. The 'apple' was the head of it—and eating the fruit surely meant swallowing the seed. Both myths *sound* like perfect metaphors for sucking cock and swallowing cum, but over the years, I've decided that it's what happens inside your own body while you're having sex, that keeps you young. Hormones and all that. Maybe cum is like gravy, just the topping—after all.

"And, of course, you're helping the other guy get his gonads working, while he works on yours. It's a win-win party for both guys.

"Or Gals. I believe the same principles apply. As long as you can keep your body in the baby-making mode—but not making babies—you too can stay young as long as you want to. It takes two, at least to make the magic happen. Give each other longevity.

"I believe that, as far as *Mother Nature* is concerned, the human body is nothing more than a reproduction machine. Procreation! That's all she cares about—us reproducing our own kind—over, and over, and over— endlessly. That's what everything does. That's what keeps *everything* going. We're all hard-wired fuck-machines. Our bodies are genetically programmed to start growing old as soon as we stop making babies. Gets us out of the way naturally, so the younger ones can take over and make more and more babies. So, one way to stay young is to fool Mother Nature into thinking you're still making babies, and she lets you stay young to keep fucking. Nature doesn't know if you're shooting your seed into a woman or another man—as long as you keep shooting it, Mom-Nature is satisfied.

"But I don't really want to live forever—just long enough to enjoy loving a few dozen more men. Several hundred years would work just fine for me. *'So many men! So little time.'* Who said that? Mae West? Well, well, one way or the other, I keep having sex with men—and keep drinking their elixir, *just in case*—so I keep feeling young, and looking— well, I know I look a lot better than a lot of other men my age. I try *hard* to keep it that way. I must be doing something right—most other men my age are dead!"

LAST WORDS FROM DIRK: During my lifetime, I have watched this principle at work. As long as I stayed sexually active, I stayed young. I looked and felt young. There were urban legends then that "Gay boys" looked younger than their straight peers, and that seemed to be true of the

Gay men I'd met. After Herb died and I stopped having Gay sex, I started growing old, noticeably. Then I discovered the early newspaper version of CraigsList, *The Naughty Personals*, and bi-guys! I started meeting and servicing—and sometimes being serviced by—husbands and daddies and grandfathers, none of them Gay swingers, all wanting safe blowjobs. The more sex I had, the better I felt.

I once asked a hunky Bi-guy: "What do a couple of Bi guys do when they get together." He said "The same things you Gay guys do—except no kissing." Kissing was reserved for women. He didn't know what he was missing.

For a few years I had a steady stream of middle-aged men, several times a week, grateful for what one called my "Awesome blowjobs." People remarked about how young I seemed.

After I'd had the second seizure, one or more of the prescription drugs my doctors were giving me, caused a sudden end to my sex-drive. Suddenly I lost interest—in other men, in porn, in horny emails and in sex, period. I could no longer perform. I remember the day when I decided I'd probably had my last sexual encounter—and felt a sadness like I'd never felt before—and it seemed like a switch had been turned in my head to >GET OLD NOW. I have watched myself daily in the mirror, getting older and older, and I'm certain that I could stop the process if I started having sex again. But my legitimate prescription drugs make this impossible. My doctor's pills are making sure I die on schedule. I hate doctors! They are always so right and I am always so wrong!

PART SIX: REBIRTH

MILESTONE 28: The End—or a New Beginning?

1968-2012, 55-79

After Herb died, I sold our large three-bedroom house and half-acre "farm," and rented a much smaller house and yard, using the money from the sale to pay the bills until I could figure a way to make a living. During the last eighteen years I had worked with and for Herb, so had no training for any available job I could think of, and no legitimate job-history. I had also spent most of my own savings, taking care of Herb. The sale of our home had been relatively easy; our realtor was an older woman, a widow who had taken up real estate sales when her husband died. I decided to follow her footsteps and enrolled in a series of free classes, taught by Great Western Real Estate, which taught us how to pass the state exams and get our licenses—if we promised to go to work at Great Western. The classes taught nothing about the actual process of selling real estate, only how to pass the test. In June, 1988, I passed well enough to get my license, and started trying to sell real estate.

In September, 1988, Ernie died after a long, expensive illness.

On July 31, 1989, I had an "acute inferior wall myocardial infarction"—a heart attack. In the ER, the resident cardiologist gave me an injection of "Activase," a new drug at $1800 a shot, and saved my life. He also threw away my pack of Marlboros, saying "you've got to stop smoking or the next time it will kill you." He suggested that I also quit whatever high stress job had caused the heart attack after raising my smoking habit to three packs a day. I stopped smoking on the spot. I couldn't quit trying to sell real estate; it was my only source of income.

Shortly before Thanksgiving, 1989, Mother's neighbor saw her through the window of her small retirement unit lying in the middle of the floor unconscious. Mercy Hospital called me early in the morning, telling me that my mother had been admitted and requesting that I come in and help calm her down.

The doctors' theories were that she had over-self-medicated, but they hadn't a clue what med or meds had caused the seizure. They had learned that the drug they gave her to calm her down had instead badly interacted with those in her system, requiring them to put her in a strait-jacket and tie her to the bed, her arms crossed in front of her. When I went into her room, she started screaming and yelling at me to go away! "They'll get you too!"

When the dust settled, it turned out that she had tried to get rid of one of her terrible headaches, and had taken too many pills and had a seizure as a result. Her experience in the hospital turned into a story she could tell the rest of her life: the time she was kidnapped and held for ransom in the Hotel Hollywood, where she could look out of her window and see the HOLLYWOOD sign on the hill. Alan Alda was her doctor, and he kept telling her that everything would be all right. Then her only son paid the ransom, and they sent her back to Mercy Hospital, and eventually to her son's house.

She couldn't be trusted to live by herself any longer. She was eighty-six at the time. She had never fit in at the retirement community, even though she had lived there, by herself, for ten years after Dad died. She was the only widow in the complex who didn't have grandchildren, and whose only son was living with another man and had dogs instead of children. She moved in with me and Frankie on Thanksgiving Day. Her doctors fully expected her to die fairly soon. She didn't.

Frankie died in December, 1990, and I asked his Vet what kind of dog I should get next. I'd had three German Shepherds for over twenty years, but they'd all had health problems. Without hesitation he said "Australian Shepherd." He had two of his own and recommended them highly. I went home from the pet hospital and looked in the Sacramento Bee's Classified ads, the Pets for Sale column. The top entry under Dogs was "Adorable Aussie Puppy, six-months old. $400."

When I went to pick him up, the breeder explained that she had kept this one puppy from the litter, planning to train him as a show-dog, but due to financial problems, she'd decided to sell him. The first question I asked was "What happened to his tail?"

She looked at me with haughty disdain and said, "Aussies don't have tails." Actually, as I discovered later, they do have tails when they are whelped, little stubby things that get trimmed to look like a large hairy fig-leaf covering what is too often a dog's most prominent feature. The stump wags like a real tail when they are happy or excited.

I didn't quit trying to sell real estate but changed brokers and worked with a Lesbian realtor in another of Sacramento's many bedroom communities, Rancho Cordova. There the pressure was relieved but I eventually decided that I was not a good real estate salesman and started trying again to figure out what to do next. Real estate had almost killed me.

In July of 1994, Mother had another fainting-spell and fell on top of me, twisting my leg under me, causing a limp that required using a cane and took many months to recover from. It sent Mother to the hospital, and finally to the Heritage Convalescent Hospital on Hemlock Ave., in Carmichael—another of those bedroom communities—to spend her last remaining days. I was able to get her accepted on MediCal, which paid all expenses that Medicaid didn't cover. Her doctors gave her a few months at most.

I moved to a duplex close to her hospital, and started looking for another way of making a living. I had managed to save a fairly large nest-egg from the sale of our home, but I was starting to think I might not die soon after all, and knew I'd need a steady source of income to keep going.

In 1995 an unexpected letter arrived from Gayle Rubin, PhD, Author/ Historian, a Lesbian who taught Gay Lit at San Francisco State College. After explaining how she got my current address, she got to the point of her letter:

"Early on in the course of my work, I ran into the Dirk Vanden novels. They are quite fabulous, beautifully written, and give a unique sense of the Folsom/SF Leather experience in the late 1960s-early 1970s…

I just want you to know how much these books have meant not only to me but to many of the men I've known and/or interviewed. Despite the fact that the books have been so long out of print, they are fondly remembered and quite influential."

She encouraged me to get the books republished, especially the *All Trilogy*. It was my first indication in almost twenty years that my books were even remembered, much less "influential." In our exchange of letters that followed, she told me about my inclusion in several reference books, chiefly *The Gay and Lesbian Literary Heritage* by Claude J. Summers, a very handsome volume published by Henry Holt, in which my books were mentioned in two separate essays.

It seemed to me that this was the answer to my quandary of what to do next: republish my books. I started by sending letters to the publishers Dr. Rubin had recommended, only one of which responded that he had a long queue of books scheduled for publication, but that he might be able to do it in two years. Meanwhile he suggested I rewrite the *All* books with more emphasis on S-and-M and Leather.

After re-reading *I Want It All* for the first time after twenty-five years, I decided that it did, indeed, need rewriting, but not as suggested. I didn't want my books to be more angry and nasty, but less. The hero, Warren, in the first book, swore like a sailor and was meaner than I wanted him to be. That quality worked better for Bill Thorne, in the second book, *All Or Nothing*. Also, I realized that none of my books had any Black characters, and I wanted to change that. So I rewrote *I Want It All*, cutting the main character's gratuitous swearing and changing the character of Kurt the bartender into a black ex-marine, a possible potential partner for Warren.

I found a book called *The Gayellow Pages*, published by my old editor from Olympia, Frances Green, and sent queries to all of the Gay publishers listed in her directory, suggesting they publish the three *All* novels in one book, to be called *All Together*. No one responded.

It had seemed like such a good idea that I decided to publish the books myself, separately, and then to present the three of them together to some future publisher—after the books had become bestsellers for Brass Ring Books, Dirk Vanden's new publishing company!

I bought a book on self-publishing and followed their formula in finding a publisher and then a distributor. Houghton Mifflin published *I Want It All*, revised, and three different distributors agreed to distribute it nationally. I had painted the cover in color, but my money ran out before the final printing, so I had to let them do the cover black and white.

The smallest number of books one could order was two thousand, so I used all my bank funds, then maxed-out my several credit cards. I was blindly trusting on the income from sales of my books to pay the bills, especially all of my dog-doctor bills. Buddy had developed a skin condition that made it uncomfortable for him if anyone tried to pet him, and no test could determine the cause. I was learning that thoroughbred dogs have the most congenital problems, mainly hip dysplasia, very common in all of the Shepherd breeds—unfortunately my favorites.

I sent free review copies of *I Want It All* to all of the Gay publications I could find in Gayellow Pages, trusting that the inevitable good reviews would sell the books without advertising. It turned out that those few Gay magazines or newspapers that responded, all required the purchase of an ad before they would review the book. I couldn't afford advertising. I was broke.

There were fifteen hundred copies of unsold books in unopened cartons, filling one corner of my spare bedroom. My dog was sick. Mother had been diagnosed as having dementia. I'd got her on MediCal, so her hospital bills were no longer a financial burden, but still I had to visit her weekly in the nursing home and see the results of her lifelong self-hatred for having given birth to me. I was depressed and, again, only remained alive because Buddy needed me.

My health-provider at the time was Kaiser Health, and membership included psychiatric care. One of their tests indicated that I was severely depressed, so they sent me to one of the psychiatrists on staff, for sessions of fifteen minutes per week—all but the first week were conducted by the doctor's assistant, a psychiatric nurse. One of the first things my new psychiatrist recommended was bankruptcy.

I found an attorney who would take my case in exchange for an oil-portrait of his three daughters. In 1996, I became officially bankrupt. I applied for welfare and lived on food-stamps for several months—which qualifies as one of the most humiliating experiences of my life—while I found a new psychiatrist, one not connected with Kaiser, who would see me for more than fifteen minutes per week—in return for painting portraits of his son and daughter. One of his final suggestions was that I join a temp agency to find work as a clerk-typist, my only marketable skill. He died of a heart attack shortly after our last session in 1997.

I took his advice and registered with a service called CalStaff, specializing in office-replacements during vacations and temporary fill-ins for sick workers. I spent a month in a State of California temporary building, in the licensing department, sending permits for hunters to kill elk, deer, and bears. When hunting season ended, CalStaff sent me to another company where I transferred information from index cards onto a computer all day long. I was able to continue the mind-numbing task for a month, until I asked for a change and the agency sent me to another computer-related company called Quest, out in the boondocks of Sacramento, on a road paralleling the railroad tracks called Roseville Road, in a giant warehouse that had been refurbished into a series of cubicles and offices that were the central part of the operation, which designed, installed and maintained large installations of computers for corporations, banks, hospitals, and the like; I was hired to help the files-manager catch up with a huge backlog of invoices.

The current file/mail clerk had been overwhelmed and on the verge of quitting—or being fired—and my more-competent "help" pushed him over the edge. He quit and I was offered the job, permanently, on December 10, 1997.

Mom died on June 16, 1999; she had been in the convalescent hospital—a warehouse of dying, sick and crazy people—for five long years. I was convinced that she didn't let-go sooner because she thought that Van was "over there, on the other side," just waiting to make Eternity miserable for her as he had her life on earth. She was definitely not eager to join him on some planet, far away in another galaxy, where the two of them would become a God and watch over their own version of humanity, bringing those souls to Jesus. In the last few months she was completely out of touch with reality—she was convinced that the Russians were invading the country, and were camped right outside her window. She didn't recognize me as her son, but thought I was one of the Mormon "Ward Teachers," who came to visit her regularly. She often talked of her imaginary trips home, back to the old Vernon homestead in Vernal, with all of her young brothers and sisters, back when everyone was happy. In the end she slipped into a coma and they had her hooked up to a whole bunch of machines. I finally commented to her doctor, "It's too bad we don't have Dr. Kevorkian here," and she said, "We don't need Dr. Kevorkian. Go home and rest." I kissed my unconscious mother on her forehead and went home. The doctor called the next day to tell me Mom had "passed away" during the night. She was ninety-six-and-a-half when she finally gave up the ghost. One of the last things she said to me, in one of her lucid moments, was "I am so tired."

She is encrypted with "Dad" in the Mount Vernon cemetery in Fair Oaks.

One final irony: Mormons believe that Mormon souls can't get into Heaven unless they are wearing Mormon "Garments" (aka "holy underwear"), flimsy nylon jump-suits that fit both sexes, buttoned down the front with a barn-door in the rear. They had to be specially "marked" with carefully hand-stitched little holes above the breasts that looked like button-holes. For many years, Mama had kept a box under her bed marked "Burial Garments," but when I gave them to the local Mormon mortuary, they told me they couldn't use them for some reason and insisted that I buy new garments, purchased from ZCMI, in Salt Lake City, which manufactured holy underwear for the Mormon world. I often wondered if someone sewed those holy-buttonholes in Mama's burial garments so they would let her into Heaven.

In 2001, Buddy started having "twitches," little tics, for no apparent reason. His face and his whole body would twitch at unpredictable times. It didn't seem to bother him, but his vet suggested that I take him to the University of Davis Veterinary Hospital to diagnose his problem. I had to borrow a thousand dollars from Quest to pay for his exams. They diagnosed "Idiopathic Epilepsy," and gave me a prescription for phenobarbital to give him for the rest of his life. The drug made him drunk and stupid and he stopped being Buddy, my companion and substitute child. He died June 6, 2002.

I quickly replaced him with Andy, an Australian Shepherd mix, from a shelter in Nevada City. They told me he was probably around six years old. My regular Vet revised his age to more-nearly ten or eleven. He had all sorts of physical problems, which was probably the reason he had been abandoned in the first place. Andy was the only unhappy dog I have ever known. He lived with me, and I took care of him, for a year, but there was no bond between us. All he wanted was to go home. He was obsessed and determined. Every time we went for a walk, he would strain at the leash to go up each driveway we passed, desperately sniffing to find his old markers. Every time we met a family of walkers with children, he would go wild, trying to get to what looked like his old family. I could tell he got angry with me for not letting him go. I didn't dare let him out of my sight, for fear he would run as fast as he could in a direction he had decided pointed him home. When we finally got back from our walk and he saw where we had come, he was disappointed and sad.

In June, an email arrived from the Rescue service in Nevada City which had helped me adopt Andy. A new rescue needed adopting. Since I had stated a preference for Australian Shepherds, they gave me first dibs on an Aussie mix (they theorized that part of the mix was an Aussie Cattle Dog or Queensland Heeler) who looked so much like Buddy that I said yes on the spot, and renamed him on my drive up the hill to pick him up: Buddy Jr.

When I took him to a new Vet, here locally, I asked about heart-worm medication, specifically the kind Buddy Sr. had been taking all of his life, and was told that the medication in question was now "contra-indicated" for Australian Shepherds. It caused idiopathic seizures! She gave Buddy Jr. a different brand of pills.

Living with a new dog was the final straw for Andy. He refused to eat, got stumbling-down weak, and finally had to be carried to the car and then into the Vet's for euthanasia. His ashes are among the growing stack of small wooden boxes in my spare room, waiting for mine—and that lilac bush.

MILESTONE 29: More Troubles

On the first day of January, 2006, I woke up in the hospital with my right arm and shoulder immobilized, and I was strapped to the bed so I could barely move. The nurses explained that I'd had a seizure shortly before midnight on December 30, had managed to attract the attention of my duplex neighbor, who called 911 and brought Buddy inside after the ambulance had taken me unconscious to the hospital, leaving him standing in the street looking after them. I had been unconscious in the hospital for two days and an operation was already scheduled to repair the damage the grand mal epileptic seizure had caused.

One of my co-workers at Quest took care of Bud while I was in the hospital and nursing home.

It turned out that the seizure had crushed the rotator cuff in my right shoulder, requiring an operation to replace it with surgical steel, then three weeks in a convalescent hospital and six weeks physical therapy. My arm never recovered a hundred percent, but I was able to go back to work at Quest in July, 2007. Most of the expenses were covered by various personal and company insurance and State unemployment benefits, but with seven months to think about all the whys and wherefores, I became very aware of the possibility that I might have to stop sorting and filing invoices for a living, and once again find a new way to pay the rent.

I applied for Federal Disability but was turned down because I had applied after age sixty-five, even though I was actively employed when the disabling event occurred. Apparently sixty-five is the legal age of retirement, and disability is disallowed after that date, no matter the circumstances. When I called Social Security to find out why I'd been denied, the young man said, "Because you're over sixty-five. Have a good day."

During the three years it took Herb to die, I had been working on my autobiography which I called "Pissing In The Ocean." I based the title on a photograph published on the front page of *The Rolling Stone*, back in the early sixties, featuring the naked backside of a famous TV actor, taking a leak into an ocean of fish-piss. The title seemed especially apropos since all of the work and energy, anger and self-recrimination, had seemed to be accomplishing something at the time, but all it amounted to, in reality, was a reputation among Gay publishers, and surely Gay readers, as a dirty-book writer—a good one without doubt, with fantastic reviews published in national media—but a Gay dirty book writer, no matter how esoteric or grandiose I tried to make it seem.

Earl Kemp at Greenleaf, and George at Frenchy's Gay Line, had forever branded me with an invisible scarlet letter on my forehead, Fag-Hot Pioneer. My place in Gay Literary history was assured as such, and there seemed nothing in the world I could do to change what had been cemented in place for 40 years. Those seven books defined me forever.

Sometime after Herb died, I wrote to Edmund Miller, who had written some nice things about the *All Trilogy*, in *The Gay & Lesbian Literary Heritage*, asking his advice for getting my sad little story published. I had written it during the lowest part if of my life to that point, and it was thoroughly angry and cynical. He suggested that I put the biography aside for awhile and try to write something more positive and uplifting; he suggested I "fictionalize" the events of my life and use them as the basis for something more interesting than my real life story. It was a challenge, and I wrote an opening chapter and outline for a Gay murder-mystery called *All Of Me (Can You Take All of Me?)* and sent it to the same old bunch of Gay publishers, and once again, no one responded.

One of my co-workers at Quest was a "webmaster," and helped me put up a website to promote Dirk Vanden. I posted all of my old, good reviews, and put up the chapter and outline for *All Of Me*, asking anyone interested in reading the rest to please get in touch with me.

In September, 2008, a retired professor of German Literature, J. C. ("Chico") Thomas contacted me, asking for the chapters following the one I had posted, and informed me that he was "a fan," and had been for many years. He had most of my books in his library and wanted to add this one. He was also in his late seventies, retired from a university in Georgia.

Over the year that followed, the two of us wrote *All Of Me*—a "fictionalized autobiography." I called myself "Rick Vernor, Real Estate Broker, living in Sacramento, California." Chico kept encouraging and prodding me, trying to help me believe I was a better writer than I thought I was: "I think I've probably read more of you now than anyone else still alive, and have not yet been disappointed in what you can produce; you write Great Gay Art. Deal with it."

Chico tirelessly tried to repair my battered ego, and helped me begin to believe that maybe my books could be republished, and that the income from their royalties might eventually help pay the rent. He convinced me that my novels were Gay Literature, not trash. He gave me the courage to once again try tilting at windmills. The following year, trying to find a venue for *All Of Me*, was a roller-coaster ride from publisher to publisher, with high hopes again and again being dashed after weeks or months waiting for an evaluation and decision. We both thought it was a good book, but for one reason or another, none of the Gay publishers we queried were interested.

While searching for publishers, I was amazed to discover that a majority of the current publishers of Gay Erotica were women, working with stables of more-or-less heterosexual women writing Gay Romances. It kept bothering my potential editors and publishers that although my books were classic Gay Erotica, they weren't romantic enough for that publisher's audience.

I finally decided to self-publish, and bought the cheapest service I could find, one that included publishing the book in the various e-media, plus a P.O.D. (Print-on-Demand) paperback, but no promotional bells and whistles. Those were additional—and expensive. *All Of Me* was published July 2010, by RoseDog Books, a subsidiary of Dorrance Publishing. Once again, I found myself with a book to sell, but no idea of how to sell it.

A woman in Australia who wrote Gay Romances as "A.B. Gayle" came to my rescue early in 2011. She had been looking for an "authentic" Gay voice and had found my three *All* novels from a small one-man publishing company in San Francisco called GLBPubs. She suggested that I get the *All* books republished and recommended a company called loveyoudivine (lower case always) Alterotica. I had been rewriting one of my oldest Greenleaf novels which Kemp had renamed *Leather* from my original *Hatters & Hares,* referencing *Alice in Wonderland.* I sent the revised version to lyd and the CEO accepted it and welcomed me with open arms to a publishing "family," which wrote stories about just about every sexual deviation imaginable, except for "bestiality, necrophilia, underage, non-consensual, and of course, incest no matter the gender configuration."

I was welcomed as a "Grand Master of Classic Gay Erotica," but I made the mistake of quarrelling with the CEO about the term "Grand Master." I was comfortable with the title "Master of Classic Gay Erotica," but not with "Grand Master" of anything, and asked her to change it in all of the press releases, etc. Unfortunately, the phrase had been set in the "Master Catalog Page," and made it to the back cover of *Down The Rabbit Hole*—lyd's new title for *Hatters & Hares*— so my reintroduction to the reading world was as a "Grand Master," whether I wanted to be or not. Then I made another mistake by complaining that the cover for *I Want It All* didn't represent the central character, who was an "average, non-buffed" young man, not perfectly muscled and shaved. My criticism was not received kindly and I was told by the CEO that her team would take over from here and that I should back off and stop interfering. The three *All* books were published as e-books, and a compilation of the three was made available as Print-on-Demand paperbacks and as e-books. They accepted my title for the threesome: *All Together.* I must say, what they put together for me is altogether pleasing, and will serve as my contribution to Gay Literature, and look good on Gay coffee tables and bookshelves for years to come.

PART SEVEN:

The End of the Road

The French have a saying: *"Plus ça change, plus c'est la même chose!"* The more things change, the more they remain the same. The longer I live, the truer that saying becomes.

Gay Life has changed drastically since I "came out" in 1949. In the days before laws began to change—the 1970s—I was arrested twice for being Gay. I spent 18 days in the Mobile Alabama City Jail, without being charged, simply because I was Gay. Then I was released and told to get out of town and never come back because: "We don't like your kind around here."

In those days, there were only a small handful of publishers willing to publish my novels; now there are hundreds—but, surprisingly, as I said, many of these are operated by heterosexual or bisexual women, with variously sexual women authors writing Gay Romances for a mostly heterosexual female audience. Gay consciousness has changed; same sex marriage and serving in the military are now the political issues of Gay activists in an effort, supposedly coming from the "Gay community," to make us just like everybody else. There is little place for an author like me, who still thinks that being Gay is being "special." That is a joke to my ex-publishers who consider my books on a level with "The Vampire Lesbians from Hell," and are not interested in anything new I might write, only the "Retro-Queer" stuff that tells what it was like, back at the beginning of Gay erotica, in 1969. (I consider the beginning to be Richard Amory's book *Song of the Loon*, first published in 1965; that was what inspired me to write and publish my own books in '69-'73.) Richard

Amory would be laughed out of town by these publishers. I was told by one of those straight publishers that I was completely out of touch with today's market, and to shut up and stand back, and let their crews do what was necessary to publish my "classics."

In the old days I fought with straight men who published and wrote "fag-hots," who insisted that my books have "hot sex on the first page and as often thereafter as the plot would permit." If I didn't make the sex scenes hot enough, my straight editor added his own idea of fag-hots, such as "pulsating purple cock-heads spurting volleys of creamy ambrosia!" Nowadays I am fighting with female publishers, who also think they know better than I how to edit and publish my books. The sexes of my antagonists have changed, but the fighting has not.

I've had a number of Gay relationships, two of which lasted long enough to be significant, but all of them were "illegal." The idea of "Gay marriage" would have seemed insane in those days. Winn and I lived together in Sacramento and Hollywood for 6 years; Herb and I spent 18 years in San Francisco, then Sacramento, as a Gay couple. When he died of AIDS I had to get a lawyer's help to let me settle Herb's affairs. Because his illness ate up all of the money we both had in separate accounts, I was eventually forced to declare bankruptcy, and then to apply for work at a temp agency as a file clerk. My college education and my BFA in Theatre Arts meant nothing to any possible employers. My status as a "Pioneer" of Gay Erotica was something I didn't dare mention, and my seven published books brought in almost no royalties, even though three of them were still on the market.

Looking back now it seems appropriate that I started out as a bastard and managed to stay something of a bastard my whole life, but now, of course, with a very different meaning from what my "Dad" meant when he spewed out his hatred at me for ruining his life. From the point of view of "the system," a bastard is an independent thinker and a free man who follows his own path. Championing free sex, homosexual sex, drugs and free thinking, I was being a real bastard in the staid Mormon world I would have become part of, if not for my homosexuality. Still am.

In 1969, because of an Acid Trip, I figured out what Jesus meant by "The Son of Man." It was the same thing I was talking about as the next step in human evolution. The "new" humans " replacing Homo-sapiens are "Homo-sexuals" with a new and different kind of intelligence. "An enhanced capacity for abstract thinking." All my life I've been an abstract thinker and believed I was crazy. I called it "paying attention." I saw things no one else saw. I made connections nobody else made. I could look at current happenings and extrapolate the future. When I first figured out and started believing that Gays were going to save the world, I was quite sure I was certifiably insane—and so did Herb and everybody else around me.

In a sane world, I should be able to retire to a comfortable Gay community, and write my memoirs in an accepting, encouraging environment, but there is no place for me to go where I can be among other Gays and Lesbians or at least non-homophobic "friends," in these last few years of my life. I've been trying for three years to find a Gay retirement facility, but there is nothing even close to Sacramento, and certainly nothing I could afford in my financial condition. I am a "Pioneer of Gay Literature," and a "Master of Classic Gay Erotica," but currently that seems to mean just that I've been around for a long time. It is my hope that with the republishing of those old books and the publishing of this new one, "Pioneer of Gay Literature" will take on a new and fuller meaning.

They say Gay men with AIDS—my lovers among them—were like the canaries in the mine whose deaths alerted the world to the catastrophe of HIV. It's true that there are near-cures for AIDS now (I believe there has been a cure available since before the beginning of "Homocaust") and that Gay community visibility and activism helped bring these about. Surely, my efforts to tell the world about Gay life back in the old days helped bring about that visibility and activism. To the extent I've feared that my work lured men into the world where they got infected, I now see that same work gave them the ability to respond to the crisis with pride and power. Still, I miss Herb and our life together more than I can say and hate that AIDS happened during my lifetime. Being out here on the cutting edge of evolution is painful and scary.

It's almost as though I'm being another kind of canary myself these days, demonstrating the very serious need for retirement options for Gay elders. We need someone to save the canaries!

I have an article on the Internet that appeared in Lambda Literary, November 23, 2010, titled: *What Happens When You're Old & Gay? Gay Pioneer Asks, "Where Do We Go From Here?"*

It begins:

> The Gay Community has a huge potential problem facing it that very few people are currently even aware of—or want to think about! I ran headlong into it when I woke up in the hospital six months ago, after an "idiopathic" seizure at age 77, possibly caused by a brain-tumor, or cancer, (it wasn't) with a $75,000 hospital bill for a weekend visit. Fortunately I had Medicare!
>
> But I had no family to support me and only a few close and very busy friends to help me, when I needed help more than I ever have. It has turned out that two idiopathic seizures, two years apart, have been caused by medication my doctors prescribed, which I've been taking for 15 years—but no matter the cause, I can no longer physically take care of myself and can't even drive my own car to the store.

Ironically, when I was forced to retire from filing invoices and delivering mail at Quest—caused by my Personal Care Physician's prescription medicines—I saw the need to keep earning money as an author, so I set out to publish my autobiography and sent out the usual plethora of query letters to various kinds of publishers, expecting the usual plethora of rejections that have been one of the banes of my life. I received a note back from Toby Johnson, an editor at Lethe Press, saying he was interested in my spiritual wisdom. "Spiritual wisdom"—I wasn't expecting that! One working version of my title had been *"Why Me?" "Why Not?" The unlikely life of a Gay Pioneer, from Mormon Miracle Baby to Homosexual Atheist, in 78 Years.* I didn't think of myself as a "spiritual writer." And yet, there was my fascination with the mystery of Jesus. That would be considered "spiritual" of some sort.

Lethe Press is a small Gay Print-on-Demand publisher that specializes in what's now called "Spec Fic," i.e. speculative fiction, the kind of mix of fantasy, science fiction, horror, parallel universes, with ironic twists and quirky moral lessons, etc. that we used to see on TV on "The Twilight Zone"—along with the radical concept that homosexuality is a gift, not a curse. Another of their specialties is "Gay spirituality." Lethe Press also uses this "state-of-the-art" P.O.D. technology to bring Gay classics back into print that had been orphaned when their publishers closed (or when the mainstream publishing houses decided they had experimented with Gay titles long enough and dropped their Gay lines). The editor at Lethe wrote that he was interested in Gay men's spiritual/mystical/psychedelic experiences, not because they were religious, but because they offered an alternative to religion altogether.

Those "crazy" insights of mine that I used to have to hide or at least downplay with Herb and with my friends who thought my Gay Jesus and Gabriel Horny were signs I was nuts is what Lethe Press thought was the boon I had to offer the world at the completion of my "hero's journey" through this life as Dirk Vanden. Now all those crazy ideas will finally be published as *The Wit and Wisdom of Gabriel Horny*—the real conclusion to my little story.

Thus, in an unexpected way, Dirk Vanden has been reborn from a "fag-hot" pornographer to a writer of wisdom and insight. My *All Trilogy* was reprinted in 2011 and was nominated for a Lambda Literary Award, the closest thing the Gay genre has to Oscars. (Imagine Oscar with an erection.) Just being nominated is an honor; winning a Lammy would be the perfect cap to my "literary career." It pleases and amuses me to see that some of the "Best Gay Erotica of 2012" was written in 1969. Those porn pulps from the '60s are being highlighted in library exhibits; college professors give Gay Lit courses and write books about these books' role in the creation of Gay genre. Wayne Gunn and a Lesbian co-author are currently preparing a new book about the Neglected Gay and Lesbian Pulps of the '60s and '70s, including mine.

The whole literary industry has been transformed by digital books—"throwaway literature." Until I found Lethe Press, I worried that my new digital books from lyd would vanish into a great electronic trash heap in a couple of years (the length of my contract.) But now, Dirk Vanden will stay "in print" virtually forever. Print-on-Demand has allowed Gay presses, like Lethe—with a positive vision of sexuality and homosexuality—to serve up a whole range of literary fiction, adventures and romances. Now there are novels with Gay protagonists that don't need any "fag-hot" passages. It's as though my original idea of being a writer of serious literature about the lives of real homosexuals has finally come true. Homosexuality is being assimilated into mainstream culture, but these are not the "Queens" and "Dykes" I knew in the '60s. We've "normalized" ourselves. Gay life has changed, but it is not quite what I was expecting.

The Gay men and Lesbians who are now fighting for the right to be soldiers, to get married and to raise children (hopefully to adopt, not to have their own—that would just add to the population problem) are the leaders of the reformation—although not necessarily aware of the role they are playing. They are "different " in ways their predecessors were not, and "special" in ways their followers might not be. "You don't have to be Gay to be Queer!" could be their motto. It doesn't matter. The problem to solve is the begetting of children.

Humanity has become the earth's "cancer" and is quickly killing its own host. Spurred by Religion, it keeps reproducing and reproducing and will go on reproducing until there is nothing to eat and nowhere to live. Queers of all sorts are like a neutered virus, stopping the infection, showing the world it is possible to contribute to society and to have Love and a Family without making babies.

I still believe in my "vision" 40 years ago, that homosexuality will eventually save the world from Religion and Overpopulation. I have watched things change for over sixty years, and they are getting better—maybe not in time to help me—but definitely better. That progress will continue. Mankind's oldest scourge, Religion, is being relentlessly examined, being proven false, and is losing the control it has had over us for thousands of years. We are finally learning that the real power lies, not in the high priests from the cathedrals or temples or church houses, but within *us*. The power is called "Love."

Many years ago, I wrote an author's note as a preface to *All Is Well*:

AUTHOR'S NOTE

In all of my previous books, sex has necessarily been the predominant theme, because whether or not their assumptions were correct, my publishers insisted on "hot sex" and lots of it, the kinkier the better, with a little plot and characterization tossed in here and there for good measure. Olympia has allowed me far more freedom in writing *All Is Well*; the sex is still there (as it must be in Gay novels as well as Gay lives) but only as one of many aspects of the story. Some readers may find the sex scenes less masturbatory as a result. I've had to make a decision—to write "just another sex book" or to test my convictions that Gay people want to understand themselves and one another more than they want to jack off. After all, there are thousands of books which supply masturbatory fantasies for those who want them; there are very few books which advance the idea that being Gay isn't as wretched and sinful as we've all been taught to believe it is.

There is a tremendously exciting reformation going on, all over the world, and I feel that Gay people are going to wake up and find themselves in the vanguard of that reformation. But in order to "wake up" we must first understand ourselves—and that, more than anything else, is what *All Is Well* is all about."

That is also what *It Was Too Soon Before...* is all about.

Putting this book together, I have decided that, in the end, after all, it has been worth the struggle to get here. I believed in myself enough to keep going, one disaster after another, because I knew I had something to say to the Gay World. I had tried to say it forty years too soon, when the world wasn't ready for my radical theories and insights. I wrote six different "how to come out" manuals for different kinds of men, inviting them to explore and expand and indulge their sexuality. Those have become part of the foundation of Gay Literature—not just a handful of masturbation fantasies, as my original publishers tried to make them.

"Plus ça change, plus c'est la même chose" also applies, with a nice twist of meaning, to the love of dogs. That has been an unchanging constant in my life, no matter how wild and unpredictable it was otherwise. A pattern has repeated itself once again: four weeks ago I lost Buddy Jr., my best friend and substitute child for 10 years, and for many days afterward, I felt like I was dying myself. But my "dog-luck" continues: I have rescued and adopted "Buddy III," a four year old Australian Shepherd/ Spaniel mix, the smartest and sweetest dog I've ever known, who has adopted me as much as I have him. He has effectively brought me back to life, my personal "resurrection." He's my "Happy Ending!"

One final note from the author: Attentive readers will have noticed that I capitalize what I consider a proper noun, the name for what I am: "Gay." I'm not gay, small g. Never have been, and surely, at my age, I never will be. But I have been "Gay" all my life. It is not a word I would have chosen to describe me, but the shoe definitely fits so I am compelled to wear it. It is more appropriate than "Queer," since, now, Queer has taken on a whole bunch of variations-on-a-theme of different-from-normal—bisexuals, transsexuals and gender-queers. I think the capitalized Gay makes a statement that I am proud of what I am, and if Mormons and Catholics and Baptists and their ilk can capitalize their names, then so can I because Homosexuality has essentially become my "religion." (Semen is my sacrament!) I am not a gay Californian; I am a Gay Californian, and an ex-Mormon!

Herb Finger, 1969

Herbert The Good peddles
his "Magic Jools," 1971

Herb, 1970

Herb & Luv 1970

Herb Finger, Sacramento's Celebrity Chef, on TV

CHEFONE — 1982

Brewster House Restaurant, Davis, California, 1984

The Finger/Fullmers at home on Leedy Lane.
Dirk and Ernie and Frankie and Herb

Herb's final companions, Frank & Ernie.

NEWSWEEK
(see top right, fourth from left)

A panel from The AIDS Quilt, 1990

Buddy, 1990

Buddy Jr, 2003

Buddy Jr, 2010

Buddy III, 2012

"Mike Davis" in COLT brochure,
circa 1980

"Mike Davis" in the Movies
at last.

"Mike" and his best
friend "Al Parker" in the
Good Old Days. Photos courtesy of COLTstudiogroup.com

Reprise

Many years after we split in Las Vegas, 1969, I learned that Winson Strickland had become a famous Porn Star who called himself *Mike Davis!* He had joined Colt Studio sometime in the early seventies and appeared in a long list of Colt and Halstead movies.

An old friend who knew us both in the early sixties found my website and sent email to inform me of Winn's death by AIDS, Jan. 21, 1986. He was forty-one when he died.

I have heard from several of his fans, who adore him even twenty years after his death, requesting more information about him, or pictures, anything. There are a number of websites devoted to him, so he must have had many adoring fans and friends. Everybody loved Winnie!

I have to say: *He achieved his dreams!* That's what he wanted more than anything else. He became a famous movie star, and it killed him. But he did it—*his way.*

Someone made an *AIDS Quilt* panel for him.

According to *Clone: The Life and Legacy of Al Parker Gay Superstar* by Roger Edmonson, Parker and his lover took care of Winn while he died. I suspect that he and Parker had a love affair both on and off screen. I'm glad he had someone who loved him with him when he died.

He always had good taste in men.

I loved him very much. And so did a great many others.

—

The last I heard from Richard Amory came on a postcard from New York City, where he had been invited by Olympia, to attend a party in his honor, upon the publication of *Willow Song*:

July 9, 1974,

Dear Dirk—Out here on a visit—Frances told me you'd written her. Saw Maurice and managed to pry some $$$ out of the SOB. New York is weird. Autograph party for me next Sat. Imagine!

According to his son, Cesar, who mans his website, Richard Amory died in the late summer of 1981, of liver failure due to long-term alcohol use. His lover Matt had died, probably of AIDS, in '79 or '80. Richard had been *"devastated and very bitter."*

—

For publishing the Greenleaf Classics "illustrated" edition of *The Presidential Report of the Commission on Obscenity and Pornography* in 1970, Earl Kemp was sentenced to one year in prison for "conspiracy to mail obscene material." He served only the federal minimum of three months and one day. But his career as an erotician was over. He now lives in the Arizona desert and is known primarily as a editor and publisher of science fiction.

—

I had attempted to return to college in Berkeley in 1960, and get my degree in Psychology instead of Theatre Arts. I had an idea for a Master's thesis called "A Matter of Lost Innocence," which postulated that homosexuals were people with a certain kind of intelligence, (which should be measurable) who saw through the rules and regulations of religion and society and became homosexuals as a reaction against those rules, etc.. That professor I befriended in the coffeeshop, Richard Alpert, told me: "The cause of homosexuality is already known. Freud has told us."

I did read some of Freud's theories on homosexuality and was amazed at how much I agreed with. He believed that humans are basically bisexual and can go either way, or maybe both, depending on their life-experiences growing up. My theory of intelligence explained why the malleable bisexuals go Gay. But the professor dismissed my opinion as though it was completely without merit, and unnecessary.

I quit school, went back into Theatre, met Winn, got fired, moved to Hollywood to get Winn into the movies, started writing books about homosexuals.

Dr. Richard Alpert returned to Harvard where he got together with another professor named *Timothy Leary*, and started conducting experiments with *LSD*. Eventually they were both fired from Harvard and Dr. Leary became famous for coining the slogan: *"Turn on, tune in and drop out."* Dr. Alpert forsook his Jewishness and Freud and became *Baba Ram Dass*, and then just *Ram Dass*—whose best-known advice is *"Be Here Now."*

Ironically, Ram Dass has admitted to being Gay and to have been having Gay sex at the time he was teaching at Berkeley; he's also acknowledged fathering a son at that same time, perhaps, in some sort of effort to avoid being Gay. It would seem he has proved Freud's theory all by himself.

But, if the future Ram Dass hadn't shot me down, I might be sitting in some rented office right now, treating homosexuals who have problems with being homosexual. I would never have written the books I did which have probably had much more impact on Gay Life than I ever could have had as a psychologist. Thank you very much!

I am also grateful to Doctors Alpert and Leary for having delivered a new version of Shewbread to the modern world: "Window pane." It explains so much! You might even say that Ram Dass (the guru with the *Freudian slip* for a name) introduced me to my own alter-ego Gabriel Horny.

Gabriel says: "Heaven is a state of mind." Be there now.

Self portrait, ICDLITE,
oil on canvas, 1973

CONCLUSIONS:

THE WIT & WISDOM OF GABRIEL HORNY

After awhile
you begin to understand the way the world works,
& it isn't at all like they told you!

* * *

In another time & place, I would have been a "Shaman,"
or "Wizard," or "Oracle,"
or whatever the oddball-misfit
("Visionary Mystic")
of the tribe was called.
I would have been singled-out early
& sent to live with the elder Wizard,
where he or she would have taught me all the magical words &
rituals, appropriate to the customs of the tribe,
and sooner or later I would have inherited the job —
or been killed by stoning for being possessed by demons.
Instead, I was born into a tribe called "Mormons,"
who didn't believe in Wizards —
so neither could I.
Instead I embraced Mormonized Christianity with the fervor
That I now assume,
only incubating Wizards feel —
certainly none of the people I knew seemed to feel it so
intensely,
or to take it as seriously as I did!
Mormons believed in saints, so I became a little saint.
They hated that!

* * *

IN THE BEGINNING:

ONCE UPON A TIME,
long, long ago
— give or take a zillion years or two —
the predecessor of the star we call "Sun"
was floating around in the galaxy,
minding her own business,
tending her offspring as usual,
when suddenly, a huge asteroid
appeared on her horizon.
There was a cosmic attraction between them
& after a brief heavenly courtship,
the asteroid, came crashing into her
& she collapsed in upon herself,
creating what astronomers now mistakenly call a "Black Hole,"
but which isn't a hole in space at all,
but is actually a "Space Pregnancy."
The "collapse" caused a kind of space-vacuum,
sucking in space-junk from all directions,
— all her old planets and moons,
comets & space-dust, even starlight —
(That's why astronomers can't see them!)
sucking everything into her center
growing denser and hotter,
until finally she exploded!
"Nova!"
Starbirth!
In the process of exploding,
the "born-again" star started spinning,
throwing off arms of burning stuff
which eventually condensed into spheres,
which continued rotating around the revitalized sun,
following the paths they had already established,
finally becoming perfectly balanced
between gravity, centrifugal force and inertia.
Slowly each sphere condensed and solidified,
variously sized and composed,
depending on what stuff

– or new combinations of stuff -
had been in the arm of fire
thrown off by the star, which had formed them.
On one particular sphere,
now called "Earth,"
conditions were just right so that,
as the exterior cooled off to become a crust,
surrounding still-burning star-stuff,
moisture condensed around the outside.
Over millions of years, enough moisture collected
to form what we now call "lakes and oceans."
"Sunlight," raw energy, interacted with the water
& created air.
Water & air, rubbing against each other caused lightning:
electricity interacting with water and minerals
from the earth,
started the first "living" thing.
Over billions & billions of years,
from that "simple" beginning,
uncountable forms of life have mutated & evolved,
— & vanished —
plants & animals,
filling the seas
& covering the habitable parts of the crust
that surrounds the still-molten star stuff
(which keeps us all from freezing to death in the winters).
One of these days, billions of years from now,
(hopefully not sooner)
another catastrophic celestial conjunction will occur
& the whole process will start all over again!

* * *

This explanation of our beginning makes much
more sense to me than
"A magic old man, living in the clouds,
reached down & zapped the dirt with his finger,
creating the first man—
then, he made a woman out of the man's rib
and then forbade them to fuck,
thus introducing Sin to the world."

* * *

You and I and all other animals begin life as an egg.
Forget that nonsense of "beginning" when one is born,
when one comes howling & protesting out of the warm, loving mother
into the cold, cruel world.
We begin as exact copies of Mom,
genetic blueprints to produce someone exactly,
precisely like her,
in every detail.
She produces many of these copies of herself every month
for many years of her life.
Were she able to impregnate herself,
she could give birth to exact duplicates of herself.
However, fortunately or unfortunately,
she needs a man to fertilize her eggs,
& thereby invites modification of her potential clone.
In the process of Getting Together,
the sperm & the egg have a contest,
the sperm being the exact duplicate
of the male, DNA-wise.
Whichever gene wins the contest,
the forming embryo will have, say,
blue eyes instead of green,
blond hair instead of auburn,
If our father's maleness triumphs
in the sex-determination department,
the original ovaries move down & become testicles;
the clitoris becomes the penis,
the lining of the vagina becomes the scrotum,
the breasts shrink,
Some muscles get larger, some smaller.
Otherwise, men & women
are pretty much the same.
We all contain bits & pieces of both parents,
& could probably be properly pigeonholed
somewhere along a scale between
All-male & All-female
& all-possible combinations in between!

* * *

Everything is in some way
Essentially parallel
With everything else:
Everything begins,
"lives,"
then ends,
and is recycled.
Fruits & vegetables,
You and me,
the Earth,
the Sun,
the Universe,
Space...

* * *

Where did the raw material of the universe come from?
There had to be something to go "BANG!" in the first place.

* * *

The globe is the most universal shape in the universe.
Liquids condense into globes in space;
so does everything else.
Surely Space is globular.
But where does Space exist?

* * *

The shape and depth of space
is no more awesome
or significant
than apple blossoms.

* * *

From the very beginning of it, the earth has been round —
but it has required millions and millions of years
for us to discover that simple fact.
What other "simple facts" don't we yet know about our world
and ourselves?

* * *

I am sunlight
mixed with earth, air and water.
I am billions & billions of little bits and pieces
of modified sunshine!

* * *

We are all made of Sunshine & Starstuff!

* * *

This year's compost
is last year's sunlight
and next year's food.

* * *

We are the end result of the earth's attempt
to see and understand and perhaps control itself.
We are the earth's consciousness, becoming aware of itself.
We must keep it alive and well, healthy and strong, or we'll lose it.
It's the only home we've got!

* * *

"Time" began when people started keeping track of it.
Time will end when we stop keeping track of it.
Time does not exist;
only the track exists.

* * *

Nature is relentless.
As soon as an organism becomes less than healthy,
a process of natural recycling is begun.
The unhealthy individuals soon become
fodder for the healthy ones.

* * *

As soon as an animal or plant begins to function
at less than ideal health,
for whatever reason, real or imaginary,
then Nature goes to work to destroy that organism
and return it to "the bank" —the earth.
All sorts of beasts and birds and bugs and germs accomplish this.
When a human is emotionally depressed,
(or cat or dog or whatever — elephant, dolphin, ape or donkey)
even through there is no "real" or physical cause,
Nature begins to destroy that entity.
He or she gets sick —
with whatever disease(s) are the handiest or easiest to catch.
Hopefully, the illness gets "Mommy" to say "I love you,"
and the depression is temporarily relieved,

and the illness goes away.
But if no one says "I love you,"
more and more things go wrong,
until the organism essentially disintegrates.

* * *

Illness is a symptom of unhappiness.

* * *

We use illness as a means of getting sympathetic attention,
or of avoiding an unpleasant situation.

* * *

Illness is a highly favored form of dumping.
It is also a popular means of self-punishment.

* * *

At a very early age, we learned how to be "really" sick
when there was a test at school, or hard work to do.
Mom always said "This had better be real, or you're in trouble!"
So we learned how to catch colds,
get stomach aches,
and otherwise damage ourselves with real diseases.

* * *

Early in life, I learned
that the only way I could get anyone's attention
was by being sick.
Accomplishments didn't do it.
Being a good boy didn't do it.
In fact, the more I did and the better I tried to be,
the more people disliked and avoided me.
Being "good" annoyed people,
even though that's what they claimed they wanted me to be.
They lied.
But every time I started feeling sick,
I got all sorts of care and concern —
which, of course, went away as soon as I got better.

* * *

Cheer up!
You'll feel better!

* * *

Feeling good produces a chemical in the blood
that keeps us healthy,
"young"
and functioning properly!

* * *

When you feel good,
you generate an electromagnetic force field around you.
This can be seen by some people and has been called an "Aura."
(I've never seen one,
but it probably looks something like the aurora borealis.)
Force fields interface and interact with other force fields,
forming invisible electronic networks.
If you feel bad, you produce a negative field,
something like a "spiritual vacuum."
People sense such a dumping-ground,
and unconsciously seek it out
to dump on.

* * *

Feelgood wards off disease
while feelbad invites it.
This should be true for all living organisms!

* * *

We instinctively reach for Feelgood
whatever the brand.

* * *

It is the easiest thing on earth:
becoming addicted to something that feels good!

* * *

Drug-addiction is a symptom of unhappiness.

* * *

Drugs produce artificial well-being — all drugs:
Aspirin, Prozac, Valium, LSD, cocaine, heroin, morphine,
mescaline, marijuana, nicotine, caffeine, alcohol, etc....
They are only substitutes for the real thing.
We should be able to create well-being without help,
but no one has taught us how.

* * *

You have to feel good about yourself
before you can start feeling good.

* * *

Guilt causes cancer.

* * *

What we call "diseases" are only
Nature's cleansers.

* * *

Cancer = organic Mr. Kleen!

* * *

We truly catch an illness!
Sometimes we run ourselves ragged,
trying to capture something sick-making!

* * *

The Blues kill more people than wars.

* * *

Nature abhors pain and suffering.
Only human beings put great value on living
even though it hurts.

* * *

Medical Science has "corrected" natural population control
— survival of the fittest —
by conquering diseases with drugs.
Nature strives to maintain balance:
When we cure one disease,
another one will show up in its place —
often more than one.
We must cure the patient of the need to be sick,
or repeat the old syndromes over and over and over!

* * *

One does not avoid disease in order to become healthy;
one stays healthy in order to avoid diseases.

* * *

The more you stay healthy,
the less you get sick.

* * *

We are electro-chemical bio-computers
programmed to live and die as "human beings"—
can we change our own basic programming?

* * *

We have programmed ourselves to "grow old,"
to degenerate and to self-destruct.
Can we, by learning how to reprogram ourselves,
bypass those old habits
and live for as long as we want to?

* * *

Could it be that we are already programmed for immortality,
Or at least long-life,
but just don't know how to access and begin the program?

* * *

Immortality by hypnosis?

* * *

When you discover an elementary truth,
you must accommodate its directives;
you must incorporate it into your life,
or it won't work for you.
Intellectually knowing that illness is the result of feeling bad
does not automatically guarantee that you will stop being sick!
You must understand the process, and apply the knowledge.

* * *

The process of socialization gives us expectations;
from infancy to old age,
we are surrounded by examples of every "natural" stage of life;
we learned what to expect;
we programmed ourselves
to follow the patterns now presumed to be
in the DNA of our parents.
We believe many things are "natural" or "normal"
when they may not be that at all!
They may just seem to be because most of us believe they are!

* * *

It should be possible —
if only I knew how -
to regrow my teeth and hair and regain 20/20 vision,
by reactivating the patterns
which are still in my memory-banks,
somewhere....

* * *

You will be amazed
when you start to understand the amount of anger
that hovers hidden in our daily lives.
We wake up angry,
we have to, or we couldn't work up the aggression necessary
to go to work and spend 8 hours in the hostile world,
that "jungle-out-there."
We wake up angry at the alarm clock,
for jerking us out of a pleasant dream,
angry about everything that went wrong yesterday,
angry about grievances not addressed,
angry at having to go through the same damned thing
day after day after day...!
Anger creates energy,
which, if not released, will do great damage to you,
inside and out.
We must learn to change that anger to joy,
or we will continue killing ourselves and each other!

* * *

Being afraid will wear you out as quickly as worrying, or being angry.
Fear, anger & worry put your body on "alert!"
which drains its resources and wears it down.

* * *.

I've got good longevity genes;
If only I can keep from killing myself,
I can live for a very long time!

* * *

Love is the food of Immortality.

* * *

Happiness creates an energy; the happier you are,
the more "Alive" you feel.

* * *

I don't know how to be happy!
I've never been properly programmed for it!

* * *

We were programmed to need love, to give and receive it.
We judge ourselves according to the quantity
& the quality of our loves.

* * *

No one can have
perfect health
without love.

* * *

People get very mean when deprived of love.

* * *

Love validates;
validation energizes.

* * *

While in the womb,
& even before the moment of conception
(your parents were "making love")
You were surrounded by love;
your mother loved you
from the moment she decided she wanted you.
Unless you were somehow deprived of that love,
and were born disfigured or handicapped,
you were born needing love
as much as nourishment;
in fact, love, to you, is a nourishment!
You need it in order to go on living!
At least at the beginning of your life,
you were welcomed and loved –
by your parents & grandparents, aunts and uncles
but as you grow older
it becomes more and more difficult to find .
You can die from lack of love.

* * *

RELIGION:

Jesus died.
Peter lied.
Christianity is built on that foundation.

* * *

The entire structure of Christianity
has been built upon
The Greatest Lie Ever Told:
That Jesus rose from the dead and
physically ascended into Heaven,
Promising to return, to save the Jews from slavery
some future day,
When it was safe to be The Messiah,
The King of the World
Who would judge mankind and send all the Sinners to Hell,
And restore the earth to Paradise...
It does not compute!
The Greatest Truth Ever Told
has been perverted by
The Greatest Lie Ever Told.
"Love One Another"
has been replaced by:
"Hate and judge Sinners!"

* * *

"The Greatest Story Ever Told"
is indeed the greatest "story" ever told.

* * *

Christianity is the result of Peter's attempt
to deal with a dead Messiah.

* * *

Jesus tried to take away sin;
Peter & Paul put it back again!

* * *

The Bad News: There's no Heaven!
The Good News: There's no Hell!
The Best News: We're alive!

* * *

There's no carrot in front of us,
But no whip behind!

* * *

A mystery should be solved,
not worshiped.

* * *

A mystery as such is mysterious & frightening,
and usually doesn't make sense until it is over.

* * *

The end of a Mystery is always a surprise —
or should be!

* * *

Every time I solve one of
"Life's Little Mysteries,"
I find I have put together
Only a small piece
Of a much larger puzzle.

* * *

All of our Sacred Cows Are Pure Bull!

* * *

"Faith Healing" depends upon the faith of the healee,
not the healer.
Thus may charlatans make miracles!

* * *

We all have miracle-power,
but no one has taught us
nor allowed us to learn
how to use it.

* * *

Computers are primitive models of the human brain.
The more you learn about one,
the more you know about the other.

* * *

Think of the Bible as a computer program:
OT = DOS (strict and demanding)

NT = Windows 1.0 (user-friendly)
What's next? Vista? (for a better view)

* * *

If you were raised as a Christian,
If you truly believed all the stories,
you were programmed by your church,
your relatives, friends, et. al.,
to punish yourself whenever you enjoyed yourself!
Headaches, Colds, & "the Flu,"
are the handiest self-punishments.
Until you reprogram yourself,
you will continue to risk getting sick
whenever you have a good time.

* * *

If you know you are going to feel guilty about doing something,
don't do it!
If you do it, you will surely punish yourself!

* * *

If you "Sin," & "God" doesn't punish you,
that opens several frightening questions:
Is there really a God?
Is what you did truly sinful?
And if not, why not,
and if it isn't, what is it?
Is your religion mistaken about God & Sin?
Much easier just to punish yourself!
(& blame it on God!)

* * *

There are programs in our heads
which we put there many years ago,
which are still functioning as though they were true,
even though we have long ago disproved
the "reality" on which they were based.
We have changed part of our conscious behavior,
but those programs need to be deleted,
or they will continue to run (ruin) our lives.

* * *

The patterns you followed were faulty.
The models you based yourselves on
were those of your parents —
and they were the products
of patterns & forces
completely unknown to them,
& usually thoroughly misunderstood.

* * *

Prayer is basically Self-Talk.
Which is the same as Self-Programming.
Which is how prayer works:
You reward or punish yourself
Depending on how angry or pleased you are
with yourself.

* * *

If prayer is self-talk,
guess who God is!

* * *

We create "God" in our own minds,
using ideas and models that are popular
in the groups around us as we grow up.
In our deepest core, we posit God,
and it is that core to which we pray,
and which answers prayers.
It is that core which watches eternally,
which judges and condemns us,
or loves and forgives us,
depending on which religion
defines and governs us.

* * *

If the earth were a corporation
& "God" the C.E.O.,
He would have been fired
centuries ago!

* * *

One day I found G O D
in my alphabet soup!

* * *

Can we enforce civilization
without a boogey-man?

* * *

We are our own accusers,
our own judges, juries & jailers,
but we can pardon ourselves,
and become our own rewards!

* * *

Most of humanity is marching resolutely
into the future — facing backward!
With their fingers stuck in their ears!

* * *

Our religions are keeping us anchored in the past.

* * *

The major cause of much, if not all the violence,
gangs, drug use, murders, suicides, etc.,
the literal, veritable falling-apart of society,
is disenchantment:
Disappointment, frustration, hopelessness & rage
over unkept promises:
The Tooth Fairy, Easter Bunny, Santa Claus,
Virgin Mary & Little Baby Jesus Christ,
Prince Charming, Bambi & Peter Pan,
God, Jehovah, Allah, Zeus, Thor, Lucifer,
Justice, Equality, True Love, Happily-Ever-After...
& all the other myths & fables.
Lies, all lies.
Prayers unanswered.
Wishes unfulfilled.

* * *

How can you ever trust again
a person, family or society
which has so consistently lied to you?

* * *

If they have lied about God & Jesus,
how can you possibly believe
anything else they've said,
or ever will say?

* * *

"Happily-Ever-After"
is the Curse of our times.
Anyone who believes in it
is doomed to unhappiness.

* * *

Turning the other cheek
usually means getting slapped twice.

* * *

Christian "Sacrament"
is holy cannibalism
for Christ's sake!

* * *

Christian Sacrament began as
Shewbread and wine,
For which Mormons substitute
Wonder Bread and bottled water.

* * *

We are judging and condemning ourselves
according to a book of myths and fables,
which lives within the very fabric of our lives.
Virtually every aspect of our society
is based in some way or other upon "The Holy Bible!"
We must stop judging and punishing ourselves
as "failed Divine Creations"
i.e. "Sinners,"
and see ourselves instead
as the End Result of a long, understandable, natural process.
Then we will finally realize that we have become
The best that ever has been!
And that's much more impressive than a
"Failed Divine Miracle!"

* * *

They try to force me
to be less than I am
because they cannot,
or will not,
be more than they are.

★ ★ ★

Most of what humanity believes
are fabrications covering the true reality.
There is something under there somewhere!
It's us!
It's just us.
That's all it has ever been.
And yet, how amazing that is,
when you stop and think about it!

★ ★ ★

The human animal evolved from its predecessor
several million years ago.
It evolved into its "next step" several thousand years ago.
This "new kind" of human is to homo sapiens
as a Lexus ZX is to a Model T Ford.
That is what Jesus was talking about when he said
"You already have what you seek, but you know it not."
He called himself the "son of man," not the "son of God,"
i.e., the "next step" in the evolution of humanity.
It was Peter who appointed Jesus "Messiah,"
for which, Jesus renamed "The Rock"
"Satan."
Matt. 16:16-28

★ ★ ★

Jesus was not preaching Christianity;
He was trying to teach Evolution,
"substance abuse" and homosexuality

★ ★ ★

What you read in The Bible
are the "official 'CYA' stories"
for what actually happened.

★ ★ ★

Religion is a power trip.

★ ★ ★

Religions, Laws,
Astrology, Medical Science, Psychology,
Voodoo, Shamanism, Witchcraft, etc.,
all have been attempts to deal with the human condition.

None are all true; none are all false.
All contain errors, but all contain truths —
scattered throughout like pearls in a pigpen
after a feast of oysters!

* * *

Religion is a necessary evil.
What else would control
All the crazy people
in the world?

* * *

Religion is designed
To scare the Hell out of you!

* * *

When you closely examine a religion,
you will find a machine
churning out babies for The Church.

* * *

A closed mind is most often clenched around a religion.

* * *

"Christ-ness" is a state of mind.

* * *

"Heaven" is a state of mind.

* * *

"Apocalypse" means "Uncovering;"
"Revelation" means "Uncovering."
This is the Age of Uncovering!
Just watch television:
Civilization is being exposed!

* * *

Civilization is being stripped bare.
Not much there.
Lots of people,
very little civilization.

* * *

Our "Civilization" is based upon the greatest lies ever told:
Creation, Gods, Heaven, Hell, Christ, Satan, Virgin Mary,

et. al..
These were invented to explain things
that seemed unexplainable.
They are comforting,
but they are all myths.
This is the end of civilization as we know it.
It is crumbling and cannot be stopped.
The "New World" must be built upon Truth,
or it cannot survive.

* * *

The truth is the truth!
It does not depend upon time or place,
and it does not "belong" to anyone!
For example: "Religion is the opiate of the masses,"
does not depend on the acceptability of Karl Marx
for its trueness.
"Treat others as you would have them treat you,"
does not depend on the divinity of the Teacher from
Nazareth.

* * *

Religion is keeping the next evolutionary step from happening.

* * *

Like it or not, humanity has grown out of its "childhood."
We're "maturing," cosmically speaking,
and we have to get rid of our "childhood"
myths and obsessions
and our magical notions of how things work.

* * *

Good people are good people, with or without "God."
Bad people are bad with or without God.

* * *

"Intelligence" is always the last to evolve.
Never the first.
Everything — you, me, the earth, the universe —
All are evolving from simple to complex,
Not the other way around.
God did not create us: We are creating God!
The Universe's "Intelligence" is evolving:

We are "microchips" in the "mind" of the Universe —
But that "Mind" is still evolving
and is not yet self-aware
let alone, aware of you or me.
You are the only one aware of you.
Others are only partially aware of you,
within the schemes and boundaries of their own personal
universes.

* * *

Some people spend entire lives
hiding from each other,
and lying to each other,
and hating themselves for it.

* * *

All of my life I've been called
"too sensitive for my own good."
That was quite true,
but I didn't know what to do about it.
I couldn't just turn it off —
I had no idea where the switch was!
Whenever I was near an angry person,
I became angry.
Whenever someone was sad,
I felt like crying.
It makes shopping at the mall
like a trip into Hell!

* * *

We are the dreamers,
those seekers after truth,
the True Believers,
who, as children,
were called "too imaginative,"
"over-sensitive!"
We are the ones who saw the hypocrisy,
the blatant insanity,
which everyone else seemed not to notice,
or used for their own benefit.
We couldn't help noticing that the Emperor was naked!
And often made the mistake of saying so!

We are the ones who wouldn't settle
for a piece of horse manure
in our stocking for Christmas;
we keep looking for the pony!

* * *

It is easy getting into the Enchanted Forest.
The hard part is
in getting out again.

* * *

We are headed for mass-consciousness,
at first via radio, television and computers,
and then by our brains themselves.
We'll have to clean house in
our heads
before we let anyone in!

* * *

We have been taught to disbelieve
everything we are.

* * *

We are doomed to chase the Impossible Dream
forever and evermore.
Otherwise we could not grow.
We become that which we seek —
but the dream grows as we grow,
evolves as we evolve!

* * *

We are all Gifted Children
that someone forgot to unwrap!

* * *

Multiplicities of onenesses...

* * *

What you know of yourself
is what you allow yourself
to be conscious of —
the tip of the iceberg
compared to all you really are.

* * *

By ceasing to be what you seem to be
you become what you have been all along.

* * *

We are all fervent idealists!
So full of perfectionism
we crack if we bend,
and we judge ourselves harder
than any others.

* * *

Most of my life, I've been mad at myself!
I'm not condemning myself any more.
It feels really good to forgive yourself!
(Sort of like spiritual masturbation!)

* * *

Each of us has our own "Dream Theater,"
which is activated while sleeping,
meditating, tripping on LSD, Peyote, Mescaline,
"Out-of-body experiences,"
"Religious experiences,"
Epileptic grand mal seizures, etc..
Paul of Tarsus was an epileptic
who had a seizure on the way to Damascus—
and talked to Jesus.
Joseph Smith was an epileptic
who had a seizure in the "Sacred Grove" —
and talked to Jesus.
It is typical of a grand mal seizure
that the epileptic talks to God or Jesus —
or at very least an angel.
It was called "the falling-down sickness,"
and many Old Testament Prophets had it —
and those who didn't ate "Shewbread" for their visions.
Once you have experienced the power & seeming reality
of one of those LSD—or "Shewbread"—"visions,"
or "mystical experiences," or "hallucinations,"
you suddenly understand all of those old Biblical prophets,
all the Wizards & Seers & Witch Doctors & Oracles,
wheels within wheels,

angels & demons, Heaven & Hell, myths & religions,
& John-the-Beloved's "Revelations"!
(Now there was an acid-trip for you!)

* * *

Mormonism = compulsory mediocrity.

* * *

Mormonism (etc.) works for Mormons (et. al.)
If you can swallow that bullshit,
it seems to be very satisfying.

* * *

Mormonism is a Religion Sandwich:
Christianity wrapped in Bullshit —
which makes it bullshit within bullshit.

* * *

Concept Progression: Holey underwear=holy underwear=
holy under where?=wholly unaware.

* * *

Most people absolutely refuse
to jeopardize their beliefs
by thinking about them.

* * *

During Sunday School, Mass,
or whatever your worship ritual is called,
you "get high" on the words, the images, the singing,
& the music!
The colored lights & candles & incense & harmonious singing
cause your body to create "Endorphins"
which stimulate your body & brain, making you feel good,
safe & secure, loved, & immortal!
A group, feeling good, magnifies the sensations. ("Synergy")
You go back week after week to get high again on Jesus!
And you cannot understand,
however hard you try,
how any idiot could possibly get hooked on drugs!

* * *

Billions of people are hooked on Jesus!

* * *

It doesn't make a bit of difference what the loved object is —
a man or woman, dog or cat,
dead saint or incorporeal savior —
Loving makes you feel good,
no matter who or what you love!

* * *

Whatever the road,
whoever the teacher,
the lesson of life is Love.
(Or, hopefully: Either learn it,
or go back & do it again,
'til you get it right. Right?)

* * *

There is at least one thing which unites us:
We all believe in love!

* * *

It finally comes down to this:
Love is the only thing
that makes life worthwhile.

* * *

Love comes in all flavors.

* * *

Love has no limits!
It can include everything!

* * *

The only way we can save the world is with Love!
Nothing else can stop us from destroying ourselves.

* * *

You are born with a need for love
While growing inside your mother's womb,
you were surrounded with the physical & chemical reactions
of her love for you as you were growing inside her.
It was all soft & warm & delicious!

Love & touch were all around you for 9 months.
No wonder you cried when you were born!

* * *

If you think of something as a punishment, it is.
If you think it's a reward,
it will be that just as easily.

* * *

You are defined & limited by what you believe.
You may be being forced to think of yourself
in ways that are not true at all —
by the people & institutions around you.
As you cease to believe certain things about yourself,
you tear down the walls you have built up around yourself.

* * *

The less you are preoccupied
with all of your problems,
the more you are able to see
what is going on around you.

* * *

A Shaman manipulates other people's magic.

* * *

Christians are hung-up on crosses

* * *

Crosses are the symbols of death
not life!

* * *

We have overpunished ourselves.
We have a refund coming!

* * *

By contemplating only the imperfections,
we miss the miracles.
Stop limiting yourself
by being something
you no longer believe in.

* * *

The world is insane!
Therefore, anyone who deals successfully with the world
is necessarily insane as well!
By "the world" I do not mean the "earth,"
third planet from the sun, which I love,
but rather "the way of the world" —
the religions codified into laws,
schools & institutions
which promulgate those religions.
Also, those people who still believe in those laws,
institutions & religions.
Their lives are based upon insanity!

* * *

The very ideas of "Heaven," "Hell," & "Final Judgment"
invite murder,
Legal & otherwise.

* * *

"My God is better than your God
& I'm willing to kill you to prove it."

* * *

What most people call "Love" is an illusion,
often a delusion,
an expectation,
triggered by some aspect of sex —
the act itself, or the thought of it.
Nature has made it very difficult to not reproduce.
When people meet & feel an instinctive impulse to procreate,
"Endorphins" are produced,
and flood the brain, making the body feel good.
It is this "good-feeling"
which is popularly known as "Falling In Love."
It is much like the LSD or psychedelic experience:
For a relatively brief period of time, while "high,"
or "in love,"
one feels dynamic! Healthy! Immortal!
When that good-feeling goes away,
we try to repeat whatever action
caused the feeling in the first place:

sex, drugs, religion....
Religions are designed specifically
to produce that good-feeling,
which is what people refer to when they speak of
"Religious Ecstasy"
or "The Presence of God."
It is also the basis for "miracle power."

* * *

In the beginning, man invented God.
To get even,
woman invented The Devil.

* * *

In order to sustain & maintain itself,
The Church must prevent its followers from truly finding Heaven.
("The Priests & Pharisees are like dogs sleeping in a manger.
They neither eat, nor allow the cattle to eat.
They have been given the Keys to the Kingdom of Heaven,
but they will not enter,
nor will they let their followers enter.")

* * *

You don't know you're dreaming
Until you wake up.

* * *

"The survival of the fittest"
applies to everything in the cosmos
— & beyond.

* * *

The story of Adam & Eve in The Bible
is the result of a male-dominated society's
twisting of facts to suit the leaders.
It began as a cautionary tale about mating.
Mating was Paradise at first, but then Sex
(the Jews called sexual intercourse "knowledge."
Adam "knew" Eve with his "Tree of Knowledge,"
his "Serpent,"
& produced Cain & Able),
which at first seems heavenly,
turns into hell because it gets the wife pregnant.

The way to avoid pregnancy,
says the old pre-biblical old-wives' tale,
is to abstain.
Otherwise, you get kicked out of Paradise,
with children,
& have to earn a living or somehow bring food & comfort
to the little ones,
who end up killing each other.

* * *

Scaring you into accepting
Their leadership & laws
Is what Religion & Politics
Are all about.
"Fear & Guilt."
Two sides of a coin named "Power & Control."

* * *

Religion is the cause, not the cure.
Religion turns good, decent people
into bigots & hypocrites.

* * *

Each of us sees God in his own image.
A Mormon imagines his man-like God living on a planet called Kolob,
with many wives and many children.
The Pope believes in a God who chose him Pope.

* * *

GAY LIFE:

While searching for myself
I found a multitude.

* * *

Inside drab and ugly outer shells
we are creatures of exquisite beauty
hiding from each other
and ourselves.

* * *

The Gay lament:
"How can I respect anyone
who wants to have anything to do
with someone like me?"

* * *

We try to get somebody else to love us
before we can love ourselves.

* * *

People who do not love themselves
do not allow themselves to be loved.

* * *

If you don't believe in yourself
nobody else will either.

* * *

We are all good little boys and girls
pretending to be bad big boys and girls,
acting out roles that have been prescribed for us,
trapped inside our own pretending.

* * *

We are called "Gay"
not for what we are
but for what we will be
when we discover what we are.

* * *

When they call you
"the scum of the earth"
remember:
The scum of milk is cream!

* * *

The "scum of the earth"
is the "cream of the crop."

* * *

You must like yourself
before you will permit yourself
to enjoy yourself.

* * *

There are those who believe that "Gay Lib"started on
Christopher Street in 1969.
That is like believing
that a flower can bloom
without having been planted.

* * *

Human population is out of control,
literally exploding!
The earth simply cannot sustain so many people.
There will continue to be wars and plagues and pestilences
until we stop reproducing ourselves so abundantly!
Might homosexuality save the planet?
Organic Birth Control?

* * *

Don't be afraid of becoming
what you already are.

* * *

We are pain-savers!
We collect outrages and injustices
the way other people accumulate
paper bags and rubber bands!

* * *

We are humanity blossoming.

* * *

The "Poor Little Me" method:
First you set yourself up;
Then you knock yourself down;
Then you say:
"Now look what you made me do to myself!"

* * *

I'm in the habit of feeling rejected.
I go through the old syndrome
whether it is valid or not.

* * *

Help!
I'm trapped in a syndrome
& can't get out!

* * *

The practice of homosexuality is being drastically altered
from what it has been, up until very recently
to what it will soon be for a huge number of people
in the very near future:
It will become the lifestyle of choice
for much of the world's population
early in the twenty-first century.
Legalized organic birth control.
The idea of bringing children
into a world such as this
turns off a vast number of young people,
who would gladly be Gay
if it wasn't such a "bad" thing to be.
Television is turning that current unreality
into future reality
all around the world.
Most Gay men and lesbians on TV
are like "the boys & girls next door."
No big deal.

* * *

MISCELLANEOUS APHORISMS

All I can give you is me.
I'm all I've got.

* * *

I'm glad I am!
I celebrate myself!

* * *

Fight ugliness with beauty!

* * *

"Never in a Million Years" was day-before-yesterday

* * *

If nobody knows where we're going,
How will we know when we get there?

* * *

Modern music:
("I can torture you and call it art!")

* * *

When everybody else believes you're crazy,
sometimes you're tempted to wonder
if maybe they might be right.

* * *

The history of humanity
is an incessant, almost imperceptible
movement toward perfection.

* * *

I am a perfectionist continually frustrated
by the impossibility of perfection!

* * *

More often than not,
the people who are the least talkative
have the most to say.
And the opposite is even truer.

* * *

I now believe that every single step of my life
has been necessary,
for one valid, logical reason or another,
in order for me to become what I am supposed to be:
Me!

* * *

There are reasons for everything
if only we knew them;
there are no effects without causes.

* * *

Plan, but don't worry.
Planning assumes success.

Worrying assumes failure.
Remain flexible.
Do not get angry or upset
by a necessary change of plans;
You cannot foresee a multitude of particulars.

* * *

Change is as predictable
as it is inevitable;
we must simply learn
what to look for.

* * *

By attempting to impose order and sanity
upon an un-sane and disorderly universe,
are we merely driving ourselves crazy?

* * *

Instead of using "time" simply as a measuring device,
we have allowed it to incorporate a "Mystical Quality"
with which it "shapes our lives."
Actually it does no such thing —
so long as we do not allow it to.

* * *

I am the only one paying attention to my life.
Everyone else is too preoccupied with their own lives
to do more than fleetingly notice mine.

* * *

I must follow the path I'm on,
no matter where it may take me.
Wherever it goes is where I should go,
to give me whatever it is I should have
when I'm finished,
when the path ends
and I get where I'm going.

* * *

My memory allows me to be me.
I wouldn't know what to do without it!

* * *

It takes at least 2 people,
believing in something,
to make it real.

* * *

Worry is a measure of doubt.
The more worried you are,
the more you doubt
the thing you want to happen.

* * *

One of the first tricks we learn as children
is to recreate Mommy and Daddy inside our "imaginations."
Thus we could anticipate what they would do
under certain imaginary circumstances.
Eventually, everyone important to us
takes up residence inside our heads
and are up there, at this very moment,
chattering away at us,
complaining and criticizing,
making us feel guilty
even though we don't know why!

* * *

I was never taught how to "control" my "imagination."
Only to put it away very quickly,
whenever I was caught playing with it!

* * *

The "pendulum of change" swings each way
from "liberal" to "conservative"
approximately every 10 - 20 years.
each set of swings
moves us ultimately forward;
we never go back all the way.

* * *

Up until now, wars have helped control population growth.
Many of the prime breeders were killed in the fighting.
Many of those young people
who would otherwise have joined gangs
and killed people at home,

joined the biggest gangs of all
— the Armed Forces —
and killed people in other countries.
Now they roam the streets.

* * *

Suppose dogs socialized humans rather than the opposite.
After all, dogs have been around a lot longer than people!

* * *

If you've never experienced
the love of a dog,
You've never known Love
in its purest form.

* * *

Dogs and old people get on very well together
because they truly love each other,
and neither requires intellectual companionship.

* * *

The human race is currently undergoing spiritual circumcision!

* * *

I have heard Truth singing!

* * *

Perseverance makes winners out of losers

* * *

Television is homogenizing humanity.

* * *

When you feel bad, you see the worst in people;
when you feel good, you see the best!

* * *

Even if you've got the best equipment in the world
What good is it if you never use it?

* * *

Once you have tasted how delicious Life can be
you can never forget or be satisfied with less.

* * *

The ultimate failure is to fail at failing.

* * *

In the land of the blind,
a one-eyed man is thoroughly distrusted!

* * *

We see and hear the world
through a filter of our (mis)conceptions.

* * *

Most people are too busy to be introspective.

* * *

Politics is the "art"
of making your opponents truths
sound like lies
while making your own lies
sound like truths.

* * *

Knowledge understood becomes Wisdom.

* * *

Wisdom is a treasure which cannot be hoarded,
but must be shared to have any value.

* * *

I am like a hidden fountain,
flowing endlessly,
whether anybody drinks or not.

* * *

I would rather be an enigma
than a disappointment.

* * *

Once you open the door of Doubt,
That let's all the hot-air out

About the Author

Dirk Vanden was one of the heroes, the pioneers of the gay pulp movement. Between 1969 and 1971, he published seven novels—works that were viewed seriously enough to cause them to be listed by Ian Young in his great bibliography and by two different contributors to Claude J. Summers's *Gay and Lesbian Literary Heritage*. Of course, Vanden, like all the other pulp writers, has been mostly ignored by literary critics.

—Drewey Wayne Gunn, review of *All of Me*
Lambda Literary, September 18, 2010